Counter-Democracy

T0384780

Democracy is established as a generally uncontested ideal, while regimes inspired by this form of government fall under constant criticism – hence the steady erosion of confidence in representatives that has become one of the major political issues of our time. Amidst these challenges, the paradox remains that, while citizens are less likely to make the trip to the ballot box, the world is far from entering a phase of general political apathy. Demonstrations and activism abound in the streets, in cities across the globe, and on the internet. Pierre Rosanvallon analyzes the mechanisms used to register a citizen's expression of confidence or distrust, and then focuses on the role that distrust plays in democracy from both a historical and theoretical perspective. This radical shift in perspective uncovers a series of practices – surveillance, prevention, and judgment – through which society corrects and exerts pressure. The Seeley Lectures are established as a unique forum to promote the finest political thought of our time, and *Counter-Democracy* is a powerful and provocative addition to this distinguished series.

PIERRE ROSANVALLON is Professor and Chair of Modern and Contemporary Political History at the Collège de France. He is also professor at the École des Hautes Études en Sciences Sociales as well as the President of the international intellectual workshop "La République des idées."

ARTHUR GOLDHAMMER, a translator specializing in French history, literature, philosophy, and social science, has translated more than a hundred works by many of France's most noted authors. He is on the editorial board of the journal *French Politics, Culture and Society*, and in 1996 was named Chevalier de l'Ordre des Arts et des Lettres by the French Minister of Culture.

The John Robert Seeley Lectures have been established by the University of Cambridge as a biennial lecture series in social and political studies, sponsored jointly by the Faculty of History and the University Press. The Seeley Lectures provide a unique forum for distinguished scholars of international reputation to address, in an accessible manner, themes of broad and topical interest in social and political studies. Subsequent to their public delivery in Cambridge the University Press publishes suitably modified versions of each set of lectures. Professor James Tully delivered the inaugural series of Seeley Lectures in 1994 on the theme of *Constitutionalism in an Age of Diversity*.

The Seeley Lectures include

(1)   Strange Multiplicity: Constitutionalism in an Age of Diversity
      JAMES TULLY
      ISBN 978 0 521 47694 2 (paperback)
      Published 1995

(2)   The Dignity of Legislation
      JEREMY WALDRON
      ISBN 978 0 521 65092 2 (hardback) 978 0 521 65883 6 (paperback)
      Published 1999

(3)   Woman and Human Development: The Capabilities Approach
      MARTHA NUSSBAUM
      ISBN 978 0 521 66086 0 (hardback) 978 0 521 00385 8 (paperback)
      Published 2000

(4)   Value, Respect and Attachment
      JOSEPH RAZ
      ISBN 978 0 521 80180 5 (hardback) 978 0 521 00022 2 (paperback)
      Published 2001

COUNTER-DEMOCRACY

Politics in an Age of Distrust

PIERRE ROSANVALLON
Collège de France

Translated by
ARTHUR GOLDHAMMER
Harvard University

 CAMBRIDGE
UNIVERSITY PRESS

CAMBRIDGE
UNIVERSITY PRESS

University Printing House, Cambridge CB2 8BS, United Kingdom

Published in the United States of America by Cambridge University Press, New York

Cambridge University Press is part of the University of Cambridge.

It furthers the University's mission by disseminating knowledge in the pursuit of education, learning and research at the highest international levels of excellence.

www.cambridge.org
Information on this title: www.cambridge.org/9780521713832

Originally published in French as *La contre-démocratie* by Éditions du Seuil 2006 and © Éditions du Seuil, Paris. First published in English by Cambridge University Press 2008 as *Counter-Democracy*. English version © Cambridge University Press 2008.

First published 2008
3rd printing 2012

A catalogue record for this publication is available from the British Library

Library of Congress Cataloguing in Publication data
Rosanvallon, Pierre, 1948–
[Contre-dimocratie. English]
Counter-democracy : politics in the age of distrust / Pierre Rosanvallon ; translated by Arthur Goldhammer.
  p.   cm. – (The Seeley lectures; 7)
Includes bibliographical references.
ISBN 978-0-521-88622-2 (hbk.) – ISBN 978-0-521-71383-2 (pbk.)
1. Democracy.   2. Legitimacy of governments.   3. Political participation.
I. Title.
JC423.R616813   2008
321.8–dc22

2008036970

ISBN 978-0-521-88622-2 Hardback
ISBN 978-0-521-71383-2 Paperback

CONTENTS

vii

FOREWORD

This book is based upon the Seeley Lectures delivered in
Cambridge in 2006. Pierre Rosanvallon, who is a Professor,
both at the *Collège de France* and at the *Raymond Aron Centre
for Political Research* in Paris, has attracted much attention in
France and elsewhere for his work on the intellectual history of
French politics since the Revolution, on contemporary questions of social justice, and on the definition and trajectory of
modern democracy. His historical studies of French politics,
incorporating a fundamental and pioneering re-evaluation
of French liberalism, include *Le Moment Guizot* (1985). His
examination of contemporary problems of social justice is
most powerfully represented by *La Nouvelle Question sociale:
Repenser L'État-providence* (1995), which was translated into
English in 2000 as *The New Social Question: Rethinking the
Welfare State*. His third area of concern, work most relevant to
the present volume, has focused upon the intellectual history
of democracy in France. This has been published as a trilogy:
Le Sacre du citoyen: Histoire du suffrage universel en France
(1992); *Le Peuple introuvable: Histoire de la représentation
démocratique en France* (1998); and *La Démocratie inachevée:
Histoire de la souveraineté du peuple en France* (2000).

Rosanvallon believes that there are significant differences between American and European conceptions of democracy, dating back to the second half of the nineteenth century.
In the United States, democracy has been viewed from a

ix

globally fundamentalist perspective and treated as a unique, universal, and intrinsically good political form, destined to spread throughout the world, once offered to its different peoples. This has been a vision not only articulated in works of political science, but also tirelessly preached by successive American presidents from Woodrow Wilson and Franklin Roosevelt to J.F. Kennedy and George W. Bush. In this utopian and quasi-religious perspective, the supposed ethos and institutional form of democracy has remained relatively constant and uniform. So has the political ambition: to ensure a concordance between political practice and this pre-formulated democratic norm, and to further its diffusion throughout the world.

But such an approach has been beset by increasing pessimism. It has found itself confronted by an intractable set of problems, creating an apparently unbridgeable gap between the democratic ideal and a discouraging political reality. Numerous studies have lamented an endemic distrust of politicians, low levels of electoral participation, the decline of political parties, and widespread political apathy or passivity.

In Europe, by contrast, conceptions of democracy and expectations of its progressive improvement have from the beginning been more realistic and low-key. 'Real democracies,' Rosanvallon notes, have always involved 'tension and conflict.' The problem with the conventional notion of democracy, he thinks, is that it elides questions of legitimacy (abiding by the procedural rules of democratic representation) with questions of trust (the assumption that politicians will act for the common good). But according to Rosanvallon, not only is any convergence between legitimacy and trust ever more than purely temporary, but durable forms of *dis*trust have been an inherent component of all democracies, however legitimate. Therefore his alternative conception of democracy encompasses not only the formal, legal, and constitutional practices of democratic regimes, but also all those limiting and corrective devices – whether constitutional or extra-constitutional, including those which date from pre-democratic epochs – by which the people have attempted to impose control over the political processes carried out in their name. This is what Rosanvallon calls 'counter-democracy'.

Rosanvallon believes that conventional definitions of democracy, which restrict it to the electoral process, are too narrow. A more adequate account would include the various ways in which the people are able to check or hold to account their representatives or the government, irrespective of the electoral process. In particular, he picks out for detailed discussion three ways in which distrust may be expressed: powers of oversight or 'surveillance,' forms of prevention, and the testing of judgments.

Conceived in this way, democracy, or rather the forms, which Rosanvallon assembles together as 'counter-democracy,' can be said to possess a history much longer and more multifaceted than that recognized by conventional democratic theorists. For such a history can include practices which enforce forms of popular control or veto, ancient as well as modern, extra-European as well as western. Such an approach also makes possible a more optimistic account of contemporary democracy than that found in many English-speaking accounts. For it suggests that a citizenry may be no less (or more) active than before, simply that it has chosen to exercise these 'counter-democratic' powers in different and less familiar ways.

But, as Rosanvallon concedes, there are also dangers in this account. Although the modern citizen may not be as 'passive' as the conventional account maintains, Rosanvallon accepts that levels of political distrust have increased, especially in relation to scientific expertise or economic forecasting, and that there now exists a great distance between civil society and political institutions. It is a situation in which there is a heightened danger of the unwanted appearance of all sorts of populism. Furthermore, if the price of enlarging the contemporary definition of democracy is to accord to all forms of 'counter-democracy' – whether institutional or extra-institutional – the status of 'an authentic political form,' it is difficult to see how such populism could be excluded from a recognized place in the formal political system.

How effectively Rosanvallon deals with this difficulty is for the reader to judge. Clearly, the implications of some of Rosanvallon's arguments are controversial, but that is only to be expected of an arresting and original approach to the understanding of contemporary political life and of a more positive conception of the prospects of political change.

Gareth Stedman Jones

Introduction

The democratic ideal now reigns unchallenged, but regimes claiming to be democratic come in for vigorous criticism almost everywhere. In this paradox resides the major political problem of our time. Indeed, the erosion of citizens' confidence in political leaders and institutions is among the phenomena that political scientists have studied most intently over the past twenty years. National and comparative research has yielded a clear diagnosis. The literature on voter abstention is also abundant. Significantly, even the newest democracies suffer from this affliction, as a glance at the formerly Communist countries of Eastern Europe and the erstwhile dictatorships of Asia and Latin America shows. How are we to understand this situation, which has been variously described as a "crisis," a "malaise," a "disaffection," and a "breakdown"? Most explanations invoke a series of factors, including the rise of individualism, anxious retreat into the private sphere, decline of political will, and rule by elites increasingly cut off from the broader public. We hear frequently about the "decline of politics," and blame is said to lie with rulers who cannot see or abdicate their responsibilities as well as with people who have become discouraged by or indifferent to the political. Something is missing, critics say; something has gone wrong. Today's democracies have somehow deviated from an original model, somehow betrayed their original promise. Such judgments are commonplace nowadays: a bleak or bitter appraisal of the present is linked to nostalgia for a largely idealized civic past. In some cases what emerges from these expressions of disappointment is a muted or partially concealed hatred of democracy.

This work takes a different approach to understanding the current state of democracies. In particular, I propose to expand the scope of analysis by attending to the ways in which different societies have responded to the dysfunctions of representative regimes. Historically, the rise of democracy has always represented both a promise and a problem: a promise insofar as democracy reflected the needs of societies founded on the dual imperative of equality and autonomy; and a problem, insofar as these noble ideals were a long way from being realized. Wherever democracy was tried, it remained incomplete – in some places grossly perverted, in others subtly constricted, in still others systematically thwarted. In a sense, there has never been a fully "democratic" regime, if we take the word in its fullest sense. Actual democracies have failed to develop as fully as they might have done, and some have been snuffed out. Thus disappointment has always coexisted with the hope of liberation from dependence and despotism. The idea of basing the legitimacy of government on election has nearly always gone hand-in-hand with citizen mistrust of the powers-that-be. The famous "Agreement of the Free People of England," published in London on May 1, 1649, was the first modern democratic manifesto, yet already we can see a duality of trust and distrust in its text. Guarantees of civil and religious liberties, trial by jury, universal suffrage, limited terms of office, strict subordination of the military to the civilian powers, and universal access to public office – all the principles on which the revolutions of the seventeenth and eighteenth centuries would thrive can be found here. Significantly, however, the document also refers to the "woeful experience" of corruption, to the risk that special interests might, in spite of all precautions, seize power and turn representative government to domination of a novel sort. Thus, even as the terms of legitimate government were set forth, a "reserve of mistrust" found expression in the same breath.

The society of distrust

The history of *real* democracies has always involved tension and conflict. Thus legitimacy and trust, which the theory of democratic-representative government has tried to link through the electoral mechanism, are in fact distinct. These two political attributes, which are supposedly fused in the ballot box, are actually different in kind. Legitimacy is a juridical attribute, a strictly procedural fact. It is a pure and incontestable product of voting. Trust is far more complex. It is a sort of "invisible institution," to borrow a well-known formula from the economist Kenneth Arrow.[1] Its functions are at least three in number. First, it represents an expansion of legitimacy, in that it adds to a mere procedural attribute both a moral dimension (integrity in the broadest sense) and a substantive dimension (concern for the common good). Trust also plays a temporal role: it implies that the expansion of legitimacy *continues into the future*. Thus Simmel observed that

[1] See Kenneth J. Arrow, *The Limits of Organization* (New York: Norton, 1974), p. 26.

3

trust is essentially "an hypothesis about future behavior."[2]
Finally, trust is an *institutional economizer*, in that it eliminates
the need for various procedures of verification and proof. The
gap between legitimacy and trust has been a central problem in
the history of democracy. The existence of such a gap has been
the rule, its elimination the exception. (One sometimes speaks
of a "state of grace" to describe the brief period following an
election, during which the two attributes merge into one, but
this is an exception.) In reaction to this general situation,
democracies have developed in two directions. First, a variety
of measures have been proposed to strengthen the constraints
of procedural legitimacy. For instance, the frequency of elections has been increased, and various schemes of direct
democracy have been employed to limit the independence of
elected representatives. What all these initiatives have in common is that they seek to improve the quality of "electoral
democracy." At the same time, however, a complex assortment
of practical measures, checks and balances, and informal as
well as institutional social counter-powers has evolved in order
to *compensate for the erosion of confidence, and to do so by
organizing distrust.* It is impossible to theorize about democracy or recount its history without discussing these organized
forms of mistrust.

---

[2] George Simmel, *Sociologie: Études sur les formes de la socialisation* (Paris:
Presses Universitaires de France, 1999), pp. 355–356. He writes: "Certain
enough to furnish the basis of practical action, trust is also an intermediate
state between knowledge and ignorance of others. A person who knows
everything has no need of trust. One who knows nothing cannot
reasonably bestow his trust."

If we wish to comprehend the variety of *democratic experiences*, we must therefore consider two aspects of the phenomenon: the functions and dysfunctions of electoral-representative institutions on the one hand and the organization of distrust on the other. Until now, historians and political theorists have been primarily concerned with the first aspect. I myself have explored this dimension of the problem in a series of works on the institutions of citizenship, representation, and sovereignty.[3] Now it is time to explore the second dimension. To be sure, various expressions of democratic distrust have been treated in any number of monographs dealing with subjects such as the history of resistance to the extension of public power and the reactions such resistance provoked, or the sociology of forms of civic disaffection and rejection of the political system. Various specific forms of action and particular attitudes have thus come in for careful scrutiny, but these have never been combined in a more general framework, apart perhaps from some very broad and quite vague attempts to view these phenomena in the context of the struggle for a freer, more just world. In this work, by contrast, I propose to view the manifold manifestations of mistrust in a comprehensive framework in order to bring out in a systematic and coherent way the most profound characteristics of the phenomenon. In short, I wish to understand the manifestations of mistrust as *elements of a political system*. I further intend to use this as

---

[3] See my trilogy *Le Sacre du citoyen: Histoire du suffrage universel en France* (Paris: Gallimard, 1992); *Le Peuple introuvable: Histoire de la représentation démocratique en France* (Paris: Gallimard, 1998); *La Démocratie inachevée: Histoire de la souveraineté du peuple en France* (Paris: Gallimard, 2000).

the basis for a broader understanding of how democracies work and a deeper knowledge of the history and theory of democracy.

In order to place the problem in its proper context, I should first point out that the expression of distrust took two main forms: liberal and democratic. Liberal distrust of power has often been theorized and commented on. Montesquieu gave it its canonical expression,[4] and the Founding Fathers of the American regime gave it constitutional form. Throughout the period during which the American Constitution was debated, Madison was obsessed with the need to prevent the concentration of power. His goal was not to establish a good strong government based on the confidence of the people; it was rather to constitute a weak government in which suspicion would be institutionalized. It was not to crown the citizen but to protect the individual from the encroachments of public authority.

In France, men like Benjamin Constant and the economist Jean Sismondi, who was also one of the leading political theorists of the early nineteenth century, took similar positions. For Sismondi, the cornerstone of every liberal regime was "the constant disposition to resistance."[5] For these writers,

---

[4] Recall the formulation in *De l'esprit des lois*, book XI, chap. 4 (1758): "It is an eternal experience that any man who wields power is likely to abuse it; he will proceed until he encounters limits. Who would have guessed? Even virtue needs limits. If power is not to be abused, things must be arranged so that power checks power."

[5] See Jean Charles Léonard Simonde de Sismondi, *Études sur les constitutions des peuples libres* (Brussels, 1836), p. 230: "All institutions must be placed under the guarantee of this disposition."

the memory of the *ancien régime* was decisive. They sought to block any possible return to despotism. Hence more democracy automatically meant greater suspicion of governmental power.[6] Similarly, Benjamin Constant went so far as to argue that liberty depends on the public's systematic opposition to the agents of government. He even spoke of the need for "surveillance in hatred."[7] His true originality lay elsewhere, however: he was the first to distinguish clearly between an "ancient" form of distrust deriving from a refusal to accept the imposition of arbitrary powers on society and a "modern" form stemming from the recognition that even new regimes based on the general will could go astray. Pointing to the "terrifying example" of Robespierre, he noted that France had been shattered in 1793 when "universal trust" in the political process "brought respected men into administrative positions," yet those same men "allowed murderous groups to organize."[8] He therefore argued that limits had to be placed on democratic confidence itself. In 1829, shortly before the charter of the parliamentary monarchy established a regime of the type he had always favored, he praised the proposed text by asserting bluntly that "every [good] constitution is an act of distrust."[9] Liberal distrust can be seen as a form of "preventive power," to borrow an expression of Bertrand de

---

[6] See Mark E. Warren's introduction to *Democracy and Trust* (Cambridge University Press, 1999).

[7] Benjamin Constant, *De la force du gouvernement actuel de la France et de la nécessité de s'y rallier* ([Paris], 1796), p. 66.

[8] *Ibid.*, p. 67.

[9] *Courrier français*, November 5, 1829, in Benjamin Constant, *Recueil d'articles, 1829–1830* (Paris: Champion, 1992), p. 53.

Jouvenel's.[10] It therefore belongs with an anxious and pessimistic view of democracy. Distrust here takes the form of suspicion of the power of the people, fear of its expression, and doubts about universal suffrage.

The second type of distrust can be called democratic. Its purpose is to make sure that elected officials keep their promises and to find ways of maintaining pressure on the government to serve the common good. In this book I shall be concerned with democratic distrust, which is the primary form of distrust in the post-totalitarian era. Democratic distrust can be expressed and organized in a variety of ways, of which I shall emphasize three main types: powers of oversight, forms of prevention, and testing of judgments. Operating within electoral-representative democracy, these three counter-powers describe the broad outlines of what I propose to call *counter-democracy*. By "counter-democracy" I mean not the opposite of democracy but rather a form of democracy that reinforces the usual electoral democracy as a kind of buttress, a democracy of indirect powers disseminated throughout society – in other words, a durable democracy of distrust, which complements the episodic democracy of the usual electoral-representative system. Thus counter-democracy is part of a larger system that also includes legal democratic institutions. It seeks to complement those institutions and extend their influence, to shore them up. Hence counter-democracy should be understood and analyzed as an authentic *political form*, which it is the purpose of this book to describe and evaluate.

---

[10] Bertrand de Jouvenel, "The Means of Contestation," *Government and Opposition* 1, no. 2 (Jan. 1966).

The democratic form of political distrust is especially important because of the erosion of trust in contemporary society. Three factors – scientific, economic, and sociological – account for the rise of the *society of distrust*. Ulrich Beck has shed much light on the scientific factor in his book on "the risk society."[11] He begins from the banal observation that people ceased to feel optimistic about the promise of technology in the 1960s. In the current age of catastrophe and uncertainty, modern industry and technology tend to be associated more with risk than with progress. The risk society is by its very nature wary of the future, yet its citizens are still obliged to place their trust in scientists because they cannot weigh the relevant issues without the aid of specialists. Thus the role of scientists is as problematic as it is indispensable, and this is a source of resentment. Citizens have no alternative but to oblige scientists to explain their thinking and justify their actions. The strategy is thus one of institutionalizing distrust in a positive way, so as to serve as a kind of protective barrier, a guarantee of the interests of society. Beck's critics have called attention to the paradoxical nature of this strategy: "The citizen who wishes to resolve problems that specialists were able neither to foresee nor to avoid finds himself once again at their mercy. His only option is to continue to delegate authority to specialists while at the same time searching for new ways to monitor and oversee their work."[12] Thus progress in science

---

[11] Ulrich Beck, *La Société du risque: Sur la voie d'une autre modernité* (Paris: Aubier, 2001).

[12] Michel Callon, Pierre Lascoumes, and Yannick Barthe, *Agir dans un monde incertain: Essai sur la démocratie technique* (Paris: Éditions du Seuil, 2001), p. 311.

and technology has given rise to specific forms of social distrust. The "precautionary principle" is often invoked in this connection, but the term only partially succeeds in capturing the complexity of the phenomenon (which bears some similarity to the liberal notion of checks and balances in the political domain).

Confidence in macroeconomic management has also waned. If macroeconomics is a science concerned with predicting future behavior, there is no denying that our ability to make economic forecasts has diminished. Medium- and long-term predictions can no longer be relied on, either because the responsible agencies no longer have the technical means to issue them or have been mistaken so often in the past that they have lost all credibility. In France the legislature used to vote on what rate of economic growth it wished to achieve over the next five years. The very idea of setting the growth rate by legislative fiat now seems hopelessly outdated, yet it was a common practice just thirty years ago, when economic planning was still a recognized prerogative of government, at least in France. Today's economy, both more open to the world and more complex than yesterday's, seems far less predictable. Attitudes toward economic forecasting therefore reflect growing distrust as well, and this distrust is amplified by a widespread belief that public policy cannot do much about the economy in any case.

In addition to scientific and economic reasons for distrust, social changes have also heightened suspicion of authority. In a "society of estrangement," to borrow an expression from Michael Walzer, the material bases of social confidence crumble. Individuals trust one another less because they have fewer personal ties. Major comparative studies have shown that diminished trust in others is closely correlated with growing distrust of government. Brazil, which tops the charts in terms of political distrust, is also the country in which indices of interpersonal trust are lowest. The situation in Denmark is exactly the reverse, and the contrast suggests that a high level of confidence in others can be associated with a lower degree of suspicion of government.[13] It is significant, moreover, that tolerance of corruption also increases as disenchantment with democracy does.[14] Thus democratic distrust coincides with and reinforces structural distrust. Taking all of these factors into account suggests that contemporary society can be described as a "society of generalized distrust."[15] This type of society forms the social backdrop to

[13] Only 2.8 percent of Brazilians agree with the statement that "you can trust most people," compared with 66.5 percent of Danes (for France, the figure is 22.2 percent, toward the bottom of the list). See Ronald Inglehart *et al.*, *Human Beliefs and Values: A Cross-Cultural Sourcebook Based on the 1999–2002 Values Surveys* (Mexico: Siglo XXI, 2004).

[14] See Alejandro Moreno, "Corruption and Democracy: A Cultural Assessment," in R. Inglehart, ed., *Human Values and Social Change: Findings from the Values Surveys* (Leyden and Boston: Brill, 2003).

[15] For France, see the survey Euro RSCG, *La Société de défiance généralisée: Enquête sur les nouveaux rapports de force et les enjeux relationnels dans la société française* (July 2004). No doubt the perception of growing distrust has fueled the recent interest of sociologists and philosophers in the concept of trust. See especially the work of Russell Hardin, Diego Gambetta, and Mark E. Warren. In French, see Vincent Mangematin and Christian Thuderoz, *Des mondes de confiance: Un concept à l'épreuve de la réalité sociale* (Paris: CNRS, 2003), and, with Denis Harrison, *La Confiance: Approches économiques et sociologiques* (Montreal: Gaëtan Morin, 1999).

the transformation of democracy whose history will be recounted in what follows.

The three dimensions of counter-democracy

Let us begin by looking at powers of oversight. In order to understand the nature of such powers and trace them back to their inception, we must first recall that the idea of popular sovereignty found historical expression in two different ways. The first was the right to vote, the right of citizens to choose their own leaders. This was the most direct expression of the democratic principle. But the power to vote periodically and thus bestow legitimacy on an elected government was almost always accompanied by a wish to exercise a more permanent form of control over the government thus elected. People recognized immediately that the sanction of the ballot box was insufficient to compel elected representatives to keep their promises to the voters. For a while, to be sure, it was thought that representatives could be tethered by instructions issued by their constituents in the form of an "imperative mandate." But this idea proved to be incompatible with the idea of open parliamentary debate, since there can be no genuine debate unless there is freedom to change one's mind after hearing opposing arguments. Hence the imperative mandate was abandoned in favor of more indirect methods of control. If it was utopian to think that the views of representatives would always fully coincide with the views of their constituents, the latter could nevertheless maintain effective pressure on the former in a less direct, more external manner. Democracies thus continually searched for "counter-powers" that could correct their course and enhance their stability. The duality of power and counter-power is strikingly evident in the French Revolution. Already in 1789 a word had emerged to denote a complementary form of sovereignty that was seen as essential to achieving the ideal of a government embodying the "general will": *surveillance*. Perpetually vigilant, the people were to oversee the work of the government. This diligent oversight was celebrated as the main remedy for dysfunctional institutions and in particular as the cure for what might be called "representative entropy" (by which I mean the degradation of the relation between voters and their representatives).

Later, during the Terror, the term "surveillance" lost its luster when it came to be associated with tyranny exercised by revolutionary clubs and committees and was subsequently stricken from the political lexicon. Yet if the word disappeared, the thing remained. In one form or another, civil society continued to inspect, monitor, investigate, and evaluate the actions of government. Indeed, the powers of oversight expanded considerably. Although the institutions of democracy have remained more or less stable for two centuries (with respect to the conception of representation, the exercise of responsibility, and the role ascribed to elections), the powers of oversight have grown and diversified. I shall be looking in due course at three primary modes of oversight: *vigilance, denunciation,* and *evaluation.* Each of these has helped to expand the idea of legitimacy beyond that conferred by voting. This expanded legitimacy rests on reputations, of both individuals and regimes. Reputation thus became another of those "invisible institutions" upon which trust is ultimately based. These primary modes of oversight share a number of essential characteristics. First, they are permanent (whereas elections are sporadic). Second, they can be exercised by individuals as well as organizations. Third, they enhance the power of society to influence the action of government (it was John Stuart Mill who observed that no one can do everything but everyone can keep an eye on what is being done). For all these reasons, the "democracy of oversight" continues to flourish.

Society's powers of sanction and prevention have also increased, and these constitute a second fundamental form of distrust built into the very structure of what I am calling counter-democracy. In *The Spirit of the Laws*, Montesquieu drew a fundamental distinction between the ability to act and the ability to prevent. The importance of this distinction grew as citizens discovered the limits of the imperative mandate as a means of achieving their goals. Recognizing their inability to compel governments to take specific actions or decisions, citizens reasserted their influence by developing new sanctions on government. Little by little, they surrounded the "positive democracy" of elections and legal institutions with what might be called the "negative sovereignty" of civil society. The primary reason for this development was "technical": blocking government action yielded tangible, visible results. Success in blocking passage of an undesired bill was plain for everyone to see, whereas the effectiveness of pressure to implement a desired policy was generally subject to more complex and controversial judgment. Opposition to a specific measure could result in clear victory, whereas authorization to proceed on a certain course left ultimate success at the mercy of future imponderables and the vagaries of execution. The democracy of imperative mandates sought only to enforce general promises or commitments, but negative democracy aimed at specific results.

From a sociological point of view, it is also perfectly clear that negative coalitions are easier to organize than positive majorities. Negative coalitions can tolerate their own contradictions more easily. Indeed, it is their heterogeneity that explains why they are easier to organize and more likely to succeed. Reactive majorities do not need to be coherent in order to play their role. Their power is enhanced because within the order of oppositions to which they give expression, the intensity of reactions plays an essential role. In the street, in protest through the media, and in symbolic expression, something more than arithmetic is involved. By contrast, true social action majorities are much more difficult to put together. Indeed, by their very nature they presuppose either a passive consensus or a positive and deliberate agreement. They cannot be based on equivocation or ambiguity, and in this respect they differ from most electoral majorities and still more from reactive coalitions. Hence they are more fragile and volatile. Experience shows that a careless misstatement can lose a politician votes more easily than an original and courageous stand can win them. Increasingly, therefore, popular sovereignty manifests itself as a power to refuse, both in periodic elections and in repeated reactions to government decisions. A new "democracy of rejection" has thus superimposed itself on the original "democracy of proposition." The power of the people is a veto power. Democratic government is no longer defined solely as a procedure of authorization and legitimation. Its structure is essentially defined by permanent confrontation of various types of veto from different social groups and economic and political forces. This has led some scholars to propose that political regimes today are characterized not so much by their institutional structure as such (presidential vs. parliamentary, bipartisan vs. multipartisan, etc.) as by the way in which the conditions of political action depend on the ability of various actors to issue a veto.

A third factor in the constitution of counter-democracy is the advent of the *people as judge*. The judicialization of politics is the most obvious manifestation of this. It is as though citizens hope to obtain from a judicial process of some sort what they despair of obtaining from the ballot box. Judicialization should be seen against the background of declining government responsiveness to citizen demands. As *responsiveness* declines, the desire for *accountability* increases. *Democracy of confrontation* gives way to *democracy of accusation*. Over the past twenty years, it has become commonplace to remark on the increasing prominence of judges in the political order. Yet this observation comprehends only a small part of the problem. One needs to compare the respective properties of voting and judgment. The recent preference for judgment makes sense only in relation to the specific properties of decisions of the judicial type. To subject action to judicial scrutiny is to impose certain standards of proof, certain forms of theatricality, and certain rules of evidence. Judging action in this way has gradually come to be seen as a metapolitical form that many people believe is preferable to elections because the results are more tangible.

The original democratic social contract envisioned the people as voters. Increasingly, voters have been replaced as political actors by the three metaphorical figures we have just discussed: the people as watchdogs, the people as veto-wielders, and the people as judges. Sovereignty has thus come to be exercised indirectly, in ways not specified by constitutional rules. The sovereignty of which I speak is indirect in the sense that it manifests itself as a series of *effects*; it does not arise out of any formal authority, nor is it expressed through explicit decisions that might be characterized as political. If we are to understand the social appropriation of power in all its complexity, we must look at both electoral-representative democracy and the counter-democracy of indirect powers. When we do this, we see that the customary opposition between real and formal democracy is not very illuminating in this larger context. The distinction between direct and representative forms of government also loses much of its richness. These narrow categories must give way to a more diverse understanding of *democratic activity*. It then becomes possible to describe a broader grammar of government. Rousseau sought in the *Social Contract* to "complicate" the definition of citizenship. In addition to the mere right to vote, he therefore included the rights to voice an opinion, to propose, to divide, and to discuss.[16] In a classic essay, Albert Hirschman more recently suggested extending the vocabulary of collective action by distinguishing between *exit*, *voice*, and

---

[16] *Du contrat social*, book IV, chap. 1. In the seventh of the *Lettres écrites de la montagne* (Paris: Gallimard-Pléiade, 1959), p. 833, he makes a similar point: "*To deliberate, voice an opinion, and vote* are three quite different things among which the French do not distinguish adequately. *To deliberate* is to weigh the pro and the con; *to voice an opinion* is to state and justify one's opinion; *to vote* is to give one's suffrage when nothing remains to be done but collect the votes."

loyalty.[17] Taking counter-democracy into consideration suggests that it might be useful to extend this terminology by adding the terms vigilance, assessment, pressure through revelation, obstruction, and judgment. A primary objective of this book is to describe the history and investigate the theory of these various manifestations of counter-democracy.

The myth of the passive citizen

If we adopt the counter-democratic perspective, we can see the question of political participation in a new light. The old refrain of "democratic disenchantment" needs to be scrutinized anew. To be sure, all indicators of citizen trust in political institutions show a marked decline.[18] The rising rate of abstention is another observable sign of disaffection.[19] But caution is in order when interpreting these indicators.[20] It is

[17] Albert O. Hirschman, *Exit, Voice, and Loyalty: Responses to Decline in Firms, Organizations, and States* (Cambridge, MA: Harvard University Press, 1970).

[18] For a recent overview, see Mattei Dogan, ed., *Political Mistrust and the Discrediting of Politicians* (Leyden and Boston: Brill, 2005).

[19] See, for example, the data collected in Jacques Capdevielle, *Démocratie: La Panne* (Paris: Textuel, 2005), and Mark N. Franklin *et al.*, *Voter Turnout and the Dynamics of Electoral Competition in Established Democracies since 1945* (Cambridge University Press, 2004).

[20] Abstention rates have to be looked at over the long run, since these may vary according to the nature of the election. For instance, in the revolutionary years in France, rates varied considerably (Michelet observed that "the people stayed home" in 1791 after turning out en masse in 1790). The phenomenon of "electoral intermittence" is also key. One ought perhaps to speak of "trajectories of participation." On the French case, see François Héran, "Voter toujours, parfois … ou jamais," in Bruno

important to set them against a broader understanding of the ways in which citizen involvement has changed over time. For some time now, political scientists have tried to identify unconventional forms of participation, which may have increased in number as the rate of participation in elections declined. The number of people participating in strikes or demonstrations, signing petitions, and expressing collective solidarity in other ways suggests that the age is not one of political apathy and that the notion that people are increasingly withdrawing into the private sphere is not correct.[21] It is better to say that citizenship has changed in nature rather than declined. There has been simultaneous diversification of the *range, forms,* and *targets* of political expression. As political parties eroded, various types of advocacy groups and associations developed. Major institutions of representation and bargaining saw their roles diminish as ad hoc organizations proliferated. Citizens now have many ways of expressing their grievances and complaints other than voting. The increasing abstention rate and the phenomenon of declining

Cautrès and Nonna Mayer, eds., *Le Nouveau Désordre électoral: Les Leçons du 21 avril 2002,* as well as François Clanché, "La participation électorale au printemps 2002. De plus en plus de votants intermittents," *Insee Première* 877 (January 2003). Political scientists also distinguish between abstainers who are "in the game" and others who are "out."

[21] The literature on the subject is vast. See, for example, Pippa Norris, *Democratic Phoenix: Reinventing Political Activism* (Cambridge University Press, 2002). See also Pascale Perrineau, ed., *L'Engagement politique: Déclin ou mutation?* (Paris: Presses de la Fondation Nationale des Sciences Politiques, 1994), and Lionel Arnaud and Christine Guionnet, eds., *Les Frontières du politique: Enquête sur les processus de politisation et de dépolitisation* (Rennes: Presses Universitaires de Rennes, 2005).

19

trust must be studied in a broader context that takes these new forms of democratic activity into account. To be sure, voting is the most visible and institutionalized expression of citizenship. It has long been the symbol of political participation and civic equality. But the idea of participation is complex. It involves three dimensions of interaction between the people and the political sphere: expression, involvement, and intervention. *Democracy of expression* means that society has a voice, that collective sentiments can be articulated, that judgments of the government and its actions can be formulated, and that demands can be issued. *Democracy of involvement* encompasses the whole range of means by which citizens can join together and concert their action to achieve a common world. *Democracy of intervention* refers to all the forms of collective action by means of which a desired result can be obtained.

Democracy revolves around these three forms of political activity. Elections are distinctive in that they superimpose these various modes of civic existence (which also correspond to different "moments" of public life). The vote is indubitably the epitome of political involvement, the most organized and visible form of political activity. In the golden age of electoral participation, the all-encompassing, integrative aspect of the vote was inseparable from its "identity" aspect: voting at that time was not so much the expression of an individual preference as an expression of membership in a certain collectivity.[22] This feature of voting has been stressed

[22] In the 1960s, political scientists established the so-called "Michigan paradigm," named for the university in which the research was conducted, by showing that voters choose on the basis not of their

by numerous writers ranging from André Siegfried to the political sociologists of the 1960s. Democracy itself was long associated with the protracted struggle for universal suffrage as both means and symbol. More recent transformations of democracy must be interpreted in this light. Although electoral democracy has undoubtedly eroded, democratic expression, involvement, and intervention have developed and gained strength. Hence in many respects the notion of "the passive citizen" is a myth.[23] The transformations of political activity that I have in mind have now been noted by numerous scholars and political activists. Theorists have been slow to conceptualize these changes, however. Evidence of this can be seen in the vagueness of the terminology used to describe them. Over the past decade, for instance, political scientists have written of the advent of "unconventional" forms of politics, of a new "protest politics," and of "civil citizenship" (a term applied to any number of novel forms of political intervention and response). Political activists, who are more directly implicated in these changes, have also adopted a new vocabulary: "agitated left," "nongovernmental politics,"[24] and "politics of the governed,"[25] to name a few. The terms "anti-power" and

political knowledge, which is minimal, but rather of partisan identities that they acquire early in life.

[23] Note, too, that citizens are making greater efforts to inform themselves. See the data in Étienne Schweisguth, "La dépolitisation en question," in Gérard Grunberg, Nonna Mayer, and Paul M. Sniderman, *La Démocratie à l'épreuve* (Paris: Presses de Sciences-Po, 2002), pp. 56–57.

[24] In France, for example, see the journals *Multitudes* and *Vacarme*.

[25] See Partha Chatterjee, *The Politics of the Governed* (New York: Columbia University Press, 2004).

"counter-power" are also gaining currency,[26] while at the same time many activists are taking a fresh look at Michel Foucault's work on "governmentality." The concept of counter-democracy is to be understood in this context as well. It may provide these diverse worlds with a common language and a certain intellectual coherence, a systematic way of describing the manifold transformation of contemporary democracy in the context of a comprehensive theory of democratic politics.

Depoliticization or the unpolitical?

If what we are witnessing is not depoliticization, in the sense of diminished interest in public affairs and declining citizen activity, it remains true that something has indeed changed in our relation to the political. The nature of this change is different from what is usually suggested, however. The problem today is not one of citizen passivity but rather of what I shall call *l'impolitique*,[27] the *un*political, by which I mean a failure to develop a comprehensive understanding of problems associated with the organization of a shared world. The distinguishing characteristic common to the various examples of counter-democracy that we shall be examining is

---

[26] See Miguel Benasayag and Diego Sztulwark, *Du contre-pouvoir: De la subjectivité contestataire à la construction de contre-pouvoirs*, 2nd edn (Paris: La Découverte, 2002), and John Holloway, *Change the World Without Taking Power* (London: Pluto Press, 2002).

[27] I use the term literally, in a sense different from that set forth in Robert Esposito, *Catégories de l'impolitique* (Paris: Éditions du Seuil, 2005). On other uses of this term, see Etienne Balibar, "Qu'est-ce que la philosophie politique? Notes pour un topique," *Actuel Marx* 28 (2nd Semester 2000).

the increase in the distance between civil society and institutions. In each instance we find a sort of *counter-policy*, which relies on monitoring, opposition, and limitation of government powers, the conquest of which is no longer the top priority of government opponents. Counter-policy manifests itself in two ways. The initial consequence of counter-political strategies and actions is to dissolve signs of a *shared world*. Reactive in essence, these strategies and actions cannot sustain or structure collective projects. The distinctive feature of this sort of unpolitical counter-democracy is that it combines democratic *activity* with non-political *effects*. Hence it does not fall within the usual classification of regime types; it is a novel type, neither liberal nor republican, neither representative government nor direct democracy.

A second consequence of the various forms of counter-democracy is to make what is going on more difficult to perceive and still harder to interpret. But visibility and legibility are two essential properties of the political. Politics does not exist unless a range of actions can be incorporated into a single narrative and represented in a single public arena. The development of counter-democracy is therefore both complex and problematic. Complex because it combines positive elements of growth in social power with populist-reactive temptations. Problematic because the evolution toward "civil democracy" leads to fragmentation and dissemination where coherence and comprehensiveness are needed. It was my awareness of the problematic aspects of the phenomenon that led me to coin what might at first sight seem to be a rather shocking neologism: *counter-democracy*. Indeed, the disturbing connotations of the word call attention to the ambiguities inherent in the practical applications of distrust. Social distrust can encourage a salutary civic vigilance and thus oblige government to pay greater heed to social demands, yet it can also encourage destructive forms of denigration and negativity. Counter-democracy can reinforce democracy, but it can also contradict it. In some respects, this book "rehabilitates" distrust, on the grounds that it can be both deeply liberal and deeply democratic. But the rehabilitation is lucid, and attentive to the possibility that things may go wrong. This inherent ambivalence of distrust is to my mind the deep reason for the disenchantment that is a common feature of today's democracies. This disenchantment is not simply a question of disappointment that could potentially be overcome (by, say, procedural improvements in the system of representation). Rather, it reflects the impasse to which the combination of the democratic with the unpolitical leads. This insight forms the basis of the reflections that follow on the advent of a new democratic era.

Reinterpreting the history of democracy

The approach I am proposing also leads to a new way of looking at the history of democracy. The various forms of indirect power mentioned thus far are at once pre-democratic and post-democratic. They are post-democratic in the sense that they arise in response to promises unkept by the representative governments established in response to the struggle for liberty in the Netherlands, Great Britain, the United States, and France in the seventeenth and eighteenth centuries. But they are also pre-democratic, because the exercise of the powers of oversight and resistance often represented a first step toward human emancipation. For example, the right to resist tyranny was formulated in the Middle Ages, long before anyone could envision any form of popular sovereignty. Similarly, governments were subjected to oversight and judgment long before there was any notion of choosing them by election. So perhaps it is time to move beyond traditional linear histories of democracy based on the notion of gradual progress toward an ideal type, of a slow transition from subjection to full autonomy. In fact, the "old" and the "new," "liberalism" and "democracy," informal social power and regular institutions have always coexisted. If counter-democracy preceded electoral-representative democracy, their two histories are intimately intertwined, and we will seek to unravel the complexities of their relationship. Indeed, the social and institutional histories of democracy cannot be separated. "Social" in principle, counter-democracy is in fact a material force, a form of practical resistance, a direct response. Whereas electoral-representative democracy is governed by slow institutional rhythms, counter-democracy is permanent and subject to no institutional constraint. In a sense it is democratic life unmediated.

In this approach it is essential to explore the connections between history and political theory, as I tried to do in my previous books. As I have often stressed, history is to be understood as a *laboratory of the present* and not just a tool for illuminating its background. Living democracy never measures itself against an ideal model; rather, it seeks to solve problems. Hence we should be wary of the idea that there was once a clearly formulated yet overtly challenged "original model" of democracy. If we begin with the complexity of the real and its insuperable contradictions, we gain a better sense of politics "in itself." We come closer to its core and are therefore in a better position to understand how it came to be. History serves theory not just as a repository of examples but as a testing ground for representations of the world. This is the source of my ambition, which is to combine the active curiosity of the historian with the rigor of the political philosopher.

To see democracy as a testing ground is even more essential in the study of counter-democracy. While textbook descriptions may suffice for institutions, the powers of oversight and obstruction can only be appreciated in action. The idea of looking at both faces of democracy as vital, practical realities is not just of methodological significance. It also allows us to approach comparative politics in a new way. When democracy is studied in a classically normative perspective, no *useful* comparison is really possible. One can only record successes and failures, measure relative achievements, and establish typologies. The danger in this is that we risk mistaking particular values for universal and making sacred cows of specific mechanisms. Conversely, if one begins with *problems* that democracy must resolve, such as the tension between the sociological political principles of representation,[28] it is much easier to investigate different national and historical experiences in a comparative framework. The virtues of a comparative approach are even greater when it comes to the study of counter-democratic phenomena. Counter-democracy, as I mentioned earlier, is both

[28] See my *Le Peuple introuvable*.

pre- and post-democratic. It exists both as pure counter-power and as what might be called "complementary" power. By broadening our view in this way, we also "de-Westernize" it. Oversight, obstruction, and judgment are practices that exist – and existed in the past – almost everywhere. Thus a general comparative approach across space and time becomes possible. The desire to improve our understanding of the present is thus inseparable from a determination to think globally about humanity's long struggle to build a free political society.

Part 1

Overseeing democracy

The idea of a power of surveillance or oversight has a long history. The need for surveillance was invoked early in the French Revolution in reaction to the tendency of representatives to claim autonomy for themselves, to transform themselves into "a kind of *de facto* aristocracy," to borrow Mirabeau's celebrated phrase. A member of the Constituent Assembly must have had the idea in mind when he spoke of "the nation's need for an overseer of the very representatives of the nation."[1] Elsewhere, a militant editorialist for *La Bouche de fer* admonished "friends of liberty" to see to it "that eternal oversight protects us from the dangers we would face if we placed all our trust in our ministers."[2] An influential woman of letters of the period made a similar point: "Representative government soon becomes the most corrupt of all if the people cease to scrutinize its representatives."[3] The watchful eye of the people became a central image of the revolution, reproduced on countless medallions and seals and incorporated into any number of the engraved allegories of popular power that reflected the spirit

[1] *Archives parlementaires de France* (cited hereafter as *AP*), 1st series, vol. 9, p. 61.
[2] Supplement to no. 70, June 21, 1791, p. 1.
[3] Mme Roland, letter of July 31, 1791, in *Lettres de Madame Roland* (Paris, 1902), vol. II, p. 354. The French, she went on, "sacrifice everything to trust, which is how liberty is lost. True, this trustfulness is infinitely convenient: it eliminates the need to observe, to think, and to judge."

of the time. The overseeing counter-power was expected to limit the dysfunctions of the representative system and reduce disappointments due to the difficulty of establishing trust. It was understood as a way to transform distrust into an active democratic virtue. "Patriotic legislators, do not speak ill of distrust," Robespierre contended. "Whatever you may think, distrust is the guardian of the people's rights. It is to the deep emotion of liberty what jealousy is to love."[4] The French revolutionary experience thus expanded the vocabulary of political science to include this new counter-power.

The idea of surveillance was associated at the time with another imperative: namely, the consecration of the new trope of social generality, designated by the term "public opinion." Calls for surveillance of government by public opinion became common in this period because the term and its associated images were useful for resolving the great problem of popular sovereignty. "Public opinion" gave substance and legibility to Rousseau's powerful abstraction. The idea of surveillance brought sovereignty closer to the people. It became something one could appropriate, instrumentalize, and strip of its glacial majesty, just as the concept of "public opinion" made society, the new sovereign, tangible and familiar. No longer were the sovereign people a remote Olympian presence, invisible and silent.[5] The ordinary conversation of the man in the street and the commentary of countless newspapers made public opinion palpable and direct, the normal form of public

---

[4] Quoted in Lucien Jaume, *Le Discours jacobin et la démocratie* (Paris: Fayard, 1989), p. 197.
[5] On this point see my *Le Peuple introuvable.*

expression. "The word *people* is an empty word if it refers to anything other than public opinion," wrote one important political commentator.[6] But for the expression of public opinion, he insisted, "the people are without a name, they are a purely metaphysical being, not even a body without a soul but a corpse." To invoke public opinion was to resolve the problem of how the general will made itself known. For the men of 1789, public opinion was a power that manifested itself always and everywhere without being represented or instituted in any particular place. Hence it became the essential manifestation of the people as an *active and permanent presence.*

Although the word *surveillance* came to be associated (through the Committee of Surveillance) with the excesses of the Terror and was ultimately abandoned, the idea and related practices remained. Surveillance constitutes a hidden and protean aspect of modern politics, whose history I want to trace and whose forms I want to analyze in detail. I should say at the outset that the realm of power that emerges from this analysis is quite different from that described by the social science of the 1970s. Since the pioneering work of Michel Foucault, the notion of a "society of surveillance" has usually been applied to societies in which authorities have relied upon a wide range of methods to enhance their dominion over ever more intimate aspects of existence. The image of the "panopticon," which Foucault borrowed from Jeremy Bentham, stands as a symbol of certain carceral forms and methods. The idea that power derives from a variety of surveillance technologies dispersed throughout society has come to be widely accepted as an

---

[6] Fréron, *L'Orateur du peuple*, no. XXXVI, 7 frimaire, Year II, p. 284.

accurate description of reality. The use of computers, urban surveillance cameras, and other advanced devices has lent credence to this Orwellian vision, as has the development of modern management systems, which subject the behavior of individuals to ever closer scrutiny. Yet we should not on account of all this underestimate the inverse phenomenon, namely, *the surveillance of power by society.* Counter-democracy employs control mechanisms similar to those described by Foucault, but in the service of society. Vigilance, denunciation, and evaluation are its three principal modalities.

1

Vigilance, denunciation, evaluation

Vigilance

To be watchful, alert, and on guard are essential attributes of citizenship – attributes present from the beginning, since the ancient ideal of citizenship would have been unimaginable if reduced to mere periodic participation in elections. Vigilance first of all means monitoring: permanent close scrutiny of the actions of government. "A free people," wrote Anacharsis Cloots during the French Revolution, "is an argus. It sees everything, hears everything, is everywhere, and never sleeps."[1] Vigilance compensates for the arrhythmia of the ballot box. The people are always at the ready, and the "dormant people" imagined by Locke and Rousseau become a giant ready to pounce. Vigilance in this sense means presence, attentiveness. The political language of the 1960s and 70s favored the term "mobilization": a militant group was "mobilized" if it was prepared to play its role effectively. Mobilization was not so much a precondition of action as a way of describing a type of presence in the world, a kind of attentiveness to public affairs. Such a disposition is not merely a property of the agent who exhibits it: it enters into the construction of a *global property* of the public sphere.

---

[1] Anacharsis Cloots, *Écrits révolutionnaires (1790–1794)* (Paris: Champ Libre, 1979), p. 110.

33

Vigilance should also be seen as a *mode of action*. Though it "produces" nothing by itself, it cannot be dismissed as mere passivity. It defines a particular form of political intervention that involves neither decision-making nor exercise of the will. It rather creates possibilities and sets limits by imposing structure on a general field of action. In a stimulating essay, the philosopher and Sinologist François Jullien used these categories to analyze what he believes to be the essential difference between the Western and Chinese ways of envisioning action.[2] In the West, the primary task from Machiavelli to Schopenhauer was to establish an empire of the subject: a man in charge of every situation, imposing his will on the world, and treating the world as a field for experiment, a place in which to overcome resistance in a project of radical self-realization. Here, action is understood as a clash between two worlds, a matter of conquest and domestication. The Chinese vision is quite different. There, the essence of action lies in attentiveness to the world, which allows for exploiting its contradictions and capitalizing on the way things are. The exercise of power is not a display of strength but rather a readiness to be guided by minute attention to the terrain and to exploit every opportunity to the full. Rather than a psychology of the will, Jullien writes, the Chinese preferred a "phenomenology of effect." It is easy to see how this difference gave rise to different ideas of strategy. In the West, Clausewitzian confrontation leading to decisive battle; in the East, the art of avoiding battle taught by Sun Tzu, the aim being to exploit the potential in every

---

[2] François Jullien, *Traité de l'efficacité* (Paris: Grasset, 1997), and *Conférence sur l'efficacité* (Paris: Presses Universitaires de France, 2005).

situation discreetly but to the full. From this basic difference follow different ideas of effectiveness and success and, ultimately, different visions of the political. In contrast to the western art of governing from above, imposing control through force, we have the prospect of almost invisible government from below, where the aim is to induce others to strengthen one's own position by shaping the framework within which they act.

Whether this comparison between East and West is valid is a question that must be left to historians. Nevertheless, we can treat the distinction as an ideal type defining two possible modes of political action. Indeed, traces of the second or eastern mode exist also in the West. It would not be difficult, for example, to show that European liberal thought in the early nineteenth century had many of the characteristics that Jullien regards as specific to Chinese thought.[3] Harking back to my earlier discussion, one can view the distinction between traditional political decision-making and vigilance in Jullien's terms. My "vigilance" corresponds to his "avoidance of battle," yet it is not without political effects or influence on public affairs. To put the point in more contemporary terms, one might also say that we have here two contrasting types of control: "the police patrol" versus "the fire alarm," to borrow

---

[3] See my treatment of "internal government" and the "government of minds" in *Le Moment Guizot* (Paris: Gallimard, 1984). On the origins of the liberal theory of governability, see Michel Foucault, *Naissance de la biopolitique* (Paris: Gallimard-Seuil, 2004) and *Sécurité, territoire, population* (Paris: Gallimard-Seuil, 2004). In the latter work, Foucault develops the idea of "pastoral power" and "individualizing power," defined by functions of watchfulness and surveillance (pp. 130–134). Note that he also remarks that to govern is to "guide the conduct of others."

metaphors from a study by two political scientists.[4] The "police patrol" corresponds to the standard conception of public action as something that is delegated to designated agents. It is a direct, centralized, voluntaristic form of control. By contrast, the "fire alarm" is a decentralized system, which relies on the vigilance of the community at large and not just professionals. Before the firemen can be called in, civilians must sound the alarm. The firefighters' effectiveness depends on the dissemination of vigilance. It reflects the state of society itself. Yet the system's results are tangible and perhaps better than institutionalized authorities could achieve by themselves.[5]

The history of the word "surveillance" is an interesting one. It first appeared in the late 1760s in the economic writings of the Physiocrats. Baudeau and Dupont de Nemours used it for the first time in 1768 to characterize a mode of action and regulation distinct from both *police* action and *market* equilibrium: "There is surely a form of attentiveness that ought to command authority, which seeks to preserve sound order and public tranquility. It aims to prevent disputes, commotions, thefts, and assaults in the marketplace. For this, *surveillance* is essential."[6] The surveillance state they hoped for was an active state, not a laissez-faire state. It defined a novel type of power

---

[4] Matthew D. McCubbins and Thomas Schwartz, "Congressional Oversight Overlooked: Police Patrols versus Fire Alarms," *American Journal of Political Science* 28 (1984).

[5] This is the conclusion of the article cited in n. 4.

[6] Abbé Nicolas Baudeau and Pierre-Samuel Dupon de Nemours, *Avis au Peuple sur son premier besoin, ou Petits traités économiques*, in *Ephémérides du citoyen*, vol. V, 1768. The word *surveillance* is italicized in the text.

based on *attention* rather than intervention. It was a watchdog state (and not the passive "night watchman" of second-hand liberal imagery). Its surveillance was "constant and comprehensive."[7] Indirect government thus instituted a third type of regulation, that of a guiding hand between the invisible hand of the market and the iron hand of traditional public sovereignty. The essential functions of the new sovereign power that the Physiocrats sought to establish were "to watch, keep, and protect."[8] In discreet fashion it sought to put the world in order.

The Physiocratic ideal would be put into practice by early nineteenth-century liberals such as Guizot, who theorized about new approaches to governability.[9] It had already been adopted to some degree by civil society, however. As early as 1789, the term "surveillance" had been taken up by popular societies and journalists. It was obvious that vigilance had democratic potential, because everyone was involved. The Revolution therefore celebrated the power of surveillance. The Club des Cordeliers, which was centrally involved in the political and intellectual movement to find a living form of popular sovereignty, characterized itself as a "society of suspicion and surveillance." The Cercle Social, a club in which such figures as Brissot, Condorcet, and Lanthenas were involved in the period 1790–1791, proposed to become an agent of "anxious

---

[7] Abbé Baudeau, *Première introduction à la philosophie économique ou analyse des États policés* (1771), in *Physiocrates* (Paris: Édition Daire, 1846), vol. II, p. 683.

[8] Guillaume-François Le Trosne, *De l'ordre social* (Paris, 1777), p. 88.

[9] See especially the arguments developed by Guizot in *Des moyens de gouvernement et d'opposition dans l'état actuel de la France* (Paris, 1821).

daily vigilance." Many believed that because surveillance was exercised directly, it might be a way to compensate for the weakness and clumsiness of the representative system. "Public opinion is law of a kind that every individual can administer," noted *Le Tribun du peuple*.[10] Throughout the revolutionary decade, one idea was tirelessly repeated: that the defects of the representative system would be corrected if not eliminated by a vigilant press. The Cercle Social advanced this theory in one of its earliest manifestos: "The power of surveillance and opinion (the fourth censorial power, which is not discussed) is the essential element of national sovereignty, because individuals can exercise it by themselves, *without representation*, and without danger to the body politic."[11] The ordinary powers (executive, legislative, judicial, and even administrative) were exercised by a small number of individuals chosen in various ways, but the surveillance power gave "King People" a permanent, visible presence. It was also believed to be the most effective of the powers. When Brissot considered the various ways in which citizens could influence legislators, he placed the "censorial power" in the front rank, attaching less importance to the constraint of the ballot box, whereas later theorists of representative government would treat elections as paramount.[12]

---

[10] January 1, 1790, p. iii.

[11] Reprinted in *La Bouche de fer*, no. 1 (Oct. 1790), p. 9. "Executive power to the elected, administrative power to the elected, representative power to the elected, but censorial power to every individual," insisted *Le Tribun du peuple*, March 1790, vol. II, p. 134.

[12] See *Le Patriote français*, no. 45, August 2, 1791, p. 232.

Although the French Revolution extolled a vigilance of active citizens comparable to that found in ancient republics, it was only much later that such vigilance became commonplace. Indeed, along with the traditional *civic vigilance* of engaged citizens concerned with the public good, there emerged what one might call *regulatory vigilance*, the importance of which increased with time. Civic vigilance was directly political and took a variety of forms: interventions by the press, associations, unions, petitions, strikes, etc. The role of such vigilant citizens was to sound the alarm and protest, especially in times of crisis or conflict. Later, however, another, more diffuse form of vigilance emerged. It took the form of constant evaluation and criticism of the actions of government by the governed. Such evaluation is decentralized in manner and applies to public policy of all types. All areas of governmental action are subject to constant scrutiny.[13] Regulatory vigilance operates through a variety of channels, from public opinion polls to published reports, from commissions of experts to journalistic exposés. In recent years, the growth of the Internet has made it easier to transmit this information to a broad public. Regulatory vigilance focuses the public's attention. It is a quasi-institution – invisible and decentralized, to be sure, but still capable of exerting significant influence on

---

[13] In this connection, Robert Goodin has developed an interesting comparison between the elected representative and the "inspector," each embodying a different way of communicating social interests. See "The Good Inspector," in Eugene Bardach and Robert A. Kagan, *Going by the Book: The Problem of Regulatory Unreasonableness* (Philadelphia: Temple University Press, 1982).

outcomes.[14] Political scientists speak of an agenda-setting function: even if the media have little ability to change people's basic beliefs, they can play a decisive role in setting the agenda of social debate.[15] Vigilance thus helps to define the political arena and establish government priorities.[16] Hence it turns out to be more effective than many types of institutionalized participation. By exercising vigilance, the public helps to regulate political decision-making (Christopher Wlezien uses the metaphor of a thermostat to describe this process).[17]

What this new kind of vigilance makes possible is a transition to what I will call *diffuse democracy*. Change comes about not through broader political participation as such but through the advent of new forms of *social attentiveness*. If we wish to understand democratization as a process transcending the boundaries of any one nation, this transformation is a crucial factor to take into account. Indeed, practices that can be grouped under the head "vigilance" serve increasingly as levers of intervention for citizens who do not yet constitute a

[14] See Bryan D. Jones, *Reconceiving Decision-Making in Democratic Politics: Attention, Choice and Public Policy* (The University of Chicago Press, 1994).

[15] See the fundamental articles by Roger W. Cobb and Charles D. Elder, "The Politics of Agenda-Building: An Alternative Perspective for Modern Democratic Theory," *The Journal of Politics* 33, no. 4 (Nov. 1971), and Maxwell McCombs and Donald Shaw, "The Agenda-Setting Function of Mass-Media," *Public Opinion Quarterly* 36 (1972).

[16] For a survey of recent literature on this question, see Jacques Gerstlé, "Démocratie représentative, réactivité politique et imputabilité," *Revue française de science politique* 53, no. 6 (Dec. 2003).

[17] See Christopher Wlezien, "The Public as Thermostat: Dynamics of Preferences for Spending," *American Journal of Political Science* 39, no. 4 (1995).

true body politic. One of the most famous decisions of the European Court of Justice strongly emphasized this point: "The vigilance of private individuals interested in protecting their rights establishes an effective control" on governments.[18] The figure of the "vigilant citizen" covers a much wider range than that of the "voter citizen."

Denunciation

A second mode of surveillance, in addition to vigilance, is *denunciation*. Once again it was the French Revolution that introduced this term to the lexicon of civic action. Think of Marat's impassioned diatribes in his newspaper, *L'Ami du peuple*, which included daily lists of enemies of the fatherland and conspirators against the republic. And of course the Terror, with its systematization of suspicion and insistence that it was a public duty to inform on "traitors," turned denunciation into a powerful tool of repression. Alongside these pathological manifestations, however, the Revolution also witnessed the introduction of quieter, more routine forms of denunciation. Revolutionaries celebrated what they called "the electricity of denunciation" because it was seen as one aspect of an important form of civic participation, namely, the monitoring of government actions by way of publicity.[19] Mirabeau himself extolled

---

[18] Van Gend en Loss decision of 1963. See Louis Dubouis and Claude Gueydan, *Les Grands Textes du droit de l'Union européenne* (Paris: Dalloz, 2002), vol. I, pp. 440–442.

[19] See Jacques Guilhaumou, "Fragments of a Discourse of Denunciation (1789–1794)," in Keith Michael Baker, ed., *The French Revolution and the Creation of Modern Political Culture*, vol. IV: *The Terror* (Oxford:

denunciation of this sort. The regulations of the Club des Cordeliers listed as one of its primary goals "to denounce to the court of public opinion abuses by various authorities and attacks of every kind on the rights of man." The emphasis was on the *function* of denunciation, on its almost routine application in the scrutiny of individual conduct and political attitudes. To denounce was then simply, as the etymology would have it, to make known, to expose, to unveil, to reveal. Publicity was expected to restore order to the world.

This militant yet almost banal idea of denunciation receded from view in many countries in the nineteenth century, when the first priority was to claim the most basic of political rights, the right to vote. Denunciation was then reserved for exceptional cases: to point a finger at problems of such magnitude that they seemed to epitomize the failures and vices of an entire ruling class or system. Scandal thus became the only occasion for denunciation. Scandal, it has been observed, conferred a kind of "ultra-reality" on the facts.[20] The denunciation of scandal always involved two dimensions: a nihilistic stigmatization of the authorities, which were always suspected of corruption, coupled with faith in the political virtues of transparency. The first was associated with populism, and I shall have more to say about it later. For now I want to concentrate on the second. In the period between the two world wars, Marcel Aymé wrote an interesting study of the Stavisky affair called *Silhouette du scandale*. He was particularly interested in the effects of

Pergamon, 1994), as well as the chapter entitled "La dénonciation" in Jaume, *Le Discours jacobin et la démocratie*.

[20] Marcel Aymé, *Silhouette du scandale* [1938] (Paris: Grasset, 1973), p. 34.

revelation, especially in relation to moral and political education. Because the scandal "bluntly posed a banal problem of
existence,"[21] it changed the way people looked at things. In
addition to creating pressure for regulation, it also provided a
civics lesson. "Scandal," Aymé wrote, "is a fountain of youth in
which humanity washes the dirt off its habits; it is a mirror in
which societies, families, and individuals confront the violence
of their lives. Without such lessons, all morality would gasp for
air, and the world would sink into a state of stunned torpor."[22]

To denounce a scandal is first of all to "uncover" it, to
make public what had been hidden. One goal is of course to
put an end to a reprehensible situation, perhaps even to bring
the culprits to justice. But that is not the only goal. To
denounce is to reaffirm one's faith in the possibility of using
publicity to administer a direct corrective. From the editors of
French revolutionary *gazettes* to the American muckrakers,[23] a
journalistic credo thus developed. The English terms "literature of exposé" and "exposé journalism" may give a better
idea of the nature of the genre than the French "*presse à
scandales*" or the English "scandal sheet," with their pejorative
and venal connotations. In the early 1900s, magazines like
Cosmopolitan, *McClure's*, and *Every-body's* pilloried the "new
czars" who helped themselves from the public treasury. These
publications were not out solely to create a sensation and sell

---

[21] *Ibid.*, p. 15.   [22] *Ibid.*, p. 102.
[23] See the collection of essays edited by Arthur Weinberg and Lila Weinberg,
*The Muckrakers: The Era in Journalism that Moved America to Reform:
The Most Significant Magazine Articles of 1902–1912* (New York: Simon &
Shuster, 1961); see also David Mark Chalmers, *The Social and Political
Ideas of the Muckrakers* (New York: Simon & Shuster, 1964).

copies by exposing the peculations, large and small, of corrupt politicians. Their mission was also to preach, to redeem the world's sins and convert the sinners. As has been rightly observed, journalists like Lincoln Steffens, the author of the spectacularly successful *Shame of the Cities* (1904), availed themselves of the language of Protestant moralism, larding their texts with words such as "shame," "sin," "guilt," "salvation," "damnation," "pride," and "soul."[24] For them, the press had a role to play in the regeneration of the nation, a role that was inextricably spiritual and political. The editor of *Cosmopolitan Magazine* put this in striking terms in 1906: "Turn the waters of a pure public spirit into the corrupt pools of private interests and wash the offensive accumulations away."[25]

To be sure, the journalism of redemptive denunciation adapted in various ways to different political contexts. From the point of view of intellectual history, however, its history is relatively coherent. Although sensibilities have changed, a continuous thread runs from the pamphleteers of the French Revolution to the investigative journalism of today.[26] It is

[24] See Stanley K. Schultz, "The Morality of Politics: The Muckraker's Vision of Democracy," *The Journal of American History* 52, no. 3 (Dec. 1965).

[25] Quoted in *ibid.*, p. 530. In the same vein, Louis D. Brandeis, "the people's lawyer," writing in *Harper's Weekly*, observed that "if sunlight is the best disinfectant, the light of publicity is the most effective of policemen." See *Other People's Money and How the Bankers Use It* (1913), new edn (New York: F.A. Stokes, 1932), p. 32.

[26] For one approach, see John B. Thompson, *Political Scandal, Power and Visibility in the Media Age* (London: Polity Press, 2000), along with two books by Géraldine Muhlmann, *Une histoire politique du journalisme, XIXe–XXe siècle* (Paris: Presses Universitaires de France, 2004), and *Du journalisme en démocratie* (Paris: Payot, 2004).

possible to describe various objective political functions of these denunciations by the media, beyond the rather idealistic and unrealistic ways in which they describe themselves. First, there are *agenda functions*, which have been much studied recently by political scientists. But the role of investigative journalism in the broadest possible sense in setting the terms of public debate and structuring political issues was first noticed at the end of the nineteenth century.[27] In the United States, the critical writings of the muckrakers played a crucial part in shaping the issues championed by the Progressive movement.[28]

Second, denunciation has an *institutional effect*. It tends to reaffirm and deepen collective norms and values. From Durkheim to Gluckman, a whole line of anthropologists and sociologists has stressed this aspect of denunciation.[29] These scholars have shown that denunciation reinforces the collective conscience by exposing what seeks to destroy it. One author sees scandal as a kind of "test" of the solidity of community organization.[30] Another shows how the rumors and

---

[27] In England, William T. Stead of the *Pall Mall Gazette* was the first person to discuss the role of the press in structuring public policy. See Thompson, *Political Scandal*, pp. 53–58.

[28] The Progressives criticized the oligarchic tendencies in the economic and political order of the early twentieth century.

[29] See the important discussion of this in the introduction to Andrei S. Markovits and Mark Silverstein, *The Politics of Scandal: Power and Process in Liberal Democracies* (New York: Holmes and Meier, 1988). For informed comment on the sociological approach, see also Damien de Blic and Cyril Lemieux, "Le scandale comme épreuve. Eléments de sociologie pragmatique," *Politix* 71 (2005).

[30] See the fundamental article by Eric de Dampierre, "Thèmes pour l'étude du scandale," *Annales ESC* (July–Sept. 1954).

fears associated with scandal serve to maintain group values in small communities.[31] Hannah Arendt made the same point in her commentary on Kant's *Critique of Judgment*, where she showed how forming a judgment creates bonds among individual subjects.[32] In a more psychological approach to society and politics, the "civilizing force of hypocrisy" has been shown to reinforce the institutional effect by inducing accused politicians to make declarations of virtue in their own defense, thus strengthening the very values they are accused of flouting.[33]

Agenda and institutional effects are thus constants in all denunciations of scandal. In recent years, however, a new moral and political function of denunciation has begun to emerge. It is associated with the growing insistence on transparency in contemporary society. That this is a media age will of course not do as an explanation. The origins of this major change have to be sought further back, in the transformation of politics itself. The trigger was what might be called the "de-ideologization" of politics and the various forms of disenchantment to which this led. When politics was understood to be in essence a clash of mutually exclusive systems based on the class struggle, personal misbehavior mattered less. The issue for critics of the status quo was not deviance but normality, so that denunciation of corruption was no substitute for a critique of the "system." The issue was the "law of profit" in general, not the peculations of a few shady bankers. It was the

---

[31] See Max Gluckman, "Gossip and Scandal," *Current Anthropology* 4, no. 3 (June 1963).

[32] See Hannah Arendt, *Juger: Sur la philosophie politique de Kant* (Paris: Éditions du Seuil, 1991).

[33] On this point, see the work of Jon Elster.

norm itself that was deviant, not the transgression of the norm. The system with all its flaws was "the establishment," as the phrase went. It is striking to note, for example, that Marxist historians usually sought to play down the importance that others spontaneously ascribed to scandals in business and finance. Take, for example, the conclusion of one Marxist history of the Panama Affair: "Do not be misled by the notoriety of scandals ... They do not explain historical development. Political regimes and economic systems never die of scandal. They die of their contradictions, which is another matter entirely."[34] In late nineteenth-century France, a period marked by the revelation of any number of cases of political corruption, socialists were vehement in their attacks on the "moral right," which they accused of launching crusades against a few black sheep while ignoring everything else that was wrong.

These habits began to change toward the end of the twentieth century. Ideological disenchantment led to a more individualized approach to political issues. Whether politicians could be trusted became a more urgent question.[35] Scandal and, with it, the politics of denunciation thus occupied center stage. The result was a series of "affairs," which stemmed not so much from a decline of political morality as from a renewed social insistence on transparency. What changed was primarily the social measuring instrument and people's sensitivity to the issues.[36] The media did not create

---

[34] Jean Bouvier, *Les Deux Scandales de Panama* (Paris: Julliard, 1964), p. 204.

[35] This point is stressed in Thompson, *Political Scandal*, p. 111.

[36] See Suzanne Garment, *Scandal: The Crisis of Mistrust in American Politics* (New York: Times Books, 1991). On the relation between crisis and

the phenomenon but merely reflected and amplified the advent of a new politics of distrust. By the same token, political leaders exposed more of themselves to the media, opening up their private lives in an effort to enhance their credibility.[37] No longer required to demonstrate their allegiance to a camp, they were instead obliged to give proofs of personal honesty and demonstrate their proximity to voters.[38] Simplicity and transparency became cardinal political virtues. With the advent of the media age and the politician's need to put himself on display, denunciation became a key form of democratic action.

The primary effect of denunciation is to sully the reputations of individuals involved in a scandal, and reputation has become an increasingly valuable form of symbolic capital. The ability to inspire trust depends on it. Trust is an "invisible institution," an assumed stock of information. It takes the place of more formal commitments such as contracts and oaths. But it cannot exist in isolation. It is a property of a relationship between persons or groups, for example, between governors and governed. That relationship must be built

scandal, see Hervé Rayner, *Les Scandales politiques: L'Opération "Mains propres" en Italie* (Paris: Michel Houdiard, 2005).

[37] On this point, see the excellent comments by Luc Boltanski and Laurent Thévenot: "Renunciation of *secrecy* is ... the price to be paid for access to exalted status. If one wants to be *known*, one must be willing to *reveal* all and hide nothing from the public," in *De la justification: Les Économies de la grandeur* (Paris: Gallimard, 1991), p. 226.

[38] See the special issue of the journal *Mots* 77 (March 2005) on the subject of proximity, as well as Christian Le Bart and Rémi Lefebvre, eds., *La Proximité en politique: Usages, rhétoriques, pratiques* (Presses Universitaires de Rennes, 2003).

and maintained, *guaranteed* in short, if it is to endure. In "traditional" politics, it is party membership that provides the necessary guarantee (which is therefore inextricably disciplinary and ideological). The party is a "visible" institution, which bolsters the trust between voters and their representatives. In the "new" politics, reputation is the principal medium of trust. A politician's reputation becomes his *certificate of warranty*.

Reputation, one might say, is the cardinal principle in democracies of opinion, in the sense that it acts as an internal social regulator that superimposes itself on strictly institutional effects. In this respect, contemporary democracies bear a curious resemblance to older societies, which were regulated by honor. Indeed, honor is also a form of symbolic capital and is also constituted by social judgment. As Mandeville observed, "by honor one means nothing other than the good opinion of others."[39] Montesquieu of course provided the classical analysis of the logic of honor in monarchies.[40] Honor is the reflection of one's social position in the eyes of others; it derives its power from the quest for and recognition of distinction; and ultimately, Montesquieu explained, it replaced both virtue and the stable hierarchy of orders as the regulating principle of monarchy. The evolution was similar in both democracy and monarchy: the gaze of the other became the ruling power. We find the same fear of destruction through loss of reputation, the same obsessive need to avoid blame and shame, in

---

[39] Bernard Mandeville, *La Fable des abeilles* (1714), remark C. (Paris: Vrin, 1974), p. 58.

[40] See De *l'esprit des lois* (1758), book III, chaps. 5 and 6.

relations among both individuals and nations.[41] Just as honor took the place of virtue as the central social regulator in the eighteenth century, reputation tended to superimpose itself on election at the end of the twentieth century. The earliest analysts of media society anticipated this development. No one said it better than Junius, the great champion of political denunciation in eighteenth-century England.

> They who conceive that our newspapers are no restraint upon bad men, or impediment to the execution of bad measures, know nothing of this country … [O]ur ministers and magistrates have in reality … little punishment to fear, and few difficulties to contend with beyond the censure of the press, and the spirit of resistance which it excites among the people. While this censorial power is maintained (to speak in the words of a most ingenious foreigner), both minister and magistrate is compelled [sic] in almost every instance to choose between his duty and his reputation. A dilemma of this kind perpetually before him will not, indeed, work a miracle on his heart, but it will assuredly operate, in some degree, upon his conduct. At all events, these are not times to admit of any relaxation in the little discipline we have left.[42]

[41] On the effects of shame, see Martha C. Nussbaum, *Hiding from Humanity: Disgust, Shame, and the Law* (Princeton University Press, 2004); John Braithwaite, "Shame and Modernity," *The British Journal of Criminology* 33, no. 1 (Winter 1993) (which includes a general discussion of the effects of publicly stigmatizing penalties on crime). On the political effects of the "power of shame" in relations between nations, especially in regard to denunciation of human rights violations, see Jack Donnelly, *International Human Rights*, 2nd edn (Boulder, CO: Westview Press, 1998).

[42] Preface to Junius, *The Letters of Junius* (Oxford: Clarendon Press, 1978).

"The more strictly we are watched, the better we behave," Bentham summed up some years later in a celebrated formulation.

Reputation is a fluctuating value. It is fragile and can be lost much more quickly than it can be acquired. It is also cumulative, increasing with age.[43] But reputation has a temporal dimension in another sense as well, in that it is helpful in predicting future behavior. In other words, it produces an effect of anticipation.[44] What needs to be stressed here is the informational aspect of reputation: reputation conveys information and assists in rational decision-making in situations where information is incomplete. This point is well-established in economic theory.[45] Economists have shown, moreover, that reputation is a form of capital and has *value*, which in the long run always exceeds the short-term gains that might be had by neglecting the reputational dimension of action. In this light, denunciation might be analyzed as a testing of reputation with the potential to diminish or even destroy its value. It is therefore a very powerful political instrument. It becomes even more powerful when the target of denunciation is no longer corruption but simply action or behavior that is dubious but

---

[43] See chap. 10, "On Power, Worth, Dignity, Honour and Worthiness," in Thomas Hobbes, *Leviathan*.

[44] See Jonathan Mercer, *Reputation and International Politics* (Ithaca: Cornell University Press, 1996), pp. 6–9. For a discussion of the importance of this factor that develops an approach broader than the economic, see Geoffrey Brennan and Philip Pettit, *The Economy of Esteem: An Essay on Civil and Political Society* (Oxford University Press, 1994).

[45] See David M. Kreps and Robert Wilson, "Reputation and Imperfect Information," *Journal of Economic Theory* 27, no. 2 (Aug. 1982).

legal. This greatly broadens the concept of scandal to include what society considers "abnormal" or unjust.[46] Actions are thus judged against social norms, the violation of which can make or break a reputation. In other words, social norms effectively acquire attributes of sovereignty. In this way, democracy as a social state came to subsume democracy as a regime type. The power of conformism, which Tocqueville described, no longer simply regulates mores. It has also become a political force. In the old world of honor, Pierre Bayle remarked that public denunciation was "a kind of civil homicide."[47]

Evaluation

Grading, or, to put it more generally, evaluation, is the third form that the power of surveillance takes. Evaluation involves carefully researched, technically sophisticated, often quantified judgment of specific actions or more general policies. The goal is to bring expertise to bear on governmental management in order to improve its quality and efficiency. Here, too, reputation hangs in the balance, but reputation of a "technical" kind: it is the *competence* of government officials that is put to the test. Interestingly, evaluation of this sort has

---

[46] Consider the Gaymard Affair in France: a minister of finance was forced to resign in February 2005 when the media revealed that one of his perks of office was a 600-square-meter apartment. Many people found this scandalously lavish. In such cases the object is moral rather than legal condemnation.

[47] Quoted in Luc Boltanski, "La dénonciation," *Actes de la recherche en sciences sociales* 51 (1984), p. 4 (taken from Reinhart Koselleck, *Le Règne de la critique* [1954] [Paris: Minuit, 1979], pp. 94–95).

sometimes served where political criticism was impossible. In ancient China, for example, conflicts of power often manifested themselves as bureaucratic exercises in administrative and financial oversight. In the Ming dynasty, where there was no democracy or representation of any kind, Pierre-Etienne Will has shown that officials were nevertheless subject to periodic *daji*, or "great evaluations."[48] The imperial administration relied on very careful inspection to bolster its power and enhance its efficiency. Yet this supervisory, functional surveillance also served as a basis for the organization of counter-powers, through which it became possible to challenge official imperial policies. In practice, these general administrative audits, which were conducted every three years, became occasions for protest. The *yanguan*, or "officials who speak out," were in effect censors, professionally vigilant but also capable of checking the excesses of the regime. The audits were in effect a form of "social reappropriation" of the power of evaluation. Hence it should come as no surprise that Sun Yat-Sen, the father of the Chinese Republic, proposed adding the "power of surveillance" (*yuan*) to the three powers of Montesquieu.[49]

---

[48] Pierre-Etienne Will, "Le contrôle constitutionnel de l'excès de pouvoir sous la dynastie des Ming," in Mireille Delmas-Marty and Pierre Étienne Will, eds., *La Chine et la démocratie* (Paris: Fayard, 2007).

[49] Sun Yat-Sen, who became the first president of the Chinese Republic in 1912, also insisted on a "power of examination," that is, the power to choose officials on the basis of a competitive examination, in the context of his celebrated theory of the five powers. In his eyes, the West contributed three of these powers by way of Montesquieu's doctrine, while the other two were the historical contribution of the Chinese.

The evaluation function has a long history. It can, of course, be seen as an outgrowth of internal controls established by governments themselves. In the early Middle Ages, for example, the Normans established a court of accounts, which marked a first step toward routinization and professionalization of royal treasuries in Europe.[50] The English exchequer perfected this model, which became the basis of the British system of justice and public administration. The creation of the Statutory Commission for Examining the Public Accounts in 1780, followed by Gladstone's creation of the Exchequer and Audit Department in 1866, marked further decisive steps in this direction. In France, the development of the Chambre des Comptes was crucial to the emergence of a modern state with rationalized administrative and financial controls.[51] Methods of supervision and evaluation evolved with technical advances, but they also occupied a central place in a political struggle for openness, which developed along with representative government. Today's evaluation techniques are obviously quite sophisticated compared with those of the past. They grew out of efforts to redraw the boundary between the private and public sectors. Proponents of the "new public management" insist on

See Sun Yat-Sen, "La Constitution des cinq pouvoirs," appendix to *Souvenirs d'un révolutionnaire chinois* (1925) (Paris, 1933). See also Tcheng Chao-Yuen, *L'Évolution de la vie constitutionnelle de la Chine sous l'influence de Sun Yat-Sen et de sa doctrine (1885–1937)* (Paris, 1937).

[50] See Charles Homer Haskins, *Norman Institutions* (New York: F. Ungar, 1960).

[51] See Philippe Contamine and Olivier Mattéoni, eds., *La France des principautés: Les Chambres des comptes, XIVe et XVe siècles* (Paris: Comité pour l'histoire économique et financière de la France, 1996).

the need for comparison and measurement.[52] Nowadays, "benchmarking" is routine in all areas of government, and no public organization can avoid having its efficiency put to the test. The need has become all the greater as the complexity of public policy has increased, but this change has also complicated the task of measurement. That is why the years since 1970 have seen a growing number of agencies specializing in the evaluation of public policy reform.[53] No longer can any agency of government claim that its purposes and methods need no justification beyond statutory authorization. The new instruments of evaluation have transformed the nature of the state.

The same can be said of the political order as such. The development of new investigative methods and new forms of expertise has heightened the expectations citizens have of government. If evaluation and measurement are techniques of management, they also add depth to public debate and place tighter legitimacy constraints on government actions. Increasingly, citizens are demanding that government officials prove their competence and subject their actions to regular evaluation. They bring their own practical expertise to bear, making use of information not available to decision-makers remote from the place where the consequences of their decisions are actually felt. The relation between governors and governed no longer suffers from the "uneven capabilities"

[52] See P. Lascoumes and Patrick Le Galès, eds., *Gouverner par les instruments* (Paris: Presses de Sciences-Po, 2004).

[53] For France, see Patrick Viveret, *L'Évaluation des politiques et des actions publiques: Rapport au premier ministre* (Paris: La Documentation française, 1989), and Bernard Perret, *L'Évaluation des politiques publiques* (Paris: La Découverte, 2001).

that were once a key feature of all representative systems. The dissemination of technical information and expertise, coupled with a general rise in the intellectual level of the population, has been a decisive factor in the shift toward constant evaluation of government officials, who are much more vulnerable and dependent than in the past. Officials have in a sense become pupils of the people they govern, subject to constant evaluation of their performance. Using the tools of evaluation, citizens have effectively gained access to a new form of power, a power that is virtually direct and capable of being exercised without intermediaries. Democracy itself is thus being transformed in far-reaching ways.

2

The overseers

The three forms of oversight that I discussed in the previous chapter rely on agents of various types. Surveillance first developed in a context of intense civic mobilization (the French Revolution) and involved social activity of many kinds. The oversight role subsequently shifted to the media (in the broadest sense of the term). In the nineteenth century, the press embodied liberty in action and exercised counter-democratic power. The Pen and the Podium were complementary (if often antagonistic) components of a single system. Both shared the same ambition: to represent the people. Over the course of the twentieth century, the conflict between the press and the politicians ranged over a broader and broader territory. Other agents and agencies began to perform similar functions of oversight, disclosure, and evaluation. From 1980 on, these newcomers began to play an ever-expanding role. New citizens' organizations emerged, independent supervisory authorities were constituted, and new methods of evaluation were introduced. A new form of power began to take shape: the social watchdog. But this power continued to reflect a personal ethical choice, a disposition of the individual. The early twentieth-century French philosopher Alain (Émile Chartier) is a good example of the type.

The vigilant citizen

Alain exemplifies what was most generous and authentic in the nineteenth-century republican spirit. For him, the Republic was not merely a regime; it was a way of structuring and legitimating power and embodied a public morality, a code of civic behavior. Harking back to 1789, Alain called upon his fellow citizens to "monitor, supervise, and judge the dread powers [that govern them]."[1] His ideal was that "the citizen should remain, for his part, inflexible – inflexible in spirit, armed with suspicion, and always dubious of the leader's projects and reasons."[2] Alain's rigor was colored, however, by a melancholy skepticism as to the nature of politics. For him, power was doomed to go unloved, and elected powers were in the end no more lovable than any other. Hence it was all but inevitable that "the free citizen should be a malcontent."[3] Alain, an ardent republican, was at best a moderate democrat, even if popular sovereignty no longer inspired in him the fears to which the two other leading republican philosophers, Charles Renouvier and Alfred Fouillée, had given voice before him. The author of *Propos* looked upon universal suffrage as a way of exercising oversight rather than command. For him, democracy was essentially "a power of surveillance and resistance."[4] In his

[1] Alain, *Propos sur les pouvoirs* (Paris: Gallimard, 1985), p. 160, "Propos du 12 juillet 1930."
[2] *Ibid.*, p. 161.
[3] *Ibid.*, p. 204 ("Propos du 27 janvier 1934").
[4] *Propos de politique* (Paris, 1934), p. 264. "A false idea of democracy is that the people govern, but this is not, as has been said, an error of democracy. It is rather an error about democracy. Democracy gives the

eyes, the only effective sovereignty was negative. "Where, then, is democracy," he asked, "if not in this third power, which political science has yet to define and which I call the Monitor? ... This power was long exercised in revolutions, on the barricades. Today it is exercised through investigation. In this respect, democracy might be defined as the perpetual effort by the governed to curtail the abuse of power."[5] Hence Alain approved Auguste Comte's judgment that the power of the people consists solely in apportioning blame. He transformed the idea of a self-governing people into that of a distrustful people.

Though an ardent republican, Alain in many respects shared the liberal vision of democracy. Although he sounds like Condorcet, he thinks more like Montesquieu and Benjamin Constant. What differentiated him from the latter two thinkers, however, was his civic restlessness, his nostalgia for active and unremitting civic engagement, which crops up frequently in his writing, though his ambition did not impel him to invent the new political forms that might have made it possible to overcome the inertia and loss of focus that he deplored. For him, the wisest citizen was one who renounces power and holds himself aloof from government. Despite his sympathy for the Radical Party, he did not believe in progress in democratic institutions or practices. There was no point, he thought, in attempting to alter the essence of power. The only

people the power to scrutinize and to judge. Nothing more is needed" (*ibid.*, p. 324).
[5] *Propos sur les pouvoirs*, p. 215 ("Propos du 12 juillet 1910"). See the set of "propos" collected by the editor under the head "Democracy as Institutionalized Counter-Power" (pp. 213–229).

hope was to moderate, control, and limit it. For Alain, vigilance was a necessary if wearisome activity, and the vigilant citizen was one who had ceased to dream. He was content to describe the "miraculous influence of a small number of wise men who sit on the ground and judge the performance of the acrobat as he walks his tightrope."[6] The grandeur of his spirit lay entirely in his utter refusal of cynicism. Unlike many theorists of democracy, who turn low expectations into a categorical imperative, he combined skepticism with scrupulous modesty and a practical commitment to ordinary people. His English-style liberalism went hand in hand with a conception of virtue modeled on the Ancients. His republican spirit persuaded him that without vigilance there could be no liberty, and he promoted suspicion to the rank of cardinal political virtue. The vigilance he envisioned was not something he either expected or demanded. It expressed itself as aloofness rather than involvement. Alain lived between two worlds: the old and the new, liberalism and republicanism, aloofness and participation, politics and ethics. Was he an exception? Certainly not, for his very ambivalence, combining rejection of the political with impatience for political progress, signaled a fundamental trait of modern citizenship.

Alain's idea of citizenship may be taken as a touchstone in the history of democratic oversight. As the sober, melancholy heir to the revolutionary imagination of 1789 and 1793, he was neither a political activist nor a parliamentarian. Hence he left no direct offspring. At the dawn of the twenty-first century, however, his example reminds us of both the

[6] *Ibid.*, p. 185 ("Propos du 26 mai 1928").

history of democracy and the problem of democracy. After so many years in eclipse he is at last coming into his own, allowing his readers to glimpse an image of themselves that can help them to understand why it is so hard to reconcile disillusionment with refusal to resign oneself to defeat. His example points the way to later movements and institutions, to which we now turn our attention.

The new activism

If we are to understand what scholars commonly refer to as "new social movements," we need to keep the various forms of the watchdog power clearly in mind. In the 1970s, sociologists and political scientists showed that the conflict between labor and capital no longer sufficed to describe the full complexity of the social structure. New collective identities clamored for public attention: sexual minorities, generational groups, feminist movements, etc. Alain Touraine described the emergence of what he called "new fields of history," organized around novel social conflicts involving the environment, regional independence, and gender relations. Other social scientists continued to explore new forms of social mobilization and identification. In order to analyze these new social movements, one had to understand the pressing issues of the time: economic globalization, social inequality and vulnerability, and human rights. Scholars also turned their attention to the evolution of modern individualism, with its increased awareness of such questions as the right to human dignity and the complexities of sexual identity. Social scientists looked into the "springs" of collective action. In France they saw the

emergence of a new type of "moral activism" in the 1980s.[7]
There were also studies of new forms of political commitment.[8] Scholars also tried to understand the variety of modes
of political action, including "unconventional" forms of citizen
participation.[9] Finally, they sought to study what kinds of
resources were mobilized in each instance.[10]

This rich literature does a good job of explaining
the profound transformation of social and political activism
in the recent past. Little attention has been paid, however, to
the *democratic function* of social movements as such. Although
it is clear that this function is no longer, as in the classic trade
union movement, one of representation and negotiation, how
to describe the *functional specificity* of the new forms of protest
remains an open question.[11] The revival of activism (by groups
such as ATTAC and Act-Up, various "social forums," and a
range of *altermondialiste* organizations, for instance) has been
abundantly studied, but almost nothing has been written about

---

[7] Emmanuèle Reynaud, "Le militantisme moral," in Henri Mendras, ed., *La Sagesse et le désordre: France, 1980* (Paris: Gallimard, 1980).

[8] See "Devenirs militants," a special issue of the *Revue française de science politique* (Feb.–April 2001).

[9] See CURAPP, *La Politique ailleurs* (Paris: Presses Universitaires de France, 1998). See also any number of works on the changing tactics of political demonstration; for France, in particular, see the works of Danielle Tartakowsky.

[10] See Olivier Fillieule, ed., *Sociologie de la protestation: Les Formes de l'action collective dans la France contemporaine* (Paris: L'Harmattan, 1993).

[11] A partial exception to the general neglect of this question is the thesis of Daniel Mouchard, *Les "Exclus" dans l'espace public: Mobilisations et logiques de représentation dans la France contemporaine* (Paris: Institut d'Études Politiques, 2001).

62

the role of such groups in the transformation of democracy itself. The idea of "powers of oversight" can help us to understand what is happening. Indeed, the most salient characteristic of the "new social movements" is that they are organized around the three forms of action I previously described: vigilance, denunciation, and evaluation. Counter-democracy, the history and theory of which it is the purpose of this book to develop, is basically organized around action of these three types.

Clearly, new social movement organizations often function as "watchdogs" in their specific policy areas. The vocabulary of social activism reflects this fact. For instance, "whistle-blowers" are people or groups that call attention to certain types of problems. Whistle-blowing has become so widespread that a new field of sociology has developed to study it.[12] Although it is especially common in the areas of consumer protection, health, and the environment, it has lately spread to other sectors of social and political action. The names of some new activist groups reflect this development. In the 1970s, such groups tended to call themselves "collectives in struggle," "defense committees," or "mobilizations for" this and that. Now they are "watchdog groups" or, in France, *observatoires* (such as the *Observatoire des inégalités* or the *Observatoire du communautarisme*, to take just two examples). Organizations of this type rely on functional expertise (in practice, counter-expertise,

---

[12] See the stimulating work of Francis Chateauraynaud, *Les Sombres Précurseurs: Une sociologie pragmatique de l'alerte et du risque* (Paris: Editions de l'EHESS, 1999); "Qui est garant de la vigilance collective," *Environnement et société* 23 (1999); "Incontournables présences: l'exercice de la vigilance," in Claude Gilbert, ed., *Risques collectifs et situations de crise* (Paris: L'Harmattan, 2003).

to do battle with experts from the other camp) and research. In many cases advocacy groups therefore play a dual role, operating as both think tanks and pressure groups.[13] Their goal is to question prevailing rationales. At times, the boundary between editor and political activist can become rather blurred. Such organizations depend in part on what Pierre Bourdieu called "authority effects," yet they also exercise real power, in the sense of a capacity to alter or constrain the behavior of those whom they choose as targets.

The evaluation function in many ways resembles the use of counter-expertise. Take, for instance, the ratings of various countries with respect to corruption that are published regularly by the non-governmental organization Transparency International.[14] These have a political impact comparable to the ratings of bonds and other securities by organizations such as Moody's and Standard & Poor's. A country that receives a low corruption rating may find its ability to borrow from major financial institutions diminished. By contrast, countries that cooperate with Transparency International to improve their anti-corruption methods are rewarded in a variety of ways. In extreme cases, a low rating can be almost as severe a sanction on a government as an electoral defeat. Finally, denunciation comes when hidden corruption is revealed. Some groups specialize in what has been called "naming and

---

[13] See Lisa Young and Joanna Everitt, *Advocacy Groups* (Vancouver: University of British Columbia Press, 2004) for interesting analyses of general import despite the limitation of case studies to Canada.

[14] See www.transparency.org/surveys.

blaming," a description that aptly captures the nature of their activism.[15]

The various kinds of groups I have discussed thus far cover a broad ideological spectrum. Some are more radical than others. An abyss separates small groups like Act-Up, which favors highly visible and disruptive forms of political action, from sober, highly professionalized non-governmental organizations. As *political forms*, however, all of these organizations exhibit similar traits. Unlike traditional interest groups, their primary purpose is not to defend the interests of their members. Indeed, their relation to their members is completely different from that of traditional organizations. Counter-democratic movements have sympathizers and donors but do not necessarily seek members as such. In contrast to old social movements, such as trade unions, their function is not one of social representation or negotiation. Their goal is to identify issues and exert pressure on governments, not to represent groups of people. Hence they are well suited to an age in which the goal of politics is more to *deal with situations* than to organize stable groups and manage hierarchical structures. Finally, they seek influence rather than power. They see democracy not as a competition for government power but as a composite of two realms – a sphere of electoral representation and a constellation of counter-democratic organizations – in constant tension with each other. The relation between the latter organizations and the

---

[15] See William L. F. Felstiner, Richard L. Abel, and Austin Sarat, "The Emergence and Transformation of Disputes: Naming, Blaming, Claiming," *Law and Society Review* 15, nos. 3–4 (1981).

political parties has changed considerably over the years. Until the 1970s, the issue of the "political purpose" of social struggle remained paramount. A vertical, hierarchical vision of politics prevailed, and the social was merely a preface to the political. Even those who firmly rejected the radical Leninist version of this vision imagined power in fairly one-dimensional terms. This is no longer the case. The authority of the political parties has diminished as a result, while the old notion of "alternation" between two parties has lost some of its previous salience.

The Internet as a political form

Certain sociologists point out that these organizations often rely on the media, so much so that one scholar has suggested that they should be referred to as "mediacentric associations."[16] There is justice in this suggestion, even if the relations between organizations and media are complex, at once intimate and distant. Both depend on publicity. As an official of one militant group remarked, "The question of visibility is central to everything we do."[17] Many journalists would say the same thing. Yet this similarity sheds little light on our subject. It simply reminds us that "publicity" and "public opinion" need to be constructed as objects of study and that in order to do so we must begin with the variety of oversight functions. The relation between the media and social movements begins to make sense when we see both as

[16] See Erik Neveu, "Médias, mouvements sociaux, espaces publics," *Réseaux. Communication, technologie, société* 98 (1999).
[17] An official of Act-Up, in *Vacarme* 31 (Spring 2005): 23.

manifestations of the same counter-democratic functions. One way to put it would be to say that the media are the routine functional form of democratic oversight, while militant civil society groups are the activist form. The two are thus functionally complementary. This complementarity is the basis of the well-known slogan, "Don't hate the media, become the media!"

This slogan raises the question of what role the Internet is to play in the new constellation of supervisory powers. Thus far we have implicitly treated the Internet as one of a range of "new media." And surely it is that, since it serves to circulate opinions, information, and analyses. Of course it is a medium different from others in terms of access costs, mode of production, methods of diffusion, and regulation. Yet one cannot leave it at that. The Web is not only a true *political form* but also a *social form* in the fullest sense of the word. What is more, it is a social form of a new type, in that it plays a part in efforts to build unprecedented kinds of communities. The social bond created by the Web cannot be thought of in the conventional terms of economic and sociological analysis: aggregation, coordination, and identification. What counts as "social" on the Internet is pure circulation, free interaction consisting of a series of engagements, each of which holds the possibility of branching out into a series of other engagements. The works of Deleuze, Simmel, and Tarde are therefore of more help in understanding the Internet than are those of Durkheim and Marx, to put the point baldly.[18] The Internet gives expression to public opinion

---

[18] The sociologist Gabriel Tarde had the original idea, long overlooked, of conceiving of the social in terms of mechanisms of interaction, which he

in an immediately perceptible, almost physical form. The truly visionary terms in which the revolutionaries of 1789 celebrated the ubiquity and power of public opinion suddenly take on new significance. Listen, for instance, to one Bergasse, who served as a member of the Constituent Assembly in the early days of the French Revolution: "Public opinion," he wrote, "is truly a product of everyone's intelligence and everyone's will. It can be seen, in a way, as the manifest consciousness of the entire nation."[19] Today, the Internet embodies in an almost material sense this pervasive force. Everyone can participate, and no one can control the result. The Internet thus magnifies not only the promise but also the pathologies associated with public opinion – the "ruler of the world," as someone once called it. This vast new realm obviously calls for further reflection, but here I can do no more than mention it in passing.

Nevertheless, there is one way in which the nature of the Internet as a political form is of more immediate concern. In the 1980s, it was widely believed that the new technologies of communication were going to disrupt established democratic practices by enabling citizens to intervene more directly in politics. The idea was that material constraints that had historically militated in favor of representative procedures were about to be lifted overnight. Various authors celebrated the coming advent of "teledemocracy" as a

described using a series of basic concepts such as imitation, repetition, opposition, and adaptation.

[19] Bergasse, *Sur la manière dont il convient de limiter le pouvoir législatif et le pouvoir exécutif dans une monarchie*, September 1789, reproduced in *AP*, 1st series, vol. 9, p. 119.

fulfillment of the Rousseauian ideal of direct participation in all collective decisions.[20] The Internet was supposed to make it as easy to organize a large virtual community as a small group. American nostalgia for the town meetings of early American history found its fulfillment in so-called electronic town meetings.[21] Others argued that the Internet would reduce the cost of voting to the point where citizens could be frequently and easily consulted. For a brief period the idea of "televoting" enjoyed the support of enthusiastic prophets of all stripes. A whole new vocabulary emerged: there was talk of "electronic democracy," "e-government," and "cyber-democracy."[22] This initial enthusiasm subsequently waned for a variety of reasons. Its chief sponsors had been intellectuals, who argued that democracy ought to be more than just voting. But these same intellectuals later shifted their attention to the more promising and complex subject of deliberative democracy. Still, the hopes of the 1990s have continued to encourage a broadly positive view of the possibilities. Cass Sunstein's influential book *Republic.com* is a good illustration

[20] See, for example, one of the first works on the subject, Benjamin R. Barber's *Strong Democracy: Participatory Politics for a New Age* (Berkeley: University of California Press, 1984), which was enthusiastically in favor, and Christopher F. Arterton's *Teledemocracy: Can Technology Protect Democracy?* (Beverly Hills: Sage Publications, 1987), which expressed reservations.

[21] This theme was central to the campaign of the populist politician Ross Perot in the 1992 American presidential election. A good deal of activist literature took a similar view, however.

[22] See the special issue of *Hermès* (26–27) 2000, devoted to electronic democracy.

of the new, more reflective and clear-sighted approach to the problem.[23]

Setting aside the differences among these various proposals and reflections as to the political uses of the Internet, I think it is fair to say that all miss a crucial point, because all focus exclusively on applying the Internet to the electoral-representative dimension of public life. Participation and deliberation are, for their authors, touchstones of democratic progress. In my view, however, the major role of the Internet lies elsewhere, namely, in its spontaneous adaptation to the functions of vigilance, denunciation, and evaluation. More than that, the Internet is the *realized* expression of these powers. Blogs diffract the net's supervisory power endlessly, and more organized sites are constantly seeking user interaction. It is striking, for example, that on-line bookstores ask buyers to evaluate and comment on the books they buy, a practice that points toward a radical transformation of the idea of criticism. This transformation may be taken as a metaphor for what the Internet is in the process of doing to the political order, namely, creating an open space for oversight and evaluation. The Internet is not merely an "instrument"; it *is* the surveillance function. Movement defines it and points not only toward its potential but also toward its possible subversion and manipulation. It is in this sense that the Internet can be regarded as a true *political form*. Other organized modes of surveillance have

---

[23] Cass Sunstein, *Republic.com* (Princeton University Press, 2001). Sunstein offers an informed and balanced assessment of the potential costs and benefits of the Internet in regard to liberty, deliberation, and participation.

also emerged, however. Institutions of a new type have been established in many countries, along with independent oversight authorities. Their purpose is to monitor government activity in many areas.

Functional surveillance by authorities

Watchdog democracy has also taken another form in recent years: independent authorities have been called upon to exercise their judgment. Everywhere, as many observers have noted, the number of these authorities has grown rapidly over the past thirty years. Their legitimacy has been the subject of much discussion. But legal and political analysts have been interested mainly in authorities regulating telecommunications, financial markets, and the media. Other, related institutions are more exclusively devoted to the functions of vigilance and oversight. Take, for instance, ombudsmen and "mediators," who help citizens bring their individual problems and needs to the attention of otherwise rigid and inaccessible bureaucratic systems. Even more significant are the citizens' review boards that oversee the work of police departments to ensure that it conforms to ethical and legal norms. In pragmatic and symbolic terms, the police are at the heart of the state, whose primary mission is to protect basic human rights by guaranteeing the security of each and every citizen. In the United Kingdom, the Police Complaints Authority was established for this purpose in 1984. Its mission is to make sure that the police behave ethically, and it fulfills this mission either by directly supervising inquiries into police misconduct or reviewing such investigations after the fact. A similar role is played by the Conseil du Surveillance des Activités de la Sûreté (Police Oversight Council) in Quebec and the Comité Permanent de Contrôle des Services de Police (Permanent Police Monitoring Committee) in Belgium.

In France, a Commission Nationale de Déontologie de la Sécurité (National Commission on Security Ethics) was established in 2000 as an "independent administrative authority," according to the law of June 6. Its mission was to "ensure ethical conduct within France by persons charged with maintaining the security of the Republic."[24] With members nominated by the houses of parliament and leading law enforcement agencies, the commission was endowed with fairly extensive investigative powers. Its annual public report discusses what has been done over the past year in response to each of its recommendations. The function of this commission might therefore be described as one of "delegated civic oversight." The parliamentary debate that preceded passage of the law of June 6 is worth noting. Many speakers felt that there would be no need for such a commission if the courts and police internal affairs boards did their jobs properly, hence that a better way to proceed would be to enhance the effectiveness of these existing institutions. Indeed, one deputy bluntly observed that the new commission would "consecrate the failure not only of the courts and police but also of the parliament and government."[25] This comment warrants further discussion. If the bureaucracy and

---

[24] Article 1 of the law of June 6, 2000.

[25] See *Rapport fait au nom de la Commission des lois sur le projet de loi portant création d'un Conseil supérieur de la déontologie de la sécurite*, by Bruno Le Roux, deputy, February 25, 1998.

representative government functioned "perfectly," then indeed no corrective oversight power would be necessary. The problem is that in fact there is a *structural* tendency toward dysfunctionality, if only at the margin. That is why there is always a need for vigilant oversight to ensure that public institutions operate as they are intended to.[26] Furthermore, the existence of external watchdog powers contributes indirectly to institutional credibility. "Even where internal monitoring systems exist in public agencies," the legislative report remarks, "they are likely to be suspected of a self-serving bias, and such suspicion tends to diminish their effectiveness."[27] Outside monitoring agencies are useful precisely because they remedy this structural defect.

Internal audit and evaluation bureaus

Internal audit and evaluation bureaus are increasingly common in many public and governmental institutions around the world. Some observers allude to a veritable "industry" of evaluation. One survey reports that the British government boasts of some thirty-five inspection, monitoring, evaluation, and audit bureaus of one sort or another.[28] Most of these trace their origins to the advent of "rational management," the call for which has become ever more insistent as the

---

[26] See Reinier H. Kraakman, "Gatekeepers: The Anatomy of a Third-Party Enforcement Strategy," *Journal of Law, Economics and Organization* 2, no. 1 (Spring 1986).

[27] See the report cited in n. 25.

[28] See Christopher Hood, Colin Scott, Oliver James, George Jones, and Tony Travers, *Regulation inside Government: Waste-Watchers, Quality Police, and Sleaze-Busters* (Oxford University Press, 1999).

so-called New Public Management movement takes hold. Nevertheless, it would be a mistake to judge these new monitoring and regulatory bureaus solely in terms of their explicit functions. Everywhere they have broadened their mandate over time. Although there are significant differences from one country to the next, the social demand for broader supervisory powers exists everywhere, as does the tendency of supervisory agencies to escape to some extent from the control of their creators.[29] The scope of their responsibilities tends to expand inexorably, and their autonomy increases commensurately.[30] Today's societies truly exhibit an *ethos of democratic oversight*, which results from the mutual interaction of public agencies, independent monitoring organizations, and political activists. Increasingly, the same language is spoken in all three realms. Because public officials need to restore public trust by alleviating the systematic suspicion of people outside government, all democracies experience a need for *neutral watchdogs*.

If government is to be truly credible and efficient, neutral watchdogs must oversee the work of the people's representatives. In other words, democracy can flourish *only if it acknowledges the risks of dysfunctionality and equips itself with institutions capable of subjecting its own inner workings to*

[29] See Steve Jacob, "La volonté des acteurs et le poids des structures dans l'institutionnalisation de l'évaluation des politiques publiques," *Revue française de science politique* 55, nos. 5–6 (Oct.–Dec. 2005).

[30] See the conclusions in Olivier Benoît, "Les chambres régionales des comptes face aux élus locaux. Les effets inattendus d'une institution," *Revue française de science politique* 53, no. 4 (Aug. 2003). Note that evolution in this sense was a key characteristic of the "oversight power" in ancient China.

constructive evaluation. The neutral watchdog can take three forms: it can exist as a *functional capability* (in the form of internal audit bureaus, for example); as an *ethos* (as in the case of independent oversight authorities); or as a *social activity* (such as that of the media, which offer a form of pure "professional" oversight, or of small groups of "militant" activists). As the interaction among these different types of watchdogs intensifies, however, all come to share similar characteristics.

3

The thread of history

Three stages

Now that we have defined various forms and properties of counter-democracy, as distinct from institutionalized democracy, we are also in a position to take a fresh look at the history of liberty and collective sovereignty. We can divide this history into three periods. In the first period limited watchdog powers were established. These were in part liberal (limiting and regulating existing powers) and in part democratic (oversight exercised by representative bodies). These powers were themselves connected with the emergence of organized constitutional government. Self-regulation of the state (for the purpose of "rationalized" rule) was combined with "democratic" regulation of the state by society. Democratic institutions arose through competition over the power to supervise and regulate.

It would take a vast amount of research to write a comparative history of the public institutions of several countries along the lines sketched above. Obviously, nothing of the sort can be attempted here. It may be possible, however, to give some idea of what such a history would look like by concentrating on the most basic level of social power and focusing our attention on a small number of municipal and sub-municipal institutions. Conflicts over regulating the power of aldermen were common in medieval European towns. In Auvergne, for instance, aldermen and guilds were regularly at odds.

The guilds insisted that town accounts ought to be subject to scrutiny by auditors chosen from outside the small group in power. In some cases negotiations led to ordinary citizens being granted the right to examine the books of town officials.[1] Residents apparently began to think of themselves as citizens as a direct result of this practice. Guild members saw themselves as regulators before they began to think of themselves as exercising a share in sovereignty. They were monitors to whom those in power had to render their accounts. We see the same thing in Italian towns, where citizens regularly investigated the administration of the *podestas*.[2]

Similar practices have been found in rural communities in the same period. These were of course smaller in size than the towns, so that it was possible for all residents to meet and discuss decisions about practical matters affecting the entire community. In these communities, *jurats*, *consuls*, or *syndics* might be charged in one way or another with carrying out collective decisions. These officials could be chosen by lot, by rotation, by co-optation of incumbents, by direct election, or by indirect election. Yet in almost all cases they were required to report on their activities to the assembled community.[3] Here

---

[1] See "Le contrôle des comptes dans les villes auvergantes et vellaves aux XIVe et XVe siècles," in Albert Rigaudière, *Penser et construire l'État dans la France du Moyen Âge (XIIIe–XVe siècle)* (Paris: Comité pour l'histoire économique et financière de la France, 2003).

[2] For an overview, see Daniel Waley, *Les Républiques médiévales italiennes* (Paris: Hachette, 1969).

[3] See the information contained in the studies collected in *Recueils de la société Jean Bodin*, "Les communautés rurales," vols. 43 and 44, 1984 and 1986. See also *Les Structures du pouvoir dans les communautés rurales en*

again, oversight constituted the true test of legitimacy: witness the fact that regulations governing public audits were usually far more rigorous and formal than regulations governing the appointment of administrators.[4] Studies of parish administration lead to the same conclusion: wherever syndics or churchwardens were elected, their activities were overseen by parishioners in accordance with formally established procedures. In sixteenth-century Protestant communities, moreover, democratic oversight of internal administration was often an essential feature of communal identity.[5] The development of such primitive forms of oversight, incomplete and fragile as they may have been, was an essential part of the early history of representative government.

In the second phase of the construction of modern parliamentary systems, these emerging powers of oversight and surveillance were institutionalized, rationalized, and subjected to hierarchical organization. Great Britain led the way. Parliament was quick to establish auditing of government accounts; indeed, the right to investigate the actions of government was one of Parliament's most jealously guarded prerogatives. Parliamentary investigations figured in any number of reform proposals. Through investigations, the people's

---

Belgique et dans les pays limitrophes, XIIe–XIXe siècle (Brussels: Crédit communal de Belgique, 1988).

[4] Interesting comments on this point can be found in Henry Babeau, *Les Assemblées générales des communautés d'habitants en France, du XIIIe siècle à la Révolution* (Paris, 1893).

[5] See Michel Reulos, "Ressources financières et règles de gestion dans les églises réformées françaises au XVIe siècle," in *L'Hostie et le denier: Les Finances ecclésiastiques du haut Moyen Âge à l'époque moderne* (Geneva: Labor et Fides, 1991).

representatives were able to form their own judgments with sufficient technical competence to hold their own against the views of the cabinet. The British system of oversight drew praise from the more forward-looking French republicans and liberals of the early nineteenth century.[6] For them, the British Parliament was first and foremost the overseer of government. Evidence for this can be seen in speeches by French deputies in praise of Parliament's investigatory powers. A *rapporteur* on the issue said that "the rights and duties of the House [of Commons] are not limited to studying the wishes and needs of the nation, to giving it laws, or to setting its taxes. Should some grave disorder indicate a flaw in the administration, the representatives of the nation will surely find it out, scrutinize the causes of the evil, and make the results of their investigation known, regardless of the consequences."[7] To scrutinize, reveal, and denounce: representation and legislation here take a back seat to a third parliamentary function, that of overseeing the activities of the government and ensuring full public disclosure.

During this second phase, Parliament wielded any number of instruments of surveillance and other checks on the power of the government: it could conduct investigations, express opposition, debate policy, monitor routine government functions, and if need be call for a vote of no confidence.

---

[6] See Léon Faucher, "Usages du Parlement britannique en matière d'enquête," *Le Courrier français*, January 13, 1835, as well as the article "Enquête" in the *Dictionnaire politique* published by Pagnerre in 1842. See also Alain Laquièze, *Les Origines du régime parlementaire en France (1814–1848)* (Paris: Presses Universitaires de France, 2002), pp. 317–329.

[7] Report by Martin (of the Nord), April 10, 1832, *AP*, 2nd series, vol. 77, p. 416.

In nineteenth-century France, by contrast, these counter-powers were in a sense "repossessed" by the state after having been held by civil society for a time during the Revolution. To be sure, the press retained independent power, but it might be argued that liberal parliamentarism was defined by the claim that Parliament ought to monopolize the powers of oversight; in this respect it was at odds with more democratic ideas of governance. Among theorists, John Stuart Mill put this point most explicitly. In *Representative Government* he argued that action and oversight were not strictly parallel. For him, this was the real reason for the separation of powers: "There is a radical distinction between controlling the business of government and actually doing it. The same person or body may be able to control everything, but cannot possibly do everything; and in many cases its control over everything will be more perfect the less it personally attempts to do."[8] The compensation for restriction of the ability to act was thus extension of the range of control. One might say therefore that oversight is an extensive power, whereas direct action is intensive. For Mill, this asymmetry defines the distinction between the executive power and the legislative power: "Instead of the function of governing, for which it is radically unfit, the proper office of a representative assembly is to watch and control the government: to throw the light of publicity on its acts: to compel a full exposition and justification of all of them which any one considers questionable; to censure them if found condemnable, and, if the men who compose the government abuse their trust, or fulfill it in a manner which conflicts with the

[8] John Stuart Mill, *Representative Government*, chap. 5.

deliberate sense of the nation, to expel them from office, and either expressly or virtually appoint their successors."[9]

For Mill, the power of parliamentary control was passive, its function essentially negative. It was not democratic in nature, in the sense that it did not emanate from the general will. For this theorist of liberal parliamentarism, moreover, there existed an almost sociological distinction between oversight and governance, quite remote from any democratic perspective: in his view, action required a higher level of ability than oversight. For Mill, this functional distinction clearly derived from the idea that a certain distance separated the elites from the masses: "[D]oing … is the task not of a miscellaneous body, but of individuals specially trained to it; … the fit office of an assembly is to see that those individuals are honestly and intelligently chosen, and to interfere no further with them, except by unlimited latitude of suggestion and criticism, and by applying or withholding the final seal of national assent. It is for want of this judicious reserve that popular assemblies attempt to do what they cannot do well – to govern and legislate."[10] In Mill's conception, Parliament is the central voice of public opinion. His idea is clearly that it is the only "authorized" expression of public opinion, although he does not go so far as to use that adjective. As "grievance committee" and "congress of opinions," Parliament in effect becomes an adequate embodiment of public opinion in general.

This conception of parliamentarism fits quite naturally into a minimal vision of democracy: the representatives of the people perform a regulatory function and serve as

[9] *Ibid.*   [10] *Ibid.*

protectors of liberty. To be sure, Mill recognizes the need for some degree of direct intervention by the people. But such intervention is in no sense a form of participation. It is merely an "ultimate form of control" or a "power of final control."[11] For Mill, representative government is essentially an organized series of controls, and the designation of representatives by way of the ballot box is only the initial act in the constitution of such an organization. Such a political system, in which the direct exercise of democratic power (through elections) is at once *functionally negative* (in the sense that it merely gives rise to a supervisory power) and *structurally secondary*, can be called "liberal": the legitimacy that stems from the election of representatives and the appointment of a government by the elected representatives is limited by the hierarchical organization of controls. Mill's theory is thus the natural result of abandoning earlier attempts to define a dual democracy: for him, Parliament incorporates all indirect democratic powers.

Paradoxically, the Jacobin Republic in France held fast to a similar conception of Parliament as the sole embodiment of all powers of oversight. Although the French Republic was "more democratic" in the sense that it celebrated the "voting public" and made universal suffrage the "sacred ark" of collective organization, it did not conceive of counter-powers outside the framework of official institutions. In this respect it remained viscerally parliamentarian. Its triumph inaugurated a monist electoral principle of democracy. Robespierre and Bonaparte not only theorized but also embodied this principle, and later nineteenth-century republicans offered a culturally

[11] *Ibid.*

diluted but philosophically faithful version of the same idea. Active political intervention by society was firmly rejected, as in the English theory of liberal parliamentarism. On both sides of the channel, regimes invoked the authority of the "absent people." In the French case, that absence was justified by endless abstraction; in the English, it was a result of social distance and wariness of the people. In fact, however, the people may have been absent but were hardly quiet, and they sought to make their voice heard beyond the ballot box. Popular impatience with government excess and misconduct sometimes took to the streets and other times resorted to the megaphone of the "penny press" as the people regularly sought to assert themselves as a counter-power to government. Yet such expressions of popular discontent were repeatedly dismissed as "undisciplined" or "unruly."

A third phase began in the 1970s. By then, parliamentarism was in decline, and civil society had developed the means to act independently. More "socialized" forms of indirect democracy therefore merged. New powers of oversight developed, and old ones were reorganized and refocused. These changes were but a small part of a broader movement to reappropriate forms of vigilance, investigation, and evaluation that had been subsumed within the parliamentary order over the course of the nineteenth and twentieth centuries.

Democratic dualism: a long history

If election and representation are one pillar of democracy and watchdog powers another, might it not be a good idea to strengthen the latter by institutionalizing them? Establishing mature controls on government might in fact mark a fourth stage in the emergence of democratic governance. This is more than idle theoretical speculation. In fact, democratic dualism, to give a name to this complementarity of representation and oversight, has a long history. This history has largely been forgotten, so we must first pause to trace its broad outlines if we are to proceed further in our reflections. We must go all the way back to the beginning – to the Greeks, that is – in order to understand why the history of democracy took the course it did.

In classical Athens, magistrates were chosen by lot more often than by election; indeed, the casting of lots was regarded as the essence of democracy. It was more radically egalitarian than voting, since it assumed that all citizens are equally capable of discharging the duties of public office. This point has been abundantly documented and discussed.[12] All too often overlooked, however, is a second characteristic of democracy, which the Greeks regarded as equally fundamental: the institution of systematic controls over the actions of any individual discharging a public function or handling public funds. Herodotus was the first to call attention to this: "In a popular regime," he wrote, "offices are distributed by lot, magistrates are responsible for their actions, and all decisions are laid before the people."[13] Rendering accounts at the end of one's mandate was the principal way in which this type of control was exercised. As for Aristotle, although he rejected Plato's aristocratic and "technocratic" reservations regarding

---

[12] See most recently Bernard Manin, *Principes du gouvernment représentatif* (Paris: Calmann-Lévy, 1995).

[13] Herodotus, *History*.

the selection of guardians, this was not the point he empha-sized in his definition of democracy. For him, the key feature of democracy was close supervision of magistrates by citizens. Although he proposed a number of different approaches in his *Politics*, and although he seemed in doubt at times about the definition of a good regime, he never abandoned the principle of popular control. Even in cases where he granted only limited power to citizens, he did not impose limits on their power to control magistrates. Ultimately, it was this power that was the central element of the various "mixed constitutions" he saw as desirable. If democracy is first and foremost a regime of "isonomy," citizen sovereignty is based on the idea of citizens as *euthynoi*, that is, "correctors" or "overseers."[14]

The Greeks envisioned a number of different forms of democratic control. In classical Athens as described by Aristotle, various officials (chosen by lot) were assigned the task of supervising the work of other officials (either chosen by lot or elected). There were overseers (*euthynoi*), auditors (*legistai*), supervisors (*exetastai*), and public ombudsmen (*synegoroi*).[15] Most other Greek cities employed similar meth-ods down to the end of the Hellenistic era, sometimes examin-ing accounts at the end of an official's mandate and at other times conducting audits during his active tenure.[16] The type

---

[14] On this etymology, see Pierre Fröhlich, *Les Cités grecques et le contrôle des magistrats (IVe–Ier siècle avant Jésus-Christ)* (Geneva: Droz, 2004).

[15] Aristotle, *Politics* VI, 8, 1322b 7–12.

[16] See Fröhlich, *Les Cités grecques*. This major work, which incorporates the most recent epigraphic research and does not limit its attention to Athens, places special emphasis on audits conducted during an official's tenure.

of audit chosen and the participation of ordinary citizens in the monitoring of officials are the best indices we have of a city's democratization. Similarly, the diminished importance and eventual disappearance of public audits are the most visible signs of democracy's decline.

This fundamental image of the "people as overseer" also helps to explain why it was so easy to institutionalize the selection of magistrates by lot. If officials are merely performing assigned tasks under strict regular supervision, it may indeed be possible to regard their personal abilities as relatively unimportant. "Good government" is not exclusively dependent on individual virtue or talent. Effective oversight procedures are more fundamental. The casting of lots in Athens was a "weak" form of democratic legitimation; oversight was more important. Together, these complementary institutions made a strong state possible. To paraphrase Adam Smith, one might say that the Greeks did not count on benevolence and virtue to achieve the common good; they relied instead on the self-interest of individuals, since every official had a direct interest in avoiding "reproach" for misconduct (the penalties could be quite severe). The available evidence does not permit us to say how this vision of democracy arose. Nevertheless, it is plausible to assume that experience of political corruption gradually gave rise to the idea that regular audits were the best means of limiting the scourge. In any case, Aristotle seems to have been of this opinion. He says that the *gerontes* (elders) of Sparta were susceptible to corruption largely because Sparta did not audit its officials. "Many of the elders are well known to have taken bribes and to have been guilty of partiality in public affairs. And

86

therefore they ought not to be non-accountable; yet at Sparta they are so."[17]

Looked at from this angle, democracy is defined not so much by popular election of leaders as by citizen oversight. In the modern era, however, elections became such a "total democratic institution" that this duality eventually disappeared. By "total democratic institution" I mean that elections were taken to be not just a technical device for choosing leaders but also a means of establishing trust in government and a system for regulating public action. We need to explore this development more fully if we hope to grasp the origins of today's political malaise.

The eighteenth century did not see Athenian democracy as we do. Government oversight was still a central issue. Everyone who attended secondary school read Plutarch and gained some familiarity with the institutions of Antiquity. Writers therefore regularly referred to Roman censors and Spartan *ephoroi*. Montesquieu devoted considerable attention to the *ephoroi*, which etymologically means "those who look at, observe, or oversee" the powers that be.[18] Rousseau also appreciated their role and dedicated an entire chapter of the *Social Contract* to the Roman censors, who were responsible for auditing public accounts and had jurisdiction over certain kinds of lawsuits. De Lolme and Filangieri also stressed the

[17] Aristotle, *Politics*, II, 9, 26, 1271a 3–6 (Oxford translation, p. 2017). Quoted in Fröhlich, *Les Cités grecques*, p. 35.

[18] On the historical interpretation of the *ephoroi*, see Nicole Richer, *Les Ephores. Etudes sur l'histoire et sur l'image de Sparte (VIIIe–IIIe siècles avant Jésus-Christ)* (Paris: Publications de la Sorbonne, 1998).

importance of "censorial power,"[19] and the *Encyclopedia* of Diderot and d'Alembert included well-informed articles on these institutions, which were said to "counterbalance" the governing authorities. All of these authors hoped to see the emergence not only of representative institutions but also of powers of oversight based on these ancient models. The idea of counter-powers was of liberal as well as democratic inspiration. Indeed, it was liberal in essence, since its purpose was to limit government action owing to the belief that all government tends toward despotism. Montesquieu concentrated on the control of monarchical power, but he also worried about limiting potential excesses of popular power. He praised the Spartan *ephoroi* for their ability to "punish the weaknesses of kings, nobles, and people."[20] This "liberal" approach to oversight also existed in England throughout the eighteenth century. The *Independent Whig*, a major republican organ of the day, claimed that the major reason for its existence was the need to oversee the action of the government and censure it when necessary.[21]

---

[19] Jean-Louis de Lolme, *Constitution de l'Angleterre* (1778), 5th edn (Paris, 1849), p. 297, and Gaetano Filangieri, *La Science de la législation* (1780–1785), book I, chap. 8, "De la nécessité d'un censeur des lois."

[20] Montesquieu, *De l'esprit des lois*, chap. 8. The *Encyclopédie* ended its article on "*ephoroi*" by pointing out "the advantages of a magistracy designed to prevent both royal and aristocratic authority from slipping into harshness and tyranny, while preventing popular liberty from devolving into license and rebellion."

[21] "He claims a Right of examining all publick Measures and, if they deserve it, of censuring them. As he never saw much Power possessed without some Abuse, he takes upon him to watch those that have it; and to acquit or expose them according as they apply it to the good of their country, or

By contrast, other writers clearly recognized the democratic essence of oversight and saw that it could lead to new forms of popular participation in politics. This was Rousseau's view. It was shared by Richard Price, who discussed it in terms borrowed from Rousseau as well as Montesquieu.[22] But the best symbol of the democratic approach was the Pennsylvania state constitution adopted in 1776. This document was widely regarded as having established the most democratic of all American state governments: unicameral legislature; suffrage granted to all taxpayers, regardless of the amount of tax they paid; and a system of rotation for members of the House of Representatives. The most distinctive feature of the constitution was Article 47, which provided for a Council of

their own crooked Purposes." This excerpt from the pamphlets published by John Trenchard and Thomas Gordon during the reign of George I under the title *Independent Whig* (1723) is quoted in Caroline Robbins, *The Eighteenth-Century Commonwealthman: Studies in the Transmission, Development and Circumstance of English Liberal Thought from the Restoration of Charles II until the War with the Thirteen Colonies* (New York: Atheneum, 1968), p. 120.

[22] Take, for example, the "liberal" emphasis in Price's vision of surveillance in *Observations on the Nature of Civil Liberty* (1776): "There is nothing that requires more to be watched than power. There is nothing that ought to be opposed with a more determined resolution than its encroachments. Sleep in a state, as Montesquieu says, is always followed by slavery" (in Richard Price, *Political Writings* [Cambridge University Press, 1991], p. 30). Contrast this with his defense of the French Revolution in *Discourse on the love of our Country* (1789), which was directed against Burke. Here Price defends the idea that resistance to the abuse of power is a fundamental right and goes even further toward democracy by discussing the right "to frame a government for ourselves." *Ibid.*, p. 190.

Censors.[23] Elected by the people of the state's cities and counties, the censors were to ensure that the executive and legislative branches properly performed their duties as "guardians of the people." The council, which deliberated in public session, could issue warnings, bring suit in court, remove officials found guilty of wrongdoing, and recommend the repeal of laws deemed contrary to the constitution. It could also convoke a constitutional convention. Like Europeans, Americans in those days were steeped in references to Rome, Sparta, and Athens. Every high school student read Kenneth's *Roman Antiquities*. Editorialists and pamphleteers liked to sign themselves "Cato," "Cassandra," or "Spartacus." With the constitution of Pennsylvania they put their classicism into action (and the state of Vermont adopted a similar constitution a short while later). The text was widely discussed in Europe. With the help of Benjamin Franklin, the Duke de La Rochefoucauld translated Pennsylvania's constitution into French early in 1777. The *Encyclopédie méthodique* immediately devoted a long article to it. Brissot wrote a quite militant pamphlet praising the Pennsylvania text and expressing warm approval of the Council of Censors.[24]

[23] On the Council of Censors, see Lewis H. Meader, "The Council of Censors," *The Pennsylvania Magazine of History and Biography* 22, no. 3, (Oct. 1898); J. Paul Selsam, *The Pennsylvania Constitution of 1776: A Study in Revolutionary Democracy* (New York: Da Capo Press, 1971); Donald S. Lutz, *Popular Control and Popular Consent: Whig Political Theory in the Early State Constitutions* (Baton Rouge: Louisiana State University Press, 1980).
[24] Brissot de Warville, "Réflexions sur le Code de Pennsylvanie," *Bibliothèque philosophique du législateur, du politique et du jurisconsulte* (Berlin, 1783), vol. III, pp. 253–257.

Condorcet, Mably, Mirabeau, and Turgot also discussed its functions.[25] The institutionalization of governmental oversight was no less exalted than the establishment of representative government.

Less than twenty years later, the need for governmental oversight became a topic of discussion in French constitutional debates. As early as 1791, proposals to establish formal controls issued from both the Cercle Social and the Club des Cordeliers. Lavicomterie devoted a long chapter to the subject in his programmatic work *Du peuple et des rois* (1791), in which he proposed creating a group of censors. In *La Bouche de fer*, Bonneville suggested that each *département* elect twelve "tribunes of the people" to oversee the actions of government. He also discussed the possibility of a "National Censorship."[26] In the spring of 1793, censors and ephors were mentioned frequently in various constitutional proposals debated at the Convention. Daunou called for "a harmonically organized surveillance of the sovereign," while the citizens of the Unité section proposed a "tribunal of ephors". Poultier looked to an "orator of the people," whose duty it would be to denounce

[25] See J. Paul Selsam and Joseph Rayback, "French comment on the Pennsylvania Constitution of 1776," *The Pennsylvania Magazine of History and Biography* 76, no. 3 (July 1952); Christian Lerat, "La première Constitution de Pennsylvanie: son rejet à Philadelphie, ses échos en France," in Jean-Louis Seurin *et al.*, *Le Discours sur les Révolutions* (Paris: Economica, 1991), vol. II; Horst Dippel, "Condorcet et la discussion des Constitutions américaines en France avant 1789," in *Condorcet, homme des Lumières et de la Révolution* (Paris: ENS Éditions, 1997).

[26] Recall that the title *bouche de fer* (mouth of iron) was borrowed from the Venetian "mouth of stone," into which citizens could slip accusations against government officials and complaints about their actions.

any negligence, failure, disloyalty, or conspiracy on the part of government officials. Prunelle de Lierre sponsored a "tribunal of the conscience of the people," while Hérault de Séchelles envisioned a "national jury" that would sit alongside the representative body for the purpose of "avenging any citizen oppressed by abusive actions of the Legislative Body or the Executive Council." Bacon evoked a "third regulatory power," while Rouzet spoke of a "college of ephors," and Kersaint envisioned a "tribunal of censors."[27] Clearly, the delegates to the Convention had particularly fertile imaginations in this regard. Despite the variety of names and procedures that were proposed, the concern was always the same: to institutionalize social vigilance and to understand sovereignty in terms of a dynamic and potentially conflictual relationship between a representative power and a power of oversight, both emanating from the people. Daunou and Cabanis offered similar proposals later, in 1799. When the "sister republics" were organized, we again find clear evidence of similar projects.[28] The Constitution of Year VIII bore a sign of one in the form of the Tribunate. It would not amount to much, however. And eventually the constitutions of Pennsylvania and Vermont were rewritten, and the Council of Censors was eliminated. In Great Britain, the debate did not take this turn. It is important to understand why these things happened.

---

[27] See vols. 63 to 67 of *AP*, 1st series.

[28] Cf., for example, the proposals of Mario Pagano in Naples. See Mario Battaglini, *Mario Pagano e il progetto di Costituzione della Republica napoletana* (Rome: Archivio Guido Izzi, 1994).

The impossibility of institutionalization

Let us begin with Pennsylvania. Established by the 1776 state constitution, the Council of Censors met for the first time in 1783 (it was to hold one long session every seven years). This would prove to be its only meeting, for it was abolished by a new state constitution adopted in 1790. To be sure, part of the reason for its elimination was "political." Revolutionary sentiment subsided as the War for Independence faded into the past. During the ratification campaign for the federal constitution in the winter of 1787–1788, the state convention accepted the position of the moderate federalists.[29] The unicameral legislature was also eliminated in 1790 for fear that it offered no barrier to any potential outburst of popular passions. The elimination of the Council of Censors thus took place in a context of conservative reaction; the dominant sentiment emphasized the need for prudence in the defense of liberty. To leave it at that would be insufficient, however. There was also a purely institutional reason for retreat on this issue: the council meeting had been the scene of a clash between radicals and moderates.[30] The intended role of the council, which was to embody a functional counter-power, had thus been overshadowed by internal conflict. Some degree of unity is essential in an oversight agency of this type. If it becomes a political arena in which the political divisions of the larger society and the representative assembly

[29] See Merryll Jensen, ed., *The Documentary History of the Ratification of the Constitution*, vol. II: *Pennsylvania* (Madison: State History Society of Wisconsin, 1976).

[30] See Meader, "The Council of Censors."

93

are simply reproduced, then its mission is undermined to the point where it essentially becomes impossible. By 1790, therefore, the general feeling was that it was simpler to allow the majority and the opposition to interact directly, while at the same time relying on an *internal* balance of power (bicameralism, constitutional court). The problem with this solution, however, was that it made the constitution less democratic. Hence this history contains important lessons, which can be pursued further by turning next to another case, that of the French Tribunate of 1800.

The Constitution of Year VIII envisioned a complex governmental structure, shaped in part by Sieyès' fertile imagination and in part by Bonaparte's impatience.[31] It instituted three assemblies: a Senate, a Legislative Body, and a Tribunate. The Senate's chief function was to ensure the constitutionality of all laws. The Legislative Body voted on laws and budgets but without deliberation or the right to amend. It was a "body of mutes," whose only power was to judge. Bonaparte's influence can be seen here: the government enjoyed broad powers, including the exclusive right to propose new laws. The Tribunate was the body in which these proposed laws were to be discussed. It was empowered to say which initiatives it believed to be desirable. It could also call attention to "abuses to be corrected and improvements to be made in any part of the public bureaucracy."[32] It could receive petitions and

---

[31] See Jean Bourdon, *La Constitution de l'an VIII* (Rodez, 1942).

[32] Article 29 of the Constitution. On the origins of this article, see the important letter on constitutional matters from Bonaparte to Talleyrand, dated September 21, 1797, in Thierry Lentz, ed., *Correspondance générale*

denounce ministers to the Legislative Body (which could then impeach them and refer them for trial before a High Court). Finally, it had the power to consider situations in which the Constitution might be suspended. Clearly, the institution borrowed a number of ideas from 1791 and 1793 concerning the power of oversight, even if it did water them down. The very name "Tribunate" alluded directly to those earlier projects and their Roman inspiration, and especially to an institution to which Rousseau had devoted considerable attention in the *Contrat Social*. It had a democratic connotation, since it evoked the image of the "tribunes of the people" whose role had often been exalted after 1789. *Le Tribun du peuple* had also been the name that Bonneville and later Babeuf gave to their prestigious and path-breaking newspapers. But once again the experiment ended prematurely for obvious historical reasons that we need not dwell on here (the advent of the First Empire and then, in Year X, the establishment of Napoleon's Life Consulate). More interesting for present purposes, however, is the fact that the Tribunate never found its proper place, even before it succumbed to the First Consul's avaricious appetite for power. The questions and debates that arose during the Tribunate's first session will help us to gauge the magnitude of the difficulty.

No sooner had the Constitution been approved than Bonaparte (who had hoped for a plebiscite) decided to muzzle

(Paris: Fayard, 2004), vol. I, pp. 1196–1198. Bonaparte speaks of a *magistrature de surveillance* but in a very limited sense, because he sees it as a legislative power of very limited scope. Note that Bonaparte asked Talleyrand to convey this letter to Sieyès.

the Assembly lest it become a focal point of organized opposition, as almost certainly would have been the case. The first
bill he submitted to the Tribunate proposed a reform in the
"formation of the law." Tight limits were imposed on deliberation, and it was expressly stated that if the Assembly did
not vote by the "date set by the government," it would be
taken to have given its consent. The government could thus
limit debate to little more than a reading of the bill, rendering
any serious examination of its substance impossible. The nature
of the institution therefore became the subject of countless
articles and speeches. Bonaparte's action focused attention on
a key question: What was the relation between the oversight
function and the idea of opposition? Roederer, a member of the
Constituent Assembly who had approved of the coup d'état of 18
Brumaire, vigorously defended the Assembly in an article published in his own *Journal de Paris*. "Does anyone know what
the Tribunate really is?" he asked. "Is it truly the *organized
opposition*? Is it true that a tribune is condemned always to
oppose the government, without reason or measure? Must
he attack everything it does and everything it proposes?
Must he speak out against the government when he most
approves its conduct? Must he denounce when he has nothing but good to say? ... If that were the calling of the tribune,
it would be the vilest and most odious of professions. I have
a different idea. I regard the Tribunate as an assembly of
statesmen responsible for overseeing, revising, purifying,
and perfecting the work of the Council of State and contri-
buting alongside it to the public good. A true Councilor of
State is a tribune standing close to the supreme authority.
The true tribune is a Councilor of State standing amongst

the people."[33] In other words, the "functional" exercise of oversight is something different from the more "political" manifestation of organized opposition to the government. Roederer was the first to make this distinction, but he did not develop it. Benjamin Constant, a member of the Assembly, also took part in the debate. He delivered an important speech on the same theme.[34] He, too, objected to "regarding the Tribunate as a permanent opposition body" on the grounds that to do so would be to deprive it of credibility and influence. Still, it is striking that the young political thinker, who had begun to establish a reputation matched only by the hostility it soon elicited from the First Consul, also failed to elaborate the conceptual difference between political opposition and institutional oversight that defined the function of the Tribunate. His speech was filled with negations and warnings: "An opposition without discernment is also an opposition without force." "The Tribunate is not an assembly of rhetoricians whose only occupation is to proclaim their opposition from the podium." He vigorously rejected "the idea of a perpetual and indiscriminate opposition." Yet he had a hard time defining the positive basis of the Tribunate's function, appealing instead in banal moralistic terms to its "courageous tenacity" and "independence." Constant's difficulty stemmed from his inability to find a place for the power of oversight in a democratic regime. It is impossible to conceptualize such a power unless one recognizes

[33] Roederer, "Du Tribunat," *Journal de Paris*, 15 nivôse Year VIII (January 5, 1800), in *Œuvres du Comte P. L. Roederer* (Paris, 1867), vol. VI, p. 399.
[34] Speech of 15 nivôse Year VIII, in Benjamin Constant, "Discours au Tribunat," *Œuvres complètes* (Tübingen: Max Niemeyer Verlag, 2005), vol. IV, pp. 73–84.

the duality of popular sovereignty. Hence Constant had a blind spot: he failed to distinguish between the democratic potential of the Tribunate (which could have reduced representative entropy by increasing social power) and its liberal function (to protect against governmental encroachment). It therefore comes as no surprise to discover that Madame de Staël's partner later dropped all reference to an institution of such indeterminate nature and became instead the theorist of what he called a "neutral power," whose function was clearly and exclusively liberal.[35] This neutral power, still characterized as a "third power" between the legislative and the executive, or a "preservative power," is essentially a constitutional court. Constant says emphatically that it is to be "the judicial power of the other powers."[36] It was in the same spirit that Sieyès had developed the idea of a "constitutional jury" as early as Year III.[37]

Bonaparte, being an impatient man of action, found the Tribunate irritating. In the summer of 1800, for example, he asked, "Why a body of one hundred members, who are useless and ridiculous when things are going well and disruptive

---

[35] A developed version of this idea can be found in Benjamin Constant, *Fragments d'un ouvrage abandonné sur la possibilité d'une Constitution républicaine dans un grand pays*, ed. Henri Grange (Paris: Aubier, 1991). See book VIII: "D'un pouvoir neutre ou préservateur nécessaire dans toutes les constitutions."

[36] *Ibid.*, p. 390.

[37] See Pasquale Pasquino, *Sieyès et l'invention de la constitution en France* (Paris: Odile Jacob, 1998). For an overview of the idea of a third power in France in this period, see Marcel Gauchet, *La Révolution des pouvoirs: La Souveraineté, le peuple et la représentation, 1789–1799* (Paris: Gallimard, 1995).

the moment anything goes wrong, a veritable alarm bell?"[38] But it was even more as a strict Jacobin that he rejected the idea of a positive opposition and active oversight. Popular sovereignty made no sense to the First Consul unless it could assert itself in a polarized fashion. It was clear to him that the nation needed no protection from the government as long as all constituent authorities emanated from the nation. Bonaparte thus partook of the dominant anti-pluralist sentiment in France at that time. For him, democracy could not be anything but anti-liberal.[39] "Is it possible to conceive of such a thing as an opposition to the sovereign people?" he asked in January of 1802, "Can there be tribunes where there is no patriciate?"[40] At that time the mere mention of the word "opposition" evoked images of revolutionary conflict and chaos, which only reinforced the point.

The failure to establish a power of oversight in the Tribunate thus marked a turning point in France. Still, the idea

---

[38] See Roederer in Œuvres, vol. III, pp. 335–336. Thibaudeau, Mémoires sur le Consulat (Paris, 1827), p. 204, notes that he spoke even more crudely about "good-for-nothing metaphysicians, vermin who infest my robes."

[39] See Pierre Rosanvallon, Le Modèle politique français. La société civile contre le jacobinisme de 1789 à nos jours (Paris: Éditions du Seuil, 2004).

[40] Reported by Roederer in Œuvres, vol. III, p. 427. These words can be compared with an important text of 1791. In that year, the Ami des patriotes wrote: "Our government has no need of opposition, and everything that has been said and resaid about the need for a balance of powers cannot usefully be applied to it." The newspaper also denounced the opposition as a "party of intrigue, which is incapable of opposing anything other than execution of the law." Quoted in Ferdinand Brunot, Histoire de la langue française, vol. IX: La Révolution et l'Empire, part 2, p. 821.

was not given up entirely. Indeed, radical republicans enthusiastically revived it in the 1830s. For instance, the Society for
the Rights of Man and the Citizen noted in its statement of
principles that popular sovereignty required the establishment
of "a permanent council of investigation and improvement,"
among whose functions would be "the reform of public institutions."[41] The *Tribune des départements*, a Montagnard newspaper of the time that invoked the heritage of Robespierre,
made a similar suggestion. Important early socialists such as
Philippe Buchez and Charles Teste conceived of an organ of
oversight and initiative distinct from the representative assemblies. In 1840, Charles-François Chevé proposed a "Democratic
Program" in which he spelled out in detail a number of tasks
that could be assigned to a "Committee of Improvement and
Investigation," whose members were to be either elected or
selected competitively to represent certain areas of competence.
What was the purpose of such an institution to be? For Chevé,
it was to embody a "power devoid of all political authority, alien
to the concerns of the parties and the present ... which would
act as both a permanent investigative body and a diligent
workshop for the development of new and better methods, a
clearing house for popular demands and a tireless laboratory
for future improvements."[42] In other words, Chevé saw
the committee as a body performing functions of representation, initiative, and oversight distinct from the responsibilities

---

[41] *Exposé des principes républicains de la Société des droits de l'homme et du
citoyen* (Paris: [1832]), p. 6.
[42] Charles-François Chevé, *Programme démocratique, ou résumé d'une
organisation complète de la démocratie radicale* (Paris, 1840), pp. 4–5.

ascribed to the legislature proper. Projects of similar inspiration were also discussed in 1848. For instance, the socialist
Pierre Leroux suggested establishing a "national jury" of three
hundred citizens to be chosen by lot in the *départements* for
the purpose of monitoring and judging the representatives of
the nation. This jury was thus to complement the role of the
press (with respect to oversight) and of elections (with respect
to pronouncing judgment on government actions).[43] A respected republican writer on politics, alluding to ancient institutions, proposed an "Inspectorate" to be elected by universal
suffrage. Inspectors were to "keep an eye on everything that
is done and make sure that everything necessary is in fact
done."[44] Once again, the goal was to establish "constant surveillance," which was deemed to be "indispensable to a republican regime" because it was a way for the sovereign people
to express its will. It was also seen as a democratization and
expansion of the idea of a "public ministry" exercising a
judicial function.[45]

These numerous proposals show that the idea of institutionalizing a power of oversight in one form or another was a
constant feature of French political thought in the first half of
the nineteenth century. Yet none of these ideas was seriously
considered at the crucial moment when the constitution of
the Second Republic was drafted. Jacobin monism combined

[43] See chaps. 4 and 5 of Pierre Leroux, *Projet d'une Constitution
démocratique et sociale* (Paris, 1848).
[44] Auguste Billiard, *De l'organisation de la République* (Paris, 1848), p. 272.
[45] *Ibid.*, chap. 11. Recall that the "public ministry" was to consist of
magistrates representing both the state and the general interests of
society.

with liberal as well as conservative caution to reject the idea of active democratic oversight after 1848. To be sure, there was a good deal of naïveté in the enthusiasm for surveillance in the period 1789–1848. There was also a certain suspicion of the idea owing to the excesses of the revolutionary societies, which tinged it at times with hints of totalitarian regimentation. More serious still, there was much vagueness in all these schemes, and the patriotic fervor of so many inventive soldiers of liberty led them to idealize the people as disinterested judges of the actions of the state. Nevertheless, a powerful intuition remains, an intuition that pointed the way toward a novel understanding of modern politics and marked an important step beyond previous political theories. The ancient ideal of the vigilant citizen – the citizen most clearly deserving of the appellation "active" – was once again brought to the fore. With the ubiquitous exhortation to citizens to keep an eye on everything and everyone, an idea of public morality in the democratic age began to take shape. Subsequently, however, it was quietly abandoned, because the faith it placed in public opinion made it suspect to both anxious defenders of the established order and apostles of the new scientific age. Fear of the untutored power of the masses and the turbulent passions of the multitude led the nineteenth century toward quieter waters, whether of conservative liberalism or scientific socialism. Republicans were content to make universal suffrage the sacred and sufficient touchstone of democracy.

The idea of oversight was later recycled. As we have seen, it was incorporated as a regular part of parliamentary government, which England offered as a model to the nineteenth century. The three key methods of liberal control – oversight by the opposition, parliamentary investigation, and influence of public opinion – were perfected there; only judicial review of the constitutionality of laws was missing. Some directly democratic forms of social oversight remained, as I described earlier. But the idea of institutionalizing them faded from view before they could receive adequate theoretical treatment.

4

Legitimacy conflicts

The proliferation of powers of oversight leads to what might be called *democratic competition*. The electoral-representative system must contend with various forms of counter-democracy. The resulting rivalry is partly functional: parliamentary control versus control by independent authorities, for example. But it is also a rivalry between actors of different types: elected representatives versus militant organizations and the media. Conflicts arise over representativeness and legitimacy. The resulting tension between constitutional powers and the media is not new, moreover; it has historical precedents.

The pen and the podium

If "the people *are* public opinion," as was said in 1789, then there can be conflict over how public opinion is represented. On the one hand, the people choose their representatives by voting. On the other hand, people have opinions, and public opinion finds its expression, however imperfectly, through various organs. Thus the deputy and the journalist are potential rivals. The French Revolution was an extraordinary laboratory in this regard, and by studying it we can gain a better grasp of the nature of the rivalry between the pen and the podium. In 1789, the French took to speaking and writing even as they were taking the Bastille. They believed that their new freedom of expression was just as important as the freedom to choose their own representatives. Under these conditions, newspapers established themselves as true political institutions with a duty to observe, censure, and denounce. The names of many of these papers summed up their intentions: *La Sentinelle du peuple* (*The Sentinel of the People*), *Le Dénonciateur* (*The Denouncer*), *Le Censeur patriote* (*The Patriotic Censor*), *Le Furet parisien* (*The Parisian Ferret*), *Le Rôdeur français* (*The French Stalker*).[1] The memory of the English political commentator "Junius" (the pseudonym used by the writer of a series of letters to the *Public Advertiser* on the rights of Englishmen) was also widely honored. Marat's first published text was entitled *Le Junius français*, for example, while Bonneville, in launching his *Tribun du peuple*, invoked "the example of the *public advertisers* of England," as embodied by the "unknown patriot" Junius.[2] All of these writers, from the most celebrated to the most humble, professed their faith in the most repetitious of terms. A few quotes will suffice to give the flavor. Camille Desmoulins advocated a "censorial empire" of public opinion,[3] with "the censor's album" to be kept by journalists.[4] In his *Patriote français*, Brissot insisted that "freedom of the press is the only way for the people to

---

[1] On this subject the essential reference is Claude Labrosse and Pierre Rétat, *Naissance du journal révolutionnaire* (Presses Universitaires de Lyon, 1989).

[2] Italics in the original. See Bonneville, "Adresse à l'assemblée nationale," in the *Prospectus* of June 1789 (*Le Vieux Tribun du peuple*, repr. [Paris, 1793], vol. I, p. 88).

[3] Camille Desmoulins, *Révolutions de France et de Brabant*, no. 1, November 28, 1789, p. 3.

[4] *Ibid.*, no. 2, December 5, 1789, p. 47.

oversee, instruct, and censure their representatives."[5] The paper's epigraph proudly proclaimed that "a free gazette is a sentinel that maintains a constant watch over the people's interests."

The status of the journalist changed as well. No longer was he a humble hack or a paid servant of some powerful patron. He assumed the role of key political player, untouchable and almost sacred. More than that, he became a veritable institution. Camille Desmoulins theorized about the journalist's new role: "Today, the journalist exercises a public ministry," he fills "a veritable magistracy."[6] Michelet rightly observes that journalism established itself as something like a "public function" in this period.[7] It is hardly surprising that journalists saw themselves as the voice of public opinion, but in fact they were much more than that. They also performed a representative function and exercised a share of sovereignty. They competed with the elected representatives of the people in their effort to express, day in and day out, the expectations of society. "I am the eye of the people; you are at best their little finger," was Marat's mocking and contemptuous challenge to the representatives of the Paris Commune.[8] Desmoulins repeatedly portrayed himself as a rival to the people's deputies and even asserted his superiority over them. The journalist's power was

[5] *Patriote français*, no. 10, April 7, 1789, p. 3.
[6] See Jean-Claude Bonnet, "Les rôles du journalisme selon Camille Desmoulins," in Pierre Rétat, ed., *La Révolution du journal 1788–1794* (Paris: Éditions du CNRS, 1789).
[7] Jules Michelet, *Histoire de la Révolution française*, book 2, chap. 7, (Paris: La Pléiade), vol. I, p. 240.
[8] Quoted in Rétat, *La Révolution du journal*, p. 197.

the power of surveillance. This key word of the revolutionary lexicon evoked the functions of the censors, ephors, and *euthynoi* of antiquity, which many people in the revolutionary era hoped to see revived outside the institutions of government. The powers of oversight exercised by journalists were therefore seen as democratic powers, a form of political sovereignty in the guise of an "invisible institution." In other words, they were more than just an exercise of freedom of the press. One of the most celebrated journalists of the day put it bluntly: "An unshackled press takes the place of a senate, a veto, and the whole Anglican get-up."[9] The fundamental issues of dual sovereignty that this conception posed were not dealt with during the revolutionary period, however. At the time, duality was seen only as a way of increasing civic activity in general and of regulating the representative system. This conception of politics had no legal basis. The coexistence of an elected government and a press that conceived of itself as a political institution was taken to be a consequence of the general tendency of the times, which made it possible for the two to work together efficiently.

The potential conflict of legitimacy was difficult to discern in revolutionary times, as indeed it is in any situation where political rights have yet to be secured. It came clearly into focus, however, as soon as universal suffrage was durably established. In France, the conflict emerged most clearly during the Second Empire; in fact, it took a particularly radical form because that regime invoked the legitimacy of the ballot box (symbolized by the restoration of full universal suffrage after the coup of December 2, 1851) to justify its anti-liberal

---

[9] Anarcharsis Cloots, quoted in Bonnet, "Les rôles du journalisme," p. 180.

stance. The Bonapartists' main argument for limiting freedom of the press was that the press had no democratic legitimacy, that it was not representative. Granier de Cassagnac, one of Bonapartism's chief ideologues, developed this argument at length: "The influence of the press is characterized primarily by a total absence of delegation. In contrast to all regular powers, the least of which is rooted in the constitution and delegated by it, the press is a spontaneous, voluntary power answering only to itself, its interests, its whims, and its ambitions. The number of public powers is limited; the number of newspapers is not. The prerogatives of the public powers are defined, while those of the press are governed by neither rule nor measure."[10] The press, to borrow one of his more striking phrases, was virtually "the rival of the public powers,"[11] even though it was unconstrained by considerations of legitimacy or representativeness. If the press were not contained, he argued, it would constitute "a complete and flagrant usurpation of public authority."[12] He went on: "Though it has no right to elect, it seeks to control elections. Though it has no right to sit in deliberative bodies, it seeks to influence deliberations. Though it has no right to sit in sovereign councils, it seeks to provoke and prevent acts of government. In a word, it seeks

[10] Speech of March 16, 1866, *Annales du Sénat et du Corps législatif*, p. 138.
[11] *Ibid.*, p. 139. He went on: "Is it not offensive to common sense, this idea of voluntarily and unnecessarily erecting alongside the Emperor, the Senate, and the Legislative Body, a new and immense political power that is independent in its own sphere and whose delimited and defined authority is to set itself up as a rival to the regular government established by all?"
[12] Adolphe Granier de Cassagnac, *L'Empereur et la démocratie moderne* (Paris, 1860), p. 21.

to substitute its actions for those of the established and legal powers, though in reality it is invested with no powers in the proper sense of the term."[13]

In this perspective, newspapers were described as "hundreds of small states within the larger state." A newspaper was a public power in private hands. Journalists intervened with no mandate other than that of their conscience or personal interests. No one elected them, yet they embodied a genuine social power.[14] Were newspapers a private institution? Bonapartists mercilessly attacked the press as the instrument of capital. Granier de Cassagnac formulated this accusation in terms that certain contemporary critics of the media will recognize: a newspaper, he wrote, "is a capitalist corporation [that] buys itself a pack of talented writers."[15] From this the conclusion followed logically: newspapers, as representatives of partial interests, ought to be subordinated to the general interest. They must not be allowed to usurp the place of the

---

[13] *Ibid.*

[14] "Where," he asked, "in the usual constitution of the periodical press, is political prerogative or the delegation of power by the people? Where, among these capitalists and writers bound by nothing other than their own interest or convenience, is the investiture that would make them the directors and governors of political bodies and judges of the government? Where is the priesthood of which journalists speak from time to time? Will someone explain how the periodical press can dominate all the public powers without enjoying the prerogatives of the least of them?" *Ibid.*, p. 22. Opponents of freedom of the press under the Restoration had already made this their central argument. "In order to be a deputy, one has to be elected by the voters. The journalist bestows his powerful ministry upon himself." Quoted in Emile Ollivier, *Solutions politiques et sociales* (Paris, 1894), p. 114.

[15] Granier de Cassagnac, *L'Empereur et la démocratie moderne*, p. 22.

ballot box and pretend to speak for public opinion in all its generality. Since it was impossible to imagine how journalists might be elected, a way of controlling them had to be found. Elected officials, too, needed a voice, since they were supposed to be the true expression of the general will, which elected them.[16] What was at stake in this Caesarian vision of politics was thus the very conception of the public. At no time was the public envisioned as a space within which groups and individuals could interact and reflect. It was perceived exclusively in the rigid terms established by the legal institution of elections.

For French republicans, no words were harsh enough to denounce the reign of Napoleon III. They attacked the regime's manifest illiberalism yet found nothing wrong with its democratic self-justification. The coup by which Napoleon seized power on December 2, 1851, was enough to discredit him in their eyes, so they never developed legal or philosophical arguments against Caesarism as such. They denounced his misdeeds on liberal grounds and therefore remained blind to the deeper roots of the evil. Indeed, Napoleon III and his supporters had merely radicalized a certain Jacobin vision of democratic monism, drawing the ultimate conclusions from Jacobinism's hostility to pluralism. In practical terms, the republicans would overcome the difficulty by advocating a moderate, watered-down version of the same Jacobin ideas.

---

[16] It should come as no surprise, therefore, to learn that the regime considered launching a very inexpensive newspaper to give the public its voice. On this point, see Émile de Girardin, "L'État journaliste," in *Force ou richesse. Question de 1864* (Paris, 1865), pp. 575–582. The expression "*état journaliste*" comes from Havin, the managing editor of the opposition republican paper *Le Siècle*.

To moderatism they added aristocratic caution (derived from their Orleanist forebears) tinctured with liberal prudence. This compromise formula set the terms for a pragmatic equilibrium that lacked a firm intellectual foundation. If certain illiberal tendencies have regularly manifested themselves in France ever since, the reason is to be sought here. To be sure, these illiberal tendencies do not recur in the old Caesarian form. Ideologically, however, the tendency to dismiss as illegitimate any form of social expression not consecrated by voting remains. This reluctance to accept alternative forms of social expression explains why the French are persistently suspicious of civil-society associations and why they refuse to grant the representatives of civil society any political legitimacy beyond that of reflecting certain particular interests. *What is accepted as a legitimate exercise of liberty is simultaneously declared illegitimate as a political institution.* From the restrictive statutes governing associations to the rules applicable to petitions and demonstrations, we see the same narrowly legalistic interpretation of democracy recurring again and again in French history.

In other words, powers of oversight can never be recognized as democratic powers within the Jacobin framework. "Decisionists" such as the German political theorist Carl Schmitt condemn these same powers on logical grounds. For example, in one of the most vigorous passages of his work, Schmitt attacked the concept of oversight (*Aufsicht*) as a "counter-concept" inimical to the type of political leadership (*Führertum*) he favored.[17] It was on the basis of this argument

---

[17] Carl Schmitt, *État, mouvement, peuple: L'Organisation triadique de l'unité politique* (Paris: Kimé, 1997), pp. 53–57.

that he struck his most forceful blows against the Constitution of Weimar and exhorted Germans to reject the claims of contemptible "indirect powers." Like the Jacobins, he believed that sovereignty could only be "one and indivisible." In recent years, however, watchdog powers have reasserted themselves. The time is therefore ripe for theorists to reconsider the question of legitimacy with an eye to overcoming the limitations of both the Jacobin and decisionist positions, neither of which seems adequate to contemporary practice. This question cannot be dealt with here in any detail.[18] It is worth pausing a moment, however, to sketch the framework within which an answer might be developed.

Three types of legitimacy

Any civil society association or organization enjoys "empirical legitimacy" in virtue of its practical contributions in its area of specialization. This might also be called "utilitarian legitimacy": the association's action is recognized as socially useful. But this kind of moral or functional legitimacy is a long way from political legitimacy in the strict sense. Political legitimacy requires different characteristics, most notably generality. Hence in order to advance further in regard to the question of the political legitimacy of indirect powers, we first need to explore the category of generality. In schematic fashion we can distinguish three forms in which generality may appear: as number, independence, or moral universal. Each has its own specific institutional forms.

---

[18] It will be the subject of a future work.

Generality as number is the most obvious form of generality in a democratic order. A regime is considered to be legitimate if it enjoys the express consent of a majority of the population. By convention, this majority is regarded in practice as a form of unanimous agreement, unanimity being superior in principle to a mere majority.[19] Universal suffrage is the institution that organizes this legitimacy, which might therefore be called "social-procedural legitimacy." Second, generality as independence is defined negatively, as non-particularity. The institutional form of this type of generality is the impartial body, such as a court or independent authority. If universal suffrage establishes a regime of which everyone is an owner, thus ensuring in principle that power cannot be confiscated by a few, generality as independence is another way of preventing such privatization, by establishing an institution of which *no* group can claim to be the owner. All the parties participating in this form of power are equidistant from it, and this guarantees its fully public character. It therefore represents "legitimacy through impartiality" in the strong sense of the term. The third category of generality, the moral universal, corresponds to values recognized by all. It can also be defined by a cognitive type of universal, the universality of reason, or by an "instrumental universal" of the sort embodied in law. These forms of generality can be embodied in any number of institutions, ranging from socially recognized moral authorities

---

[19] On the transition from the superior principle of unanimity to the pragmatic principle of majority, see the suggestive article by Bernard Manin, "Volonté générale ou délibération? Esquisse d'une théorie de la délibération démocratique," *Le Débat*, no. 33 (Jan. 1985).

(including emblematic personalities, religious institutions, charitable organizations, etc.) to authorities of a more intellectual sort. In these cases one can speak of a "substantial legitimacy." The table below summarizes our classification.

This typology is not simply a description of types of legitimacy. It reflects a certain history. Substantial legitimacy is the oldest form, and initially it reflected the fact that government had a place in a broader sacred order. After the introduction of natural rights theories in the seventeenth century, this idea was gradually secularized. Today it takes the form of references to the rights of man, philosophies of justice, or moral systems of one sort or another. Impartial legitimacy grew out of medieval efforts to define power in terms of the judicial function. This was later rationalized in the form of the modern idea of a state of laws, which was eventually extended to include a range of independent authorities. Note, moreover, that the term "legitimacy" first appeared in the French political lexicon in the early nineteenth century. At the time it denoted a political system defined primarily by law (and implicitly

Table 1.

Type of legitimacy	Related form of generality	Implementing institution
Social-procedural	Majority as equivalent of unanimity	Universal suffrage
Impartiality	Equidistance from all involved parties	Courts or independent authorities
Substantial	Universality of values or reason	Various private authorities

opposed to the democratic idea).[20] The social-procedural type of legitimacy is the most recent of all; it was added to the other forms of legitimacy to describe regimes subject to universal suffrage. The three forms of legitimacy are not mutually exclusive. They overlap and combine in various ways, and a hierarchy emerges from their opposition. In certain respects they cut across one another. For example, the legitimacy of the ballot box and the legitimacy of reason suggest two different interpretations of the sovereignty of number: a banally arithmetic interpretation in the first case, a supposed unity of all minds based on a yielding to the evidence in the second.[21] Many similar contrasts could also be cited.

New routes to legitimacy

The contemporary conflict between powers of oversight and electoral-representative democracy should be seen in this broader context. But the context itself has been shaped by two significant social and political facts. The first relates to a

---

[20] Talleyrand seems to have been the first to use the word in this sense. For example, Thiers remarked that the former prelate had wanted to "represent the law" after serving Napoleon; "he indicated this with a felicitous word, which has enjoyed enormous success: legitimacy," in Adolphe Thiers, *Histoire du consulat et de l'Empire* (Paris, n.d.), vol. XVII, p. 445.

[21] The latter view reflects the political rationalism developed by the Physiocrats in eighteenth-century France. Listen to Le Mercier de la Rivière: "The evidence must be the source of all authority, because it is on the basis of evidence that all wills are joined together." See my article "Political rationalism and democracy in France in the 18th and 19th centuries," *Philosophy and Social Criticism* 28, no. 6 (2002).

new sociological and political perception of the notion of a majority. The majority idea was very powerful when the struggle was against old forms of class domination or regimes based on limited suffrage. Sovereignty of the majority then seemed synonymous with collective emancipation, and the opinion of the majority could be taken to be pragmatically equivalent to unanimity, or at any rate the reflection of what could plausibly be construed as the general interest. This is no longer the case. The minority is no longer synonymous with the oppressor. Indeed, minorities today are often seen as being among the oppressed. Lack of unanimity is therefore a much more sensitive issue. Here, the idea of "substantial legitimacy" becomes important, as universal values are invoked on behalf of excluded minorities in order to restore the ideal of a coherent community, an ideal once embodied in the notion of unanimity. To put it another way, the normative content of the idea of unanimity is now parceled out between two different notions of legitimacy rather than concentrated in one.

A second, more directly political factor alters the terms in which legitimacy is understood. I am thinking of the relativization and "desacralization" of the meaning of elections. In the classical theory of representative government, as well as in practice, the function of voters was to legitimate those whom they chose to govern them; the governors were in turn granted a considerable measure of autonomy. This is no longer the case, for a very important reason: the voters grant their mandate in a world that is politically less predictable, by which I mean that it is a world no longer defined by disciplined political organizations with well-defined platforms offering a clear range of political choices. Hence there is a much greater gap than in the past between the legitimacy of governors and the legitimacy of their actions. In the past, elections tied these two dimensions closely together; today, their influence is more limited. Indeed, it is fair to say that elections are now little more than a way of *choosing* governors. The legitimacy of the policies they adopt is permanently under scrutiny and must be reconquered day after day and case by case. What I have called substantial legitimacy therefore takes on growing importance: whether or not a policy serves the common good and respects fundamental values is no longer a question that can be decided by elections alone. The powers of oversight that we have been examining are intended to close the gap between these two types of legitimacy. The legitimacy of these watchdog powers is therefore greater than in the past.

This enhanced legitimacy of contemporary counter-democratic practices should also be seen in relation to the difficulty of representing the people. We looked earlier at the legal status of majority rule, but the sociological side of the question of representation also needs to be explored. There has always been a tension in modern democracy between the political principle of popular sovereignty and the difficulty of defining the social bonds that hold a society of individuals together. The free expression of public opinion needs to be understood in this context: it helps to make sense of the social structure and thus to establish a self-representation of society. This is the functional justification of the role of the press, which I have described as one of the watchdog powers. But how is the press to be given *democratic legitimacy*? In addition to being a watchdog power, it is also a means of expressing the general will (and not just in the "liberal" sense of protecting other liberties). The press is supposed to represent public opinion. It is the organ of public opinion – and the word *organ* also suggests where the problem lies. The press is the organ of public opinion in the same sense in which jurists at one time held that elected representatives are the organ of the nation.[22] On this view, public opinion is like national sovereignty, indivisible and permanent. No one can truly claim to possess it. Because generality cannot be appropriated or co-opted, it is a legitimate power. Daunou characterized this feature of public opinion in the strongest of terms: "One of the essential characteristics of public opinion is to be exempt from imperious direction; it is ungovernable. It can perhaps be coerced, stifled, or annihilated, but it cannot be governed."[23] In other words, public opinion is always more diverse than any of the momentary views attributed to it, and no one can claim to be its sole incarnation.

Thus the conflict between the press and elected representatives, between oversight power and governing power, is also a conflict between different modes of representation. Ultimately, the media and similar organizations are the true illustration of the legal theory of organic representation: public opinion does not exist as such; it takes shape only when it is reflected by the media or when it is *organized* in the form of a poll or a survey or collective action or investigative process of some sort. The very idea of representation

[22] On the theory of representatives as "organ" in French and German public law, see Raymond Carré de Malberg, *Contribution à la théorie générale de l'État* (Paris, 1922), vol. II, pp. 227–243.

[23] Daunou, *Essai sur les garanties individuelles que réclame l'état actuel de la société* [1819] (Paris: Belin, 2000), p. 107.

takes two forms – the "old" notion of the strict mandate versus the "modern" organic notion – and the tension between them is evident in the latent conflict of legitimacy pitting watchdog powers against governing powers. The organic notion of representation should not be construed narrowly. Its significance is dynamic. It involves overt and continual *effort*. It is not substantial.[24] The media are a "moving organ" and at best an approximation to public opinion. During the French Revolution, moreover, the gap between the diffuse oversight conducted by the newspapers and the surveillance conducted by the patriotic societies gradually widened.[25] The societies were relatively closed organizations that disciplined their members through internal mechanisms of control whose effect was to diminish differences of opinion, if necessary by coercive means. By contrast, the press was defined by the idea of freedom of the press. Its role demanded diversity and openness. Thus the powers of oversight were constantly broadening

[24] Cf. Jellinek's famous formula: "Behind the representative, there exists another person; behind the organ, there is nothing." Quoted in Carré de Malberg, *Contribution*, vol. II, p. 288.

[25] The two forms of surveillance were considered identical in the abundant writing on the subject in the year 1791. At that time, Brissot and Lanthenas agreed with Robespierre. In Year III, however, the distinction was heavily stressed, as popular societies took the lead and engaged in violent actions that showed how they had confiscated social power. Hence the principle of unlimited (because inappropriable) freedom of the press was separated from the question of granting authorization to popular societies that were suspected of substituting themselves for society as a whole. The popular societies did not seek to correct representative government by overseeing its actions; they were seen rather as limiting the government's reach, as small groups of self-appointed militants granted themselves the right to override the judgment of the ballot box.

119

their purview; to rest would have been inconceivable. Their legitimacy depended on their activity, which was directed toward encouraging society to subject itself to constant scrutiny. In this respect, distrust served as the basis of a demanding and constructive vision of politics.[26]

[26] This conclusion brings me close to the views of Philip Pettit while at the same time allowing me to move beyond the tension between civic vigilance and democratic trust that underlies his work. For Pettit, vigilance is not necessarily linked to distrust. Indeed, it can be associated with trust, as long as it is defined by an "extremely high level of expectation." See Phillip Pettit, *Republicanism: A Theory of Freedom and Government* (Oxford University Press, 1997). It is on this point that his argument may be weakest (see his discussion of "trust and vigilance" on pp. 263–265).

Part 2

The sovereignty of prevention

"The *faculty to decide* is what I call the right to issue orders in one's own name or to correct orders issued in someone else's name. The *faculty to prevent* is what I call the right to nullify a resolution taken by someone else."[1] This distinction of Montesquieu's is essential if we are to understand recent political developments. It calls attention to a seldom analyzed negative dimension of politics whose importance is clearly growing. Preventive action has come into its own lately as a second type of counter-democratic political intervention. There is a long history to this negative aspect of the political. Long before ordinary citizens laid claim to a share of sovereignty, they had already demonstrated their ability to resist the powers-that-be. Through passive resistance, tactical withdrawal, or clever circumvention of rules, they endeavored to loosen power's grip. Descriptions of this type of behavior and its consequences are common. Tax resistance has been treated in numerous studies, for instance. But there have also been more direct confrontations of political authority. The history of humankind is punctuated by rebellions, riots, and other spontaneous uprisings, and the idea that there is a legal and moral "right to resist" was formulated long before anyone conceived of the right to vote. Popular intervention was thus

[1] Montesquieu, *De l'esprit des lois* (1758), book 11, chap. 6.

envisioned initially in negative terms; indeed, the absence of resistance was taken as proof of the people's consent.

With the advent of universal suffrage, the power of prevention took new forms. During the French Revolution there were intense debates about how to divide popular sovereignty by combining a positive electoral power with an organized power of opposition. Once again, the idea was that the people could not remain free and in control unless they maintained a sort of "reservoir of mistrust" in order to mount, if need be, effective opposition against a government they themselves had consecrated. Liberal as well as democratic interpretations of the power of prevention emerged. If constitutional solutions involving various dualistic versions of democracy were soon abandoned, other means of prevention remained. Democracies had to deal with the tensions between political legitimacy and social legitimacy stemming from class conflict. They therefore integrated into the very structure of government ways of challenging their own power, thereby moving away from the original conception of legitimacy derived solely from the ballot box. The development of organized parliamentary and political opposition consolidated what might be called *critical sovereignty*. This is a crucial feature of the operation of democracy that we would do well to bear in mind.

The degradation of this critical sovereignty is the overwhelming reality of the present period. The conflict that was once a constructive feature of democratic politics has degenerated into purely negative sovereignty. The people effectively assert their sovereignty not by proposing coherent projects but by periodically rejecting those in power. Elections have become occasions for sanctioning incumbents more than anything else. They no longer indicate choices concerning the future direction of society. Voters frequently appear to be "nay-sayers," while agents of various sorts increasingly exercise veto powers over social regulation. Uncertainty about the future has combined with the difficulty of conceptualizing complex democracy to make matters worse. Once vital counter-democratic activity has degenerated into narrow defense of corporatist interests or reactionary populist protest. These changes have dramatically transformed the political landscape, creating a new system whose contours I shall describe. By studying the long history of preventive powers, we can gain a better understanding of the roots of contemporary political change.

5

From the right of resistance to complex sovereignty

Medieval theories of resistance and consent

The idea that there can be no legitimate power without the consent of the governed preceded the emergence of the democratic ideal, that is, the ideal of a self-instituted, self-regulated social order. It was in the Middle Ages, at the beginning of the thirteenth century, that the idea of popular consent was encapsulated in a celebrated maxim: "That which is the concern of all must be approved by all."[1] All the great authors of that time, theologians as well as philosophers, paid homage to it. One should be careful, however, not to interpret this maxim in modern democratic terms. At the time, its constitutional implications were limited. No specific procedures of consent were called for, and there was certainly no intention to put decisions to a vote.[2] Its significance was above all moral:

---

[1] A translation of the Latin maxim *Quod omnes tangit ab omnibus approbetur* from the Justinian Code. This maxim is usually cited by the initials QOT. On its importance, see André Gouron, "Aux origines médiévales de la formule *Quod omnes tangit*," in *Histoire du droit social. Mélanges en hommage à Jean Imbert* (Paris: Presses Universitaires de France, 1989); Gaines Post, "A Roman Legal Theory of Consent, *Quod omnes tangit*, in Medieval Representation," *Wisconsin Law Review*, 1950 (one volume); Ralph Giesey, "*Quod Omnes Tangit*: a Post-Scriptum," *Studia Gratiana* 15, (1972).

[2] On this point see Arthur P. Monahan, *Consent, Coercion, and Limit: The Medieval Origins of Parliamentary Democracy* (Montreal and Kingston: McGill-Queen's University Press, 1987).

the Prince was exhorted to govern in the common interest.
The point was simply to affirm that society is the source as
well as the object of political authority. If there was any hint
of popular sovereignty at all, it was therefore purely passive.
The principle was solemnly affirmed, but without regard to its
application. For medieval commentators, the most important
thing was the nature of the good; achieving it depended on the
virtues of the Prince. The theoretical imperative was to distinguish between good and bad governors, to distinguish between
the Prince devoted to his people and the tyrant who governed
for himself alone without regard to his subjects' needs or desires.
The idea of consent was important insofar as it established
a practical criterion for distinguishing between tyranny and
service to the common good. It marked a political boundary
in theory, but how was that boundary traced in practice? The
criterion was purely negative: in the absence of opposition, the
consent of the people was assumed. Hence tyranny and tyrannicide were central concerns of medieval political thought.
Representations of the political hinged on definitions of this
evil and of the conditions under which it could be combated.

Evil, being absence, loss, and destruction, was easier
to define and recognize than good. From Bartolus and John
of Salisbury to Marsilio of Padua and William of Ockham,
the Middle Ages would gradually forge the broad outlines of a
negative political theory.[3] Policy could be perceived at points
where it changed course or reversed itself. Regimes were judged
primarily in terms of the likelihood that they would degenerate

[3] For an overview, see Mario Turchetti, *Tyrannie et tyrannicide de
l'Antiquité à nos jours* (Paris: Presses Universitaires de France, 2001).

into tyranny. The major concern of moral and political philosophy was to ponder ways of avoiding this danger. The radical solution of tyrannicide was therefore a central issue, and, with it, the more general question of the right of resistance. All politics was thus organized around the idea of *prevention*. It was the power to say no, the potential to remove the Prince or his administrators, that informed the earliest conception of legitimate and viable social intervention in the political realm.[4] And obviously intervention was unthinkable except in such extreme cases, because no other grounds for interfering with the actions of the sovereign was deemed legitimate. Consider the powers claimed by the first Estates General in France: the right to recuse certain members of the King's Council and to depose a usurping regent or tyrannical monarch were often mentioned, almost as frequently, in fact, as the right to audit treasury accounts or the demand that taxes should not be imposed without consent.[5] Historically, then, claims of preventive powers arose in parallel with the demand for powers of oversight.

The Reformation

During the Reformation, the right of resistance emerged in reaction to the Catholic camp's assertion of absolute

---

[4] This is not the place for a discussion of the *subject* of this intervention, because even when "the people" are mentioned in this period, they are never seen in sociological terms but rather as a kind of moral metaphor, represented by others. The people are never the masses or "the greater number," who might act directly, on their own.

[5] For the sixteenth and seventeenth centuries, see Arlette Jouanna, *Le Devoir de révolte: La Noblesse française et la gestation de l'État moderne, 1559–1661* (Paris: Fayard, 1989), table 301.

monarchical powers (in order to preclude power-sharing with Protestant religious authorities). Protestants then seized on medieval theories of popular consent and the right of resistance in order to defend themselves. Calvin set the tone with the twentieth chapter of book IV of his *Institutions of the Christian Religion* (1536), which was devoted to civil government. There he insisted strongly on the duty "to oppose and resist the intemperance and cruelty of kings."[6] Thus, initially, these doctrines were revived for religious reasons, but they quickly spilled over into the political arena in both England and France.

In England, John Knox proposed a rather radical interpretation of the right to disobey "liberticide" authorities. In *Apology for the Protestants* (1557), he was harshly critical of Mary Tudor, whom he accused of seeking "against equity and justice to oppress the pure but also expressly to fight against God."[7] A year later he returned to the attack and called for rebellion against a queen he deemed idolatrous and tyrannical.[8] At roughly the same time, in 1556, John Ponet, the bishop of

[6] John Calvin, *Institutes of the Christian Religion*, trans. Henry Beveridge (Philadelphia, PA: 1845). According to Calvin, the duty to resist belonged to "magistrates constituted for the defense of the people." He was thinking of the Estates General, which he explicitly compared to the Spartan ephors, Athenian demarchs, and "defenders of the people" in Rome. On this text, see Quentin Skinner, *The Foundations of Modern Political Thought* (Cambridge University Press, 1979), vol. II, part 3: "Calvinism and the Theory of Revolution."

[7] John Knox, *Apology for the Protestants in Prison at Paris* (1557), in *The Works of John Knox*, ed. David Laing (Edinburgh, 1846–1864), vol. IV, p. 327.

[8] See especially *The First Blast of the Trumpet against the Monstrous Regiment of Women* (1558), reproduced in John Knox, *On Rebellion*, ed. Roger A. Mason (Cambridge University Press, 1994).

Rochester and Winchester, published *A Shorte Treatise of Politike Power*, a work conceived in a similar spirit but more clearly structured. Ponet stressed the limits of civil authority in matters of conscience and asserted the people's right to resist and disobey governments that abused their authority. Two other Protestant leaders, Christopher Goodman and George Buchanan, also took up this theme. In *Dialogus De Jure Regni apud Scotos* (1579), Buchanan energetically argued that "the people have more power than kings, who derive whatever prerogatives they claim from the people; hence the people as a whole exercise the same power over kings as kings over any one of the people."[9]

These English and Scottish authors saw the right of resistance and the imperative of popular consent in a plainly more political light than did the philosophers and theologians of the Middle Ages. Their texts were not theoretical treatises but direct interventions in contemporary debates and conflicts. No longer content to see the issue in exclusively moral terms, they were nevertheless not really constitutional thinkers. The decisive step toward constitutional thought would be taken by the French "monarchomachs." This neologism, which literally means "opponents of monarchs," was applied mainly to Huguenot political writers who advocated the right to resist usurpative or liberticide governments. Several famous texts that appeared in the wake of the Saint Bartholomew massacres attracted considerable interest. These include *Le Réveille-matin des Français* (1574), Hotman's *Franco-Gallia* (1574), the *Vindiciae contra tyrannos* (1579) attributed to Duplessis-Mornay, and the précis that Théodore de Bèze published in

---

[9] Quoted in Turchetti, *Tyrannie et tyrannicide*, p. 407.

Geneva, *Du droit des magistrats sur leurs sujets* (1575). It was long traditional to see these writers as "precursors of the *Social Contract*" because of their persistence in celebrating the rights of the people, urging governments to work for the public good, and harshly criticizing the claims of absolutists. Yet their outlook was still a far cry from Rousseau's. They had no notion of active popular sovereignty and were intellectually closer to medieval political thought than to democratic individualism.[10] They were also far more moderate than Knox and the others, and their tone far less radical than Calvin's. The Huguenot theorists were also careful to separate themselves from the Anabaptist leaders of the Peasants' War and other uprisings that had marked the early years of the Reformation in Germany. What they all had in common, however, was the search for a constitutional theory of the right to resist. Therein lay their true originality.

Unsurprisingly, the monarchomach literature emphasized the role of the Estates General. Hotman's *Franco-Gallia* presented itself as a constitutional history of France, arguing that, after the Franks joined the Gauls (as the title suggested), the first real kings had been put in place by a representative general assembly. Hotman looked to a "restoration" of this early parliamentarism to give organized institutional form to the right of resistance and consent of the people. Bèze, for his part, suggested that "inferior magistrates" (by which he meant certain categories of "high-born" nobles as well as certain elected magistrates from large cities) could exert control over

---

[10] On this point, see my *Le Sacre du citoyen: Histoire du suffrage universel en France* (Paris: Gallimard, 1992), pp. 21–38.

the Prince. The most original of the Huguenot writers was the author of *Vindiciae contra tyrannos*, who envisioned a dual power within the state. In addition to the royal power, which could act directly, there were other bodies that exercised control over it; together they constituted the government. The idea was thus one of shared power, or at any rate of complementary and related powers. The words with which this idea was expressed are worth noting. The author referred to "ephors" and "public controllers," whom he viewed as "guardians" of the people and a check on the monarch.[11] With this reference to the Spartan ephors, an institution familiar to contemporaries steeped in ancient culture, *Vindiciae contra tyrannos* laid the groundwork for an institutional conception of the power of prevention vis-à-vis an active government.[12] Although La Boétie's *Contr'Un* later established itself as one of the emblematic texts of the right to resist, one that has frequently been reprinted ever since, it was not really a part of this literature, even though Calvinists did try to appropriate it by publishing several pirated editions.[13] The work in fact contains no concrete constitutional proposals.

A few years later, in the very different intellectual context characterized by the earliest formulations of the theory of natural right, Althusius devoted an entire chapter of his *Politica Methodice Digesta* (1603) to the idea: "The administrators of

[11] *Vindiciae contra tyrannos*, French translation of 1581, p. 233.
[12] See "La Sparte Huguenote" in Maxime Rosso, *La Renaissance des institutions de Sparte dans la pensée française (XVIe–XVIIIe siècle)* (Aix: Presses Universitaires d'Aix-Marseille, 2005), pp. 84–101.
[13] The first complete edition was published in 1576. The work would later be published under the title *Discours de la servitude volontaire*.

the universal association are of two sorts: ephors and supreme magistrate."[14] The ephors, Althusius argues, exercise a power of checks and prevention. They see to it that the supreme magistrate is neither negligent nor idle and make sure that his personal penchants do not induce him to act against the public interest.[15] The nature of the power of prevention changes when seen in this light. No longer is it seen solely as an extreme type of action, a radical and ultimate form of resistance to what is itself an extreme form of power, namely, tyranny. Althusius incorporated it into the ordinary hierarchy of powers, a hierarchy with a modern democratic aspect, since he called for the ephors to be elected by the people as a whole.[16] The ephors were to be legally sanctioned champions of liberty and defenders of the people's interests against the supreme magistrate; they were to act as regents during interregnums and as guarantors of the separation of powers within their sphere of action. As Althusius envisioned them, in short, they were not limited to the role of deposing the sovereign if he became tyrannical.[17] His writing thus marks a significant advance over the medieval conception. Althusius represents a turning point in political thought and stands as a precursor to Rousseau and the idea of democratic sovereignty. He was also innovative in another way: he rejected

[14] Chap. 18, "The Ephors and Their Duties," in the abridged English edition edited by Frederick S. Carney (Indianapolis: Liberty Fund, 1995), p. 99.

[15] *Ibid.*, pp. 99–100.

[16] Althusius considered different types of selection, since he mentions the possibility of selection by lot, voting within constituted bodies, and election based on straightforward arithmetic division of citizens. *Ibid.*, p. 102.

[17] This was only one of five functions he assigned to them. *Ibid.*, pp. 103–109.

Bodin's idea of sovereignty as one and indivisible.[18] In both respects he was the first thinker to envision a dualist democracy in which government and power of prevention would work together to ensure that public affairs were well managed.

The Enlightenment, the negative power, and the tribunes of the people

The question of powers of resistance was still central to the political philosophers of the eighteenth century, but by then it had moved into a basically constitutional context. Liberals were concerned with setting strict limits to power, while democrats were looking for the best means by which the people could express their sovereignty. Writers turned to Roman antiquity for answers to these questions. Many took an interest in how the Roman tribunes of the people exercised powers of prevention. Whether Enlightenment accounts of this ancient institution were accurate or not is not my concern here. I am interested solely in the way in which eighteenth-century writers understood it and described it. Bear in mind, too, that these writers often treated the Spartan ephors and Roman tribunes as if they were the same. Powers of oversight and powers of prevention, which I have tried to distinguish, were frequently confused. For instance, the Tribunate of Year VIII was closer in spirit to the ephorate than to the tribunate,

---

[18] See his critique of Bodin's *Six livres de la République, ibid.*, pp. 104–105. Althusius also had some very critical things to say abut William Barclay's *Politica*. He quotes from the English Catholic absolutist's *De Regno et Regali Potestate* (1600) and criticizes his conception of the sovereign power (*ibid.*, pp. 109–116).

whereas Althusius assigned to his ephors roles similar to those played by Roman tribunes. Most of the authors we will examine confused "tribunes of the people" with "tribunes of the plebs," moreover, when in fact the plebs constituted a distinct social class.

Veto, intercedo: I oppose, I intervene. It was this essential function of the Roman tribunes that drew the attention of eighteenth-century writers.[19] "Their power is one of prevention more than of action," was the way the *Encyclopédie* of Diderot and d'Alembert summed it up.[20] For the *Encyclopédie méthodique*, "the tribunes of the people were magistrates charged with protecting the people from the oppression of the great, with defending their rights and liberty from the projects of the Consuls and Senate."[21] Montesquieu and Rousseau included chapters on the tribunes in their major works.[22] Both were critical of what became of the institution, which in the end usurped the executive power rather than merely containing it. Yet both writers were also fascinated by the idea of a constitutional power of negation: a single tribune could halt a project simply by pronouncing the word *veto*. As Rousseau put it: the tribune "can do nothing yet prevent anything." The Tribunate

[19] For an overview of the way in which tribunes were seen at the time, see Pierangelo Catalano, *Tribunato e resistenza* (Paravia: Turin, 1971).

[20] Article "Tribun du peuple," vol. 34.

[21] *Encyclopédie méthodique*, series *Économie politique et diplomatique*, by M. Démeunier (Paris, 1788), vol. IV, p. 569.

[22] See Montesquieu, *De l'esprit des lois* (1758), book V, chap. 8; Rousseau, *Contrat social*: book IV, chap. 5. On Rousseau, see Jean Cousin, "J.-J. Rousseau interprète des institutions romaines dans le *Contrat social*," in *Études sur le Contrat social de Jean-Jacques Rousseau* (Paris: Les Belles Lettres, 1964).

was not strictly speaking a constitutional power in Rome (Rousseau called it "a special magistracy not consubstantial with the others"), yet it was necessary if the other powers were to function properly because "it set each element of the system in its correct relation to the others." Might it be possible to preserve the benefits of the institution without its potential to wreak havoc? Rousseau raised this question and suggested that a preventive power should only manifest itself intermittently. In the *Social Contract* he did not pursue this argument to its logical conclusion, but he would take it up a few years later, admittedly in a quite different context, in *Letters Written from the Mountain*.[23] In that text, Rousseau opposed the use of the "negative power" that the Small Council of Geneva (which was the executive branch of the city's government) claimed for itself over legislation and citizens' petitions to the General Council. Here, the power of prevention was completely perverted, since it reinforced the executive. It institutionalized a certain inertia but did nothing to protect liberty or the rights of the people. Because Rousseau's letters were part of a polemic directed against certain technical features of Genevan institutions, it is hard to discuss his argument without delving into details, and it would be out of place to do so here.[24] For our purposes, the important point is

---

[23] Rousseau's *Lettres écrites de la montagne* (1764) were a response to Jean-Robert Tronchin, *Lettres écrites de la campagne* (1764).

[24] See Céline Spector, "Droit de représentation et pouvoir négatif: la garde de la liberté dans la constitution genevoise," in Bruno Bernardi, Florent Guénard, and Gabriella Silvestrini, *La Religion, la liberté, la justice: Un commentaire des "Lettres écrites de la montagne" de Jean-Jacques Rousseau* (Paris: Vrin, 2005).

that this episode shows how central the idea of negative power was in this period.

Although Rousseau was interested in exploring the possibility of an essentially democratic negative power as an instrument for expanding the effective scope of popular sovereignty, it was in a different perspective that negative power was most often considered in the late eighteenth century: as a means of regulating the separation of powers. The very meaning of the term "veto" changed in this period. During the period 1750–1770 the *Encyclopédie* used the word exclusively with reference to Roman history. After 1770 it took on a different constitutional meaning. In the United States it became a synonym for "qualified negative," and the Founding Fathers used it to name the power granted to the president to prevent a bill passed by Congress from becoming law (although his veto could be overridden by a two-thirds vote of both houses). In France, the Constitution of 1791 used the word in connection with the "royal sanction," the power granted to the executive to suspend any law. Both the French and the American versions of the veto reflected Montesquieu's distinction between the power to make laws and the power to prevent their implementation. In both cases, the idea was clearly to establish a proper separation of powers between branches of government, reflecting the "liberal" hope that each would check and balance the power of the other.[25] Such a limited conception of the preventive power did not satisfy the French revolutionaries for long, however. Remembering the Roman tribunes, they sought to reinterpret it

---

[25] See Christian Bidegaray and Claude Emeri, "Du pouvoir d'empêcher: veto ou contre-pouvoir," *Revue du droit public*, no 2 (1994).

in a more democratic light yet never really succeeded in giving it a more constitutional form.

The French revolutionary experience

The question of the tribunate came up again in France in the spring of 1790, when it was discussed by the Cercle Social and Club des Cordeliers. These revolutionary societies were interested in establishing a broader conception of popular sovereignty than that based on parliamentary representation alone. Abbé Fauchet, one of the more astute readers of the *Social Contract*, spoke for example of establishing an elected "moderating power" whose specific function would be to suspend actions and laws deemed contrary to the general will, pending appeal to the sovereign for final disposition. The purpose of such a step, he explained, would be to ensure that "the whole watches over the whole."[26] Lavicomterie devoted a chapter of his democratic treatise *Du peuple et des rois* (1791) to describing what modern tribunes might be, namely, "guardians of the sovereignty of the people," ever watchful to prevent any attempt to usurp delegated powers.[27] The same magistrates were also supposed to "temper" the powers-that-be and "preserve" the rights of the people. Like Rousseau, Lavicomterie was conscious of the danger that such an institution would represent if it were to turn its power of prevention into a more

[26] "Treizième discours sur l'universalité d'action du Souverain dans l'État," *La Bouche de fer*, second supplement, 1791, vol. 7, p. 60.

[27] *Du peuple et des rois*, chap. 10, "Des Éphores ou des Tribuns," pp. 78–90. The following quotes are all from this chapter.

comprehensive power. He used Rousseau's own words to emphasize the need for absolute independence from the various constituted bodies. He also indicated that "impermanence and impeachability" should be characteristics of the tribunes in order to eliminate the danger that they might abuse their power. His solution to the problem of how to create a modern tribunate was thus to create a non-institutionalized power, a power that would be purely functional and impersonal. Was such a thing possible? The experience of the Revolution suggests that the answer is no. The constitutional debates of 1793 are instructive as to the intellectual and political bases for this conclusion and will help to shed further light on the long history of the power of prevention.

In the previous chapter I discussed many proposals to institutionalize powers of oversight in 1793. The idea of a constitutional power of prevention was also in the air, as can be seen in a proposal by Hérault de Séchelles that served as the basis of debate in the Convention.[28] Consider two articles from the section "On the Sovereignty of the People": "Article I. The people exercises its sovereignty in primary assemblies. Article II. It directly chooses its representatives and members of the national jury." Any citizen may have recourse to the national jury to seek sanctions against the powers-that-be and block government action in order to "protect citizens from oppression by the Legislative Body or Executive Council." The

---

[28] Convention presentation of June 10, 1793, *AP*, 1st series, vol. 66, pp. 256–264. Quotes that follow are from these pages. For a more extensive treatment of the debates surrounding this proposal, see my *La Démocratie inachevée: Histoire de la souveraineté du peuple en France* (Paris: Gallimard, 2000), pp. 66–81.

jury was to consist of one elected representative from each *département*. Thus two parallel powers were said to stem directly from the will of the people: the representatives constituted one of these powers and the jury that was to oversee them constituted the other. The proposed jury was democratic and exercised a share of sovereignty. It was not merely a protective shield of liberal inspiration, imposing limits on the power of government. The Convention overwhelmingly rejected this bicephalic version of popular sovereignty, however. It was impossible to overcome the Jacobins' devotion to total control. France never really succeeded in developing a non-unitary conception of sovereignty. The idea of a controlling body elected at the same time and under the same conditions as the legislature was attacked as likely to lead to a dual government that would sow confusion and discredit popular sovereignty. A critic of Hérault de Séchelles summed up the objections: "You have decreed that the legislature would exercise sovereignty. It is ridiculous to seek to erect alongside it a superior authority."[29] Robespierre had already raised a similar objection to a tribunate: "What do we care about combinations to balance the power of a tyrant? It is tyranny itself that must be rooted out. The people shouldn't need to depend on disputes between their masters for the right to breathe free for a few moments. It is their own strength that must be made the guarantee of their rights. ... There is only one tribune of the

---

[29] Speech by Thuriot, June 16, 1793 (*AP*, vol. 66, p. 577). On June 11, Chabot said: "Let us not establish two powers that may become rivals. Let us not leave the people vulnerable to a divergence of opinion between the legislative body and the national jury," *AP*, vol. 66, p. 284.

people that I can admit, and that is the people themselves."[30] As these arguments remind us, it has always been difficult for French public law to admit anything but a single sovereign power; any attempt to decompose or subdivide sovereignty is automatically seen as a source of weakness. In the end, the revolutionaries not only defended the most orthodox form of representative government but combined it with an exalted vision of the people's representatives, who were taken to be nothing less than an embodiment of the people themselves.

Writers like Condorcet[31] and Hérault de Séchelles tried to imagine a more complex notion of sovereignty that would have integrated some form of preventive power into the structure of government itself. They saw this as a possible alternative to alternation between passive consent and rebellion. They did their best to define "means of resistance" short of insurrection. "When the social body is oppressed by the legislative body, insurrection is the only means of resistance," wrote Hérault de Séchelles. "But it would be absurd to organize it. It is impossible to fix in advance the nature or character of an insurrection. One must rely on the genius of the people and count on their justice and prudence. But there is also another case, when the legislative body oppresses a few citizens. Those citizens must then find a means of resistance in the people."[32] François Robert hit upon the most striking way of putting the issue. Adapting the much dis-cussed idea of a fourth power, he, too, tried to define a mode of

[30] Speech of May 10, 1793, *AP*, vol. 66, p. 430.
[31] See Lucien Jaume, "Condorcet: droit de résistance ou censure du peuple?" in Dominique Gros and Olivier Camy, eds., *Le Droit de résistance à l'oppression* (Paris: Le Genre Humain-Seuil, 2005).
[32] *AP*, vol. 63, p. 139.

action somewhere between the ballot box and the streets. If the legislature grabs too much power, "What is to be done?" he asked. "The people are no longer active in large numbers and cannot be turned out. Is an insurrection therefore necessary? No, it is not. *What is necessary is an institution that takes the place of an insurrection*, that takes the place of the people, that is supposed to be the people, and that provokes or checks the action or inaction of all the constituted powers."[33] An institution that would take the place of insurrection and of the people: the radical quality of this extraordinary formulation perfectly captures what was at stake in this attempt to define the shape of democratic government. Robespierre and his friends opposed this approach. The Incorruptible forthrightly summed up their position: "To subject the resistance to oppression to legal forms is the ultimate refinement of tyranny."[34] To say this was to concede that he had no notion of any middle ground between politics as usual and politics as insurrection. It was to suggest that there was no room for intervention, no form of opposition or negotiation, between submission to the established order and rebellion.[35] To be sure, the very word "insurrection" became almost a commonplace in this period. So often invoked as a "sacred duty,"[36] insurrection

---

[33] *AP*, vol. 63, p. 387.

[34] Article 31 of his proposed Declaration of Rights, presented on April 24, 1793, *AP*, vol. 63, p. 199.

[35] Patrice Gueniffey pertinently characterizes the revolutionary spirit as a form of "representative absolutism coupled with insurrectional lapses into direct democracy." See *Le Nombre et la Raison* (Paris: Éditions de l'EHESS, 1993), p. iv.

[36] See Article 35 of the *Déclaration* of June 1793: "When the government violates the rights of the people, insurrection is, for the people and for each portion of the people, the most sacred and most indispensable of duties."

nearly became a normal form of politics. In the vocabulary of the *sans-culottes* of Year II, "insurrection" did not necessarily mean armed uprising. More broadly but also more vaguely it referred to various forms of resistance, various types of initiative and attitudes of watchfulness and vigilance. Some went so far as to speak of "peaceful insurrection."[37] Beyond the semantic variations, what we see is a de-institutionalization of the political. Indeed, the whole period of the Terror can be understood in these terms. Between the diffuse pressure of public opinion and insurrection, the modern term for tyrannicide and the right to resist, Jacobins saw no room for a legally sanctioned preventive power.

Fichte and the idea of a modern ephorate

It was not in Paris but in Jena that late-eighteenth-century thinking about a constitutionally sanctioned preventive power would find its ultimate expression in the writing of Johann Gottlieb Fichte, who devoted a chapter of his *Foundations of Natural Right* (1796–1797) to the idea of establishing a modern ephorate.[38] Together with the three constitutional powers, each active in its own domain, the ephorate, as Fichte understood it, was to be "an *absolutely prohibitive*

---

[37] Ferdinand Brunot mentions this shift in meaning in his *Histoire de la langue française*. See vol. IX, part 2, *La Révolution et l'Empire* (Paris, 1937), p. 855.

[38] Johann Gottlieb Fichte, *Foundations of Natural Right according to the principles of the Wissenschaftslehre*, trans. Michael Baur (Cambridge University Press, 2000). On Fichte's work, see Alain Renaut, *Le Système du droit: Philosophie et droit dans la pensée de Fichte* (Paris: Presses Universitaires de France, 1986), chap. 3, "La synthèse républicaine."

power," a power to "subject the conduct of the public authorities to constant control."[39] For Fichte, the goal was not to
oppose particular decisions, something more akin to judicial
review, but rather to institute a comprehensive power to suspend the action of government whenever necessary. The ephorate would be there "to abolish any proceeding on the spur
of the moment, to suspend government in its entirety and in
every one its parts." Fichte thought of this power as a form of
"state excommunication" and compared it to religious excommunication, which had served the Church as an infallible
means of obtaining the obedience of all who depended on it.
He saw two justifications for such a power. First, it provided
a way of overcoming the opposition between representative
democracy and direct democracy. Between a representative
democracy that risked degenerating into an elective aristocracy
and a direct democracy beset by demagogic temptations and
various practical difficulties, the ephorate provided a third
way: a *reflective democracy* that would be obliged to question
its own foundations at every turn. The ephorate would alleviate
the conservative tendencies inherent in representative democracy: although the people bestowed their trust on those whom
they elected, they retained the right to withdraw that trust and
impose sanctions. The ephorate would also remedy the defects
of direct democracy by assigning the people two different roles:
on the one hand they would form a general community of

---

[39] Fichte's italics. Note that the institution that Fichte calls "ephorate"
actually has the characteristics of the Roman Tribunate. The imprecise
terminology was typical of the period, whose relation to Antiquity was at
once close and ambiguous.

abstract citizen-voters, while on the other hand they would comprise a series of specific communities with a range of views on different issues. A regime with an ephorate could thus be both more democratic and more liberal. It would resolve the aporia of *le peuple introuvable* in democracy by imputing two distinct identities to the people, two forms of expression.[40] Each form of expression would define its own temporal frame. This would also avoid the confusion inherent in the assumption of a unified people, which inevitably results in turning the people against themselves as judge and party, master and subject.

Fichte thus developed Condorcet's insights into the idea of complex sovereignty.[41] His approach was at once more radical and more detailed. Condorcet distinguished between *delegated sovereignty* (in the form of legislative representation) and *sovereignty of control* (through constitutional oversight or assertion of constitutional power in the form of a convention). Fichte also took a radical view of the separation of powers. For him the key distinction was between "*absolutely positive* power" and "*absolutely negative* power." Executive, legislative, and judicial powers were in fact complementary, hence their separation was more apparent than real. The true central power was the executive. The liberal theory of separation of powers therefore had little importance for Fichte, except insofar as it captured the reality of a mixed regime balancing democracy, aristocracy, and monarchy (which one might rephrase in contemporary terms as a balance between liberalism and

---

[40] With the ephorate, Fichte noted, "the people are declared to be a community by the constitution in specific cases."

[41] On this point, see my *La Démocratie inachevée.*

144

democracy). In this respect he was rather close to Montesquieu. For Fichte, the more pertinent distinction was that between *positive power* (organized around the executive) and *negative power* (of autonomous critical intervention). For the latter, the ephorate was indispensable.

Fichte's text is interesting for other reasons as well. He analyzes the conditions that must be satisfied if such an ephorate is to come into existence. If the power of the ephors is to be fully legitimate, they must be elected by the people, yet no one should be allowed to propose himself as a candidate for such a position. In this respect Fichte was merely restating a central tenet of French revolutionary politics: self-nominated candidacies were banned because they were suspected of encouraging intrigue and distorting the essence of political choice, which was to identify qualified candidates in the first place.[42] By preventing individuals from presenting themselves as candidates, the revolutionaries hoped that the office would take precedence over the person.[43] Ephors were also supposed

---

[42] On this point, see Gueniffey, *Le Nombre et la raison*. In order to avoid maneuver and manipulation, or privatization of the political process, it was decided that the law should not specify how candidates were to enter the arena. Voters were thus absolutely free to vote for whomever they pleased. The system was of course viable only because elections unfolded in two stages. The revolutionary solution may have been tactically naïve, but it had its logic, which was to *personalize* elections to a radical degree, situating them in a "choice space" that could be seen as completely nonpolitical, in the sense that voters made up their minds solely on the basis of the moral and intellectual qualities of individuals.

[43] Fichte: "No one should be permitted to present himself as a candidate for the ephorate. The person who becomes an ephor will be the one to whom the people turn with confidence, the one who, in view of the

to serve for limited periods of time, so that the preventive power would be regulated by these term limits (as well as by the requirement that ephors submit their accounts to a final audit). This was another way of separating the office from the person. To the same end, Fichte suggested a carefully calculated system of rewards and punishments; this would encourage ephors to devote themselves to the public interest by linking it to their own private interest. Finally, it was essential that those wielding preventive power remain absolutely independent of the executive. Fichte proposed a strict ban on "all social relations, kinship relations, and friendly relations" with the executive.[44] Taken together, these various measures radically depersonalized the ephors, in effect reducing them to *pure function*. There was a marked asymmetry between the two powers. The positive power was by definition always involved in specific actions and vulnerable to various forms of corruption, and it was for this very reason that a negative power was needed, a negative power structurally identified with its mission so as to justify its existence. To be sure, Fichte foresaw that the ephors themselves might fail in that mission, and for that reason he envisioned the possibility of a "supplemental ephorate" in the form of popular insurrection as an ultimate check on power. Thus the author of *Foundations of Natural Right* continued to invoke theories of the right to resist. His proposal was in fact much bolder, however.

sublime choice to be made, is selected by his peers as honest and noble." *Foundations*, p. 194.

[44] Note that Fichte borrowed all the regulations that medieval Italian towns adopted in order to ensure that their *podestà* would serve the general interest.

146

Although he later came to have doubts about the viability of the governmental structure he proposed,[45] he nevertheless succeeded in identifying a major issue in magisterial fashion. Any reflection on a more complex and therefore more mature conception of sovereignty must begin with his work.

A significant oversight

Fichte marked the culmination of the era of political thought inspired by the Revolution and aimed at establishing a critical form of democratic sovereignty. His ideas were forgotten, even by most historians of ideas. To be sure, the underlying concern did not vanish, but after Fichte it found expression mainly in liberal proposals for limitations on government power. Structural checks and balances included constitutional courts, presidential vetoes, and parliamentary dissolutions. Compared with the breadth of Fichte's vision, these measures were rather limited; earlier we observed a similar shrinkage of the horizon with respect to powers of oversight. The institutions of liberal parliamentarism thus incorporated the concerns of theorists who had sought to define a more complex vision of democracy, but in doing so they radically diminished their scope. It seemed somehow impossible to incorporate this dimension of democracy, so it was banished from sight in favor of more readily assimilable

---

[45] For an idea of these doubts, see his writings from 1812: J. G. Fichte, *Lettres et témoignages sur la Révolution française* (Paris: Vrin, 2002), pp. 191–192.

theories of representative government and simplistic appeals to direct democracy.

Note, for instance, that the question of the tribunate was systematically neglected or ignored throughout the nineteenth century, even by specialists in Roman law. A striking instance of this can be seen in the monumental work of Mommsen, who labored mightily to obscure what was distinctive about the power of the tribunes. In his *Roman Public Law* he described their negative role as "abnormal," an archaic survival indicative of some sort of dysfunction.[46] Mommsen clearly recognizes the initial social function of the tribunate, namely, to represent the plebs, the forgotten class. He cannot, however, conceive that its critical institutional role has a specific political utility, so that for him the institution becomes pointless once the "Roman people" emerges as an inclusive political category.[47] Other nineteenth-century political thinkers did their utmost to interpret political history from Antiquity to the modern era in terms of "republicanism" and "democracy" in such a way as to eliminate any element that might be incompatible with representative liberal government narrowly construed. Did this imply that preventive power must henceforth be reduced to the right to resist, a "transitional concept" of no

---

[46] Theodor Mommsen, *Le Droit public romain*, new edn (Paris: De Boccard, 1984), vol. III, p. 329 (more generally, see pp. 323–357). Note that Mommsen's minimization of the importance of the Tribunate went hand in hand with his celebration of dictatorship, that is, with radical government action in exceptional circumstances. See in this edition the long, learned, and lucid preface by Yan Thomas, "Mommsen et l'*Isolierung* du droit."

[47] *Ibid.*, p. 354.

further use to a liberal democracy?[48] Of course "basic democracy" is a precious good for which men have fought ever since the French Revolution and for which they continue to fight around the world. The struggles for universal suffrage and the resistance to fascism illustrate the significance of this basic good, and of course the issue of a constitutional right to resist became a subject of intense discussion in countries where fascism took hold.[49] Although the Italian constitution of 1948 rejected the idea of a right of resistance, it was incorporated into Germany's Fundamental Law and also figures in the constitutions of Greece and Portugal. Still, setting these exceptional cases aside, a certain disenchantment with the current state of politics in many countries is reason enough to look back on the forgotten idea of "negative power" in an effort to restore vigor and substance to flagging democratic ideals.

---

[48] The phrase "transitional concept" is used by Jean-Fabien Spitz in his article "Droit de résistance," in Philippe Raynaud and Stéphane Rials, eds., *Dictionnaire de philosophie politique* (Paris: Presses Universitaires de France, 1996).

[49] Note, too, that it was in Germany that the notion of "militant democracy" (*streitbare Demokratie*) arose in opposition to the legalism of the Weimar Republic, where the rise of Hitler called into question the moral and philosophical approach to political legitimacy. For a definitive statement, see Karl Löwenstein, "Militant Democracy and Fundamental Rights," *American Political Science Review* 31, no. 3 (June 1937).

6

Self-critical democracies

In the first half of the nineteenth century, representative regimes everywhere chose institutional architectures that reflected a liberal concern with limiting the power of government. Constitutional engineering was not the focal point of democratic demands at the time, however. It seemed clear that universal suffrage was the primary goal, the central thread of the history of democracy in this period, although the precise chronology varied from country to country. Throughout this long struggle it was expected that universal suffrage would yield everything people desired. It would create a society in which each person had his or her place. It would put an end to corruption. It would ensure the triumph of the general interest. The rule of number would by itself lead to a *democratic society*. This state of mind was nicely summed up in 1848 by the *Bulletin de la République*, which greeted the advent of the vote for all in these terms: "As of the date of this law, there are no more proletarians in France."[1] Ledru-Rollin offered this lyrical comment: "Political science has now been discovered ... From now on, it is a simple matter of applying it broadly."[2] These naïve hopes were soon to be disappointed. That is why

---

[1] *Bulletin de la République*, no. 4, March 19, 1848. On this question, see also my *Sacre du citoyen*. The Chartist literature in Great Britain reveals a similar sensibility.

[2] *Ibid.*, no. 19, April 22, 1848.

the "social question" became central in discussions of political representation from this time forward. Workers, who in Blanqui's phrase felt "left out," began to assert themselves as a social force, insisting on their dignity while seeking to maintain their distance because they believed that the only way to constitute themselves as a political subject was to aspire to a certain separatism. At the same time the figures of the rebel, the resister, and the dissident limned the contours of a moral critique of undemocratic liberalism. What might be called *critical sovereignty* began to take shape. In the revolutionary period, as we have seen, some theorists had sought to institutionalize this critical sovereignty in the heart of the democratic process itself, but the dualist approach now developed in the form of social and moral criticism from outside the system. This of course altered its nature profoundly. Nevertheless, this external critique not only shaped society but obliged it constantly to question its own foundations.

The class struggle as negative politics

Although workers in France obtained the vote in 1848, they nevertheless felt that they still remained outside the system. This was in part because they believed that republican elites did not represent them, and from this belief grew a lengthy struggle to represent the working-class identity as such.[3] But it was also because workers found themselves excluded from economic prosperity. The term "proletarian"

[3] On this point see my *Le Peuple introuvable: Histoire de la représentation démocratique en France* (Paris: Gallimard, 1998).

as used at this time had both social and political connotations. Of course it referred explicitly to the lowest class of Roman citizens, a marginalized group in Roman society. The existence of class conflict confronted democracy with a challenge, and any number of authors responded as if by instinct, adopting an archaic vocabulary and speaking of helots, proletarians, and plebs in an effort to describe the new social antagonisms to which capitalism gave rise. Workers therefore reverted to older language as well, invoking the right of resistance to express their relation to the newly established order. While they may have hoped to find tribunes who could speak for them, they remained wary of those who claimed to represent them on social and economic issues, and what they wanted most of all was the right to come together in organizations of their own in order to resist their exploitation. *Social separation* was an essential feature of their vision of effective expression of their sovereignty.

Strikes were therefore doubly important, first as a means of asserting power and second as a form of political expression – what one might call a "total" social and political fact. It was through strikes that workers obtained the only true political power they wielded in the nineteenth century: the power of prevention. Jaurès cut to the heart of the matter, quoting Mirabeau: "Do not vex these people, who are the producers of everything and who can become a formidable opposition merely by remaining idle."[4] The nascent workers' movement eagerly celebrated the secession of the Roman

---

[4] Quoted in Hubert Lagardelle, *La Grève générale et le socialisme: Enquête internationale* (Paris, 1905), p. 111.

plebs.[5] It also invoked the practice of medieval journeymen, who "placed an interdiction" (i.e., a boycott) on a city or shop when they wished to make themselves heard.[6] As late as the nineteenth century, people still spoke of "damning" a city or boycotting a business. Workers asserted their power by decreeing a *social ban*. In England, the Chartists were quick to place their hopes in universal suffrage, which was achieved only gradually. In France, by contrast, workers had to confront the disappointment of universal suffrage early on and were therefore more willing to engage in negative politics. A continuous thread runs from Proudhon, the great champion of workers' separation, to revolutionary syndicalism: in social dissidence, it was argued, lay a power that could not be co-opted.

Toward the end of the nineteenth century, the idea of a general strike combined revolutionary aspirations with belief in the active virtues of a "universal and simultaneous suspension of the productive force."[7] The moral force of the refusal to suffer a debased existence was coupled with an effort to develop a true critical sovereignty. The old right to resist was thus reformulated as social protest. For the champions of this approach, it was a question of a new form of political action, a

---

[5] On this point, see Jean Allemane, *Le Socialisme en France* (Paris, 1900), p. 39. On the theme of secession, see the work of Proudhon, especially *De la capacité politique des classes ouvrières* (1865).

[6] Émile Coornaert, *Les Compagnonnages en France, du Moyen Âge à nos jours* (Paris: Éditions Ouvrières, 1966), pp. 274 and 282.

[7] The quote is from Fernand Pelloutier, *Histoire des Bourses du Travail* (Paris, 1902), p. 66. On the general strike, see Robert Brécy, *La Grève générale en France* (Paris: EDI, 1969) and Lagardelle, *La Grève générale et le socialisme*.

way of mobilizing social energy that was profoundly different from waging an electoral campaign. The goal of the movement went beyond the mere withholding of labor. The strike was said to be the most effective expression of worker sovereignty. The movement's theorists included all the great names of revolutionary syndicalism: Pouget, Sorel, Pelloutier, and Griffuelhes. But it was perhaps Émile de Girardin, that amiable jack-of-all-trades, who best expressed the ambition of the movement when he was the first to call for a general strike in response to the coup d'état of December 2, 1851. It was "with a vacuum," he argued, that Louis-Napoleon could be defeated. "The universal strike: isolation, solitude, a vacuum around this man! Let the nation abandon him. Merely by folding our arms in front of him, we can bring him down."[8] Parliamentary socialism fought against this idea. Jaurès, for example, explained that the aim of socialism was to transform the "formidable negative power" of the proletariat into a "positive power" by way of an electoral majority that was the only way of achieving progress.[9] Jules Guesde also combated the idea of a general strike, which he scornfully likened to a "barricade of idlers." What was needed instead, he argued, was a "seizure of political power by the organized proletariat."[10] The specter of Blanquism and disillusionment with the old culture of the barricades implicit

---

[8] Speech to a republican meeting on December 3, 1851. A witness reported Girardin's words, which included the first use of the phrase "general strike." See Eugène Ténot, *Paris en décembre 1851* (Paris, 1868), p. 208.

[9] Jean Jaurès, *La Petite République*, September 1, 1901, article reproduced in Lagardelle, *Grève et socialisme*.

[10] Jules Guesde, speech to the Congress of Lille (August 1904) of the French Socialist Party, *ibid.*, pp. 83 and 88.

in the Blanquist approach did much to discredit the idea of the general strike and the "power of the vacuum." The idea was linked to the insurrectional practices of the past and therefore rejected, but with rejection came a repetition of the past failure to perceive the other, critical side of negative power.

Although the class struggle was thus brought back inside the electoral framework, it nevertheless continued to exist as a social fact. Everyday opposition remained a reality, conflict became a way of life, and workers understood that they had certain resources at their disposal. Thus for a long time two forms of legitimacy coexisted in industrial democracies. The government derived its political legitimacy from the ballot box, but the representatives of the working class enjoyed social legitimacy. The latter effectively limited the former and gained practical recognition by doing so, as can be seen in the specific institutional role granted to trade unions outside the formal legal structure of government.[11] The class struggle became a structural feature of democratic politics in industrialized societies. It posed a radical and sometimes violent challenge to the very structure of society and demonstrated the inadequacy of liberal institutions. The conflict between political legitimacy and social legitimacy became a permanent fixture of social life, a source of both energy and anxiety.

---

[11] Recall that by the late nineteenth century, the trade unions were recognized as quasi-public institutions and full-fledged representatives of the working class. Pierre Rosanvallon, *La Question syndicale: Histoire et avenir d'une forme sociale*, new edn (Paris: Pluriel, 1999).

The metamorphoses of the opposition

Historically, preventive power also took another form: organized political and parliamentary opposition. The democratic role of the opposition was slow to emerge, however. At first, the opposition was seen in primarily liberal terms, as a manifestation of freedom of expression. From Benjamin Constant to Robert Dahl, political theorists treated opposition as an aspect of pluralist organization.[12] It was also associated with respect for and protection of minorities: the opposition represented minority interests while alleviating the danger of a tyranny of the majority.[13] It was also seen as one of the most effective means of limiting power: the opposition took the diffuse counter-force of public opinion and shaped it into a useful instrument. Benjamin Constant was one of the first theorists to observe that an active opposition constituted a more effective guarantee of liberty than did separation of powers. Competition of majority and opposition was for him the only effective limit on social authority.[14] What these two approaches to the role of the opposition have in common is that neither sees that role in a positive light, as an instrument of action and intervention based on shared exercise of democratic power.

[12] See Robert Dahl, ed., *Oppositions in Western Democracies* (New Haven: Yale University Press, 1966).

[13] Giovanni Sartori, "Opposition and Control: Problems and Prospects," *Government and Opposition*, vol. 1, no. 2 (Jan. 1966).

[14] See Valérie Gérard, *L'Opposition politique: Limiter le pouvoir ou le concurrencer? Deux types de légitimation de l'opposition politique: Benjamin Constant et François Guizot*, thesis, Institut d'Études Politiques de Paris, 2002.

Guizot was the first to reject this view. To be sure, he did not propose granting the opposition a share of popular sovereignty. He nevertheless pointed out that, even in its negative role, it performed a political function in the full sense of the word. In his great work "on the means of government and opposition,"[15] he showed that the opposition was a constituent part of government, to whose work it contributed indirectly. Since the opposition's goal is to replace the government, it puts that government constantly to the test. It obliges the government to explain itself, to prove its effectiveness, to justify its decisions publicly. It imposes a need for rational debate and justification. Summing up, Guizot argues that the opposition "rectifies and therefore sustains the very government that it combats."[16] The opposition is effective only when it is not content merely to denounce the action of the government in power. If reasoned criticism allows it to exercise a genuine counter-power capable of seriously constraining the majority, it also imposes obligations on the opposition, which must convince the people that it is right and the government is wrong and that it is capable of running the country more effectively. "Like any ministry," Guizot points out, "the opposition is required to have a system and a future. It does not govern, but government is its necessary goal, for if it triumphs, it will have to govern."[17] On this view of the matter, the opposition's preventive power serves an effective political

[15] François Guizot, *Des moyens de gouvernement et d'opposition dans l'état actuel de la France* (Paris, 1821).

[16] *Ibid.*, p. 307.

[17] *Ibid.*, p. 320. He also says: "The role of the opposition in a well-regulated representative government is not limited to spying on the

function and not a merely restrictive or limitative one. Guizot's constructive approach to opposition had little influence on French practice, however. French monism proved refractory to the dualist perspective behind Guizot's thought: in France, legitimacy was inevitably "one and indivisible." The consequences of Jacobinism's long-standing anti-pluralism were the same in this realm as in others. The reluctance to recognize the role of political parties, the refusal to consider the nation as a composite of different elements, and suspicion of the very idea of opposition all stemmed from the French readiness to see difference and conflict as lethal threats to the body politic.

In England, John Stuart Mill took up a number of Guizot's arguments in favor of a positive role for the opposition. He, too, held that criticism was an essential element of efficient government and looked upon government and opposition as *parts of a dynamic system.* Mill's comments drew on actual British experience, however. There, the nineteenth century saw the gradual development of practices that would lead to an institutionalized role for the parliamentary opposition.[18] At the

behavior of the government and to finding out and proclaiming its faults. Its principal mission is perhaps to point out improvements, to call for reforms that society is capable of accepting ... Free of the weight of affairs, exempt from the immediate and definite responsibility that goes with governing, the opposition generally takes the lead and proceeds boldly toward a more perfect civilization. It points out the possible benefits and achievements. It urges and exhorts the government to move forward for the good of the country." Speech of March 16, 1830, in François Guizot, *Histoire parlementaire de France* (Paris, 1863), vol. I, p. 22.

[18] See Archibald Foord, *His Majesty's Opposition, 1714–1830* (Oxford: Clarendon Press, 1964) and Robert Malcom Punnett, *Front-Bench*

dawn of the twentieth century, Lord Balfour theorized the shar-
ing of "roles" between the minority and majority in Parliament,
as well as the regular redistribution of critical and administrative
functions as a result of elections.[19] This practice became more
and more institutionalized as time went by. The "shadow cabinet" made its first appearance in 1923, after the defeat of Labour,
and the formula was finally codified and adopted in 1955. France
discovered "counter-government" in the 1970s. After 1955, one
could truly say that the opposition in Britain had achieved
official *status*. The opposition recognized the legitimacy of the
government, and the government in turn recognized the opposition and afforded it the means to function effectively. Certain
"rights" and practices were formalized: regular consultation
between majority and minority "whips"; designation of "opposition days" when the parliamentary agenda was set by the
opposition; chairmanship of financial and judicial oversight
committees; access to classified documents. Other European
countries adopted some of these practices, but Britain institutionalized them more fully than any other country.[20] One can
almost speak of a *post-majoritarian* form of democracy, in which
positive sovereignty was combined with critical sovereignty. It
remains confined within a parliamentary framework, however.

*Opposition: The Role of the Leader of Opposition, the Shadow Cabinet, and
Shadow Government in British Politics* (London: Heinemann, 1973).

[19] Arthur James Balfour, *Chapters of Autobiography*, ed. Blanche E.C.
Dugdale (London, 1930). After each election, Balfour noted (p. 133), new
and old ministers change roles when they change seats. Those who
once used to criticize are now obliged to govern, and those who had
governed now take to criticizing.

[20] See Sylvie Giulj, "Le Statut de l'opposition en Europe," *Notes et Études
Documentaires*, no. 4585, September 24, 1980.

The political history of the past two centuries shows that we must look to social-democratic regimes to find the preventive function fully integrated into the political structure. Social compromise to resolve class conflict (which requires that the existence of class conflict be recognized) is reflected in the structure of government by institutionalizing the opposition role. Implicit veto power is granted over policies to which the opposition is particularly hostile.[21] Such regimes recognize the distinction between social legitimacy and political legitimacy in their very organizational structure. To put the same point another way, they accept the institutions of liberal democracy but at the same time acknowledge the inescapable reality of class struggle.

The rebel, the resister, and the dissident

Critical sovereignty also found expression in individual *attitudes*, in refusals to accept the status quo. Earlier we saw that resistance could take a political form, but an ethos or metaphysics of opposition is also worth noticing. Albert Camus gave his version of this in *L'Homme révolté (The Rebel)*.[22] For the author of *La Peste (The Plague)*, the rebel is "a man who says no," but a "no" of intervention rather than renunciation, a "no" that marks an about-face, an affirmation of refusal. It expresses a demand, a rejection of the world's

---

[21] See Alain Bergounioux and Bernard Manin, *La Social-démocratie ou le compromis* (Paris: Presses Universitaires de France, 1979) and *Le Régime social-démocrate* (Paris: Presses Universitaires de France, 1989).

[22] Albert Camus, *L'Homme révolté* (1951), in *Essais* (Paris: Gallimard, La Pléiade, 1965).

injustice. The rebel is a man who stands up, speaks out, and prides himself on his distance from the established disorder. Camus the philosopher distinguished the revolutionary from the artist and poet. Similarly, one might imagine three types of political refusal, symbolized by the rebel, the resister, and the dissident.

Examples of rebels might include John Wilkes in eighteenth-century England, Henry David Thoreau and Ralph Waldo Emerson in nineteenth-century America, and Auguste Blanqui in nineteenth-century France. Throughout Enlightenment Europe, Wilkes symbolized the struggle for liberty. Elected to the House of Commons in 1757, he used his newspaper, *The North Briton*, to denounce the autocratic turn of the government of George III. Indicted for libel, expelled from Parliament, imprisoned, and exiled, he nevertheless remained immensely popular. Crowds besieged the prison in which he was held in London, and, after seeking asylum on the continent, he was fêted in all the capitals of Europe. He was twice re-elected to Parliament only to have the vote invalidated. His name became synonymous with the struggle for human rights and democracy against a repressive regime. He became the very type of the rebel who never flags in his effort to defend freedom against tyranny. Identified with his cause, he took the fight into the institutions of power itself in the hope of making them abide by their own rules or else replace existing rules with better ones.[23] He was thus not only

---

[23] R. Christie, *Wilkes, Wyvill and Reform: The Parliamentary Reform Movement in British Politics, 1760–1785* (London: Macmillan, 1962).

an individual unwilling to accept things as he found them but also a great champion of parliamentary government.

Thoreau's rebellion was quite different. It was by taking his distance from society that he became a radical. He gained notoriety in 1845 for refusing to pay taxes that would be used to finance the war with Mexico. He did not limit his attacks to government errors but made himself a symbol of resistance to the injustice of the law itself. The hermit of Walden was not part of any social movement.[24] Effective political intervention was not his primary concern. He was not a writer given to exalting popular sovereignty, universal suffrage, or even democracy. It was the principle of individual rebellion that he defended above all. For him, the citizen was a man who could stand on his own two feet, a man capable of defending his independence and, if need be, of withdrawing from society in order to maintain it. He did not take himself to be the representative of a people or a class. For him, the idea of "civil disobedience," which he introduced into the political lexicon, was central.[25] Hannah Arendt, fascinated by Thoreau, showed that it was impossible to deduce a political position from such a notion or to give it a legal foundation.[26] It was not Thoreau's purpose to do so. His singular heroic action was meant as a moral protest that would discredit political

---

[24] His most famous book, *Walden* (1854), recounts his two years' living alone beside Walden Pond.

[25] *On the Duty of Civil Disobedience* was published in 1849.

[26] See the essay on civil disobedience in Hannah Arendt, *Crises of the Republic* (1969). For Arendt, civil disobedience acquires legal standing only when integrated into minority politics as a "speech act" marking a dramatic turning point in the presentation of demands.

institutions. Skeptical as to the effectiveness of voting, he offered his fellow citizens this rule of conduct: "Let your life be a counter friction to stop the machine."[27] For Thoreau, all power is tyrannical and dangerous. A rebel, he is also one who would renounce politics altogether. So great is the gap between the eternal values of justice and truth and what can be achieved by the institutions of this world that no positive politics is defensible in his eyes.[28] For Thoreau, the only imaginable revolution is that which can be achieved through individual moral progress and minimal government.

One cannot discuss Thoreau without adding a word about Ralph Waldo Emerson, his Concord, Massachusetts, neighbor and comrade in the fight against slavery. Emerson, too, defended the idea of the independent individual, radically attached to his individualism, resistant to social conventions, and faithful solely to his inner truth. He, too, was tempted by a philosophy of estrangement: he urged his contemporaries to renounce all desire to imitate others and be wary of the illusion that travel is a way of discovering the world.[29] But Emerson

---

[27] Thoreau, *Civil Disobdience*. An idea of his distance from traditional politics can be gleaned from this typical passage: "Even voting *for the right* is *doing* nothing for it. It is only expressing to men feebly your desire that it should prevail."

[28] On this point, see George Kateb, *The Inner Ocean: Individualism and Democratic Culture* (Ithaca: Cornell University Press, 1992), and Jack Turner, "Performing Conscience. Thoreau, Political Action and the Plea for John Brown," *Political Theory* 33, no. 4 (Aug. 2005).

[29] "Travelling is a fool's paradise. Our first journeys discover to us the indifference of places. At home I dream that at Naples, at Rome, I can be intoxicated with beauty, and lose my sadness. I pack my trunk, embrace my friends, embark on the sea, and at last wake up in Naples, and there

formulated his rejection of government in more pregnant terms than Thoreau. Like Thoreau, he argued that faith in government connoted a lack of confidence in oneself, but he also offered a detailed political (as opposed to ethical) response that reflected his skeptical philosophy. "Whoso would be a man must be a nonconformist," he wrote in a celebrated formula.[30] His call for independence of mind was also an implicit appeal to resist. Government actions must be questioned constantly: such questioning is the essence of constructive democratic politics. Deep civic conversation enables each individual to find his place in the world and his voice in the community. Emerson founded a tradition of dissent that lives on among those who protest the decisions of government with the slogan "not in my name." But he also hoped that it might be possible to construct a more demanding and more deliberative democracy.[31]

A far cry from Wilkes, Thoreau, and Emerson, Auguste Blanqui embodied an approach to rebellion that rejected the world as it is and sought to transform it from top to

beside me is the stern fact, the sad self, unrelenting, identical, that I fled from. I seek the Vatican, and the palaces. I affect to be intoxicated with sights and suggestions, but I am not intoxicated. My giant goes with me wherever I go.

"Travelling is a fool's paradise. Our first journeys discover to us the indifference of places ... But the rage of travelling is a symptom of a deeper unsoundness affecting the whole intellectual action ... We imitate; and what is imitation but the travelling of the mind?" Ralph Waldo Emerson, "Self-Reliance," in *Essays and Lectures* (New York: Library of America, 1983), pp. 259–282.

[30] *Ibid.*

[31] On dissent in Emerson, see Sandra Laugier, *Une autre pensée politique américaine: La Démocratie radicale d'Emerson à Stanley Cavell* (Paris: Michel Houdiard, 2004).

bottom. He was the first major theorist of permanent revolution. His life exemplified a determination to rebel, a visceral hostility to compromise, and an implacable dislike of parliamentary politics. Evidence of this determination can be seen in the fact that he spent thirty-four years behind bars, earning himself the epithet "The Prisoner," despite which he continued to dream of violent uprising as the only feasible means of changing the world. He saw revolutionary action as a means of overcoming society's regrettable inertia.[32] By compressing space and time, revolutionary action makes it possible to superimpose concept upon reality. Hence insurrection is not merely one means of action among others but, as Blanqui puts it in a striking phrase, "a stunning act of sovereignty."[33] It is not only the most radical form of critical sovereignty but also the most effective, since it both destroys the old world and gives access to a new one. Like a black diamond, it thus embodies the democratic idea shorn of all disruptive contingencies: here, in action, lies the ultimate solution to the primary aporias of popular sovereignty. Insurrection is thus the mother of "utopian democracy," democracy liberated from all specific institutional arrangements. That is why Blanqui was able to look upon insurrection as an "art" (Marx would later borrow the word from him). It was a fully functional form, a

---

[32] For more on Blanqui, see the chapter I devote to him in *La Démocratie inachevée: Histoire de la souveraineté du peuple en France* (Paris: Gallimard, 2000).

[33] Louis Auguste Blanqui, "Pourquoi il n'y a plus d'émeutes," *Le Libérateur*, no. 1, February 2, 1834, reproduced in Louis Auguste Blanqui, *Œuvres*, vol. I: *Des origines à la révolution de 1848*, ed. Dominique Le Nuz (Presses Universitaires de Nancy, 1993), p. 268.

directly intelligible mode of organization, a signifier coinciding perfectly with its signified. For Blanqui, rebellion combined a political form, a social movement (or even a pure kinetics), and a moral posture. That is why he has remained an object of fascination even for those who do not share his views. His memory is intimately intertwined with the romantic image of the rebel on the barricades, who joins a warm if ephemeral community of fighters even as he commits a radical act of defiance. "The insurgent! His real name is Man ... We find him in the streets, together with his comrades on the barricades," in the description of Eugène Pottier, the author of *L'Internationale*.[34]

These three forms of rebellion (Thoreau's, Emerson's, and Blanqui's) reflect different historical inflections of critical sovereignty as a political attitude. *Resistance* is of a different order. It describes action in the much more constraining context of a foreign occupation or a situation in which it is impossible to intervene critically within the framework of existing institutions. The word is ancient: we saw earlier that the right of resistance was invoked as long ago as the Middle Ages. It took on its contemporary and symbolic meaning, however, when General de Gaulle used it in 1940.[35] The World War II resister was one who combined a moral determination to reject the established government with a hope that a new order would one day be established. His position was

[34] "L'Insurgé," in Eugène Pottier, *Œuvres complètes* (Paris: Maspero, 1966), p. 152.

[35] Henry Michel, "Comment s'est formée la pensée de la Résistance," in Henry Michel and Boris Mirkine-Guetzévitch, *Les Idées politiques et sociales de la Résistance* (Paris: Presses Universitaires de France, 1954).

therefore not merely defensive, and he did not seek simply to "put the brakes" on the actions of the existing government. He sought rather to counter discouragement and resignation with active hope; he refused to give in to fatalism and kept the light of hope alive through the darkest hours.[36] Resistance, which in the beginning implied a need for clandestine action, was associated with refusal, but it was an active, methodical, organized refusal linked to an effort of mobilization. The resister revived the principle of *political will*. De Gaulle was the living embodiment of this aspect of resistance. His famous speech of June 18, 1940, which Saint-John Perse described as having "the syntax of a bolt of lightning," breathed the spirit of resistance, the opposition of will to fate. Since then, the idea of resistance has found more ambiguous, not to say confused, expression in contexts where it signifies nothing more than hesitancy, disagreement, or intransigence.[37] Still, the ideas of a higher moral imperative, a primary legitimacy, or a sovereign decision have remained paramount.

The dissident expresses critical sovereignty in yet another form. The word *dissidence*, originally used in religious contexts, is also very old.[38] It has lately taken on a

[36] "The flame of resistance shall never be extinguished," de Gaulle said in a 1940 speech. On the use of the expression, see Arlette Farge and Michel Chaumont, *Les Mots pour résister: Voyage de notre vocabulaire politique de la Résistance à aujourd'hui* (Paris: Bayard, 2005), and Laurent Douzou, "Résister," in Vincent Duclert and Christophe Prochasson, *Dictionnaire critique de la République* (Paris: Flammarion, 2002).

[37] See Jacques Semelin, "Qu'est ce que résister?", *Esprit* (Jan. 1994).

[38] A "dissident" was a person who disagreed with or separated from a religious community. He opposed those who remained orthodox.

more political meaning, since it was used to describe intellectuals who opposed various communist governments, who identified the weaknesses in totalitarian regimes. Dissidents were unable to resist police states that maintained a tight grip over bodies and minds, but by their mere existence they demonstrated the inability of such regimes to impose their lies on all their citizens. As Claude Lefort has shown, it was the dissidents in the Soviet Union who ostentatiously refused to believe in the government, who disobeyed its orders, who exposed corruption and urged others to see things as they were. The dissident was the "superfluous individual,"[39] the person whose existence quietly discredited the regime and who drove a wedge into the seemingly solid edifice of its ideology and split it apart. Some dissidents, such as Solzhenitsyn, bore witness to actions that the regime preferred to keep hidden; others, such as Sakharov, had once been part of the apparatus but at some point refused to play along; still others, such as Havel and Zinoviev, were writers whose irony exposed the realities of the regime. Everywhere dissidents raised doubts. Hence no matter how small their numbers, they were dangerous in the long run, the forerunners of an "antipolitics" directed against the system and calling upon civil society to open its eyes and recognize its hidden strength.[40]

[39] Claude Lefort, *Un Homme en trop: Réflexions sur l'Archipel du Goulag* (Paris: Éditions du Seuil, 1976).

[40] See György Konrad, *Antipolitics: An Essay* (New York: Harcourt Brace Jovanovich, 1984), and Vaclav Havel, "Antipolitical Politics," in John Keane, ed., *Civil Society and the State* (London: Verso, 1988).

The decline of the critical dimension
in democracies

The recognition of social division, of the existence of an organized opposition, and of a vigorous moral critique of governmental power have been part of democratic life for two centuries. In consequence, democracies have found it necessary to question themselves, to look critically at their own operation and at the type of society they produce. Conflict, opposition, and even deep internal division reflect the fact that democratic and republican ideals have been taken seriously. Democratic societies have sought to bring those ideals to life, to give practical meaning to the idea that no democratic regime can exist without permanent self-scrutiny. No democratic regime is permanently defined by or fully reflected in the institutions that embody it. There is always something fundamentally indeterminate in democracy.[41] In this respect, critical sovereignty and electoral-representative mechanisms together constitute a system capable of giving adequate expression to democratic experience. Critical sovereignty is essential for giving the democratic system meaning in citizens' eyes. Even radical criticism does not lead to disenchantment. Skepticism does not turn into cynicism. Both help to make society intelligible and thus make it possible to conceive of change.

Various aspects of this critical function have eroded simultaneously, however, and thus we have entered a new political era. The lines of class conflict have been blurred by the third industrial revolution and the simultaneous

---

[41] As Claude Lefort's work has forcefully brought home.

transformation of collective identities. Workers have the sense of having lost the preventive power they once possessed. If class struggle persists, it has become fragmented and passive, and its larger meaning remains obscure. This change has been accompanied by a crisis of social and political representation, yielding the sense that a great void has opened up, that society no longer understands itself and that power has slipped away. Both forms of sovereignty – the social critical and the positive political – have collapsed. The decline of the trade unions has only amplified the effects of growing disenchantment with democracy.

As for the political order proper, the structural function of the opposition has in large part been undermined by the decline of political parties, evidence for which can be seen in the fact that it has become increasingly difficult for the parties to aggregate and reflect society's increasingly fragmented demands. To be sure, the parties continue to compete for power and to be the focal point of certain expectations, but they no longer shape people's visions of the future and no longer reflect the key cleavages of public opinion. Public opinion itself is increasingly fragmented and follows a logic of its own, without constructive ambitions. Opinion is not so much a reflection of forces that hope to govern as it is an expression of raw discontent. Hence its expressions tend to take a radically negative form, feeding the forces of obstruction. In the United States, the senatorial practice of "filibustering" allows a small number of senators to prolong debate indefinitely in order to prevent the passage of a bill. This extreme form of free expression hardly constitutes responsible opposition. In recent years the critical sovereignty of public opinion has increasingly asserted itself in such negative modes. Of course it is true that in certain countries, including France, much work remains to be done in expanding the rights of the opposition.[42] Yet institutionalization of the opposition is no longer sufficient if the ultimate goal is to give preventive power a place in the structure of democratic government.

Meanwhile, the rebel, the resister, and the dissident had largely vanished from the scene by the end of the twentieth century. Had courage diminished? Had conformism become inevitable? Had sources of new ideas dried up? Such factors no doubt played a part, but the crux of the matter lies elsewhere. With the decline of repressive governments in many parts of the world, certain forms of heroism also declined. Figures such as Aung San Suu Kyi, the tireless opponent of the Burmese dictatorship, are less numerous today because they are less necessary. Although rebellious masses may still make history by forcing a discredited government from power, this is no longer as common as it was in Europe in the late 1980s. With the completion of decolonization, the collapse of numerous totalitarian regimes, and growing international pressure to curb territorial appetites, there has been a "normalization" of politics in a relatively open setting. Simply put, it is the progress of democracy that has made committed rebels and intransigent dissidents less essential than in the past. In their place, unfortunately, pale imitations or caricatures have all too often come to the fore. Inveterate complainers and nostalgic ideologues have regrettably slipped into heroes' robes.

[42] See Marie-Claire Ponthoreau, "Les Droits de l'opposition en France: penser une oppositions présidentielle," *Pouvoirs*, no. 108 (2004).

Malcontents stand in for rebels. Militant moral rigor has given way to narrowly self-interested demands. Words have lost their luster. A constructive era in the history of critical sovereignty has thus come to an end. To be sure, a certain ability to expose deceptively soothing political programs remains, but such salutary lucidity seldom enlists the kind of support that moral fervor formerly elicited. It is often tinged with conservative nostalgia or nihilistic despair.

To sum up: the project of institutionalizing a social power of prevention was part of the political agenda of the early nineteenth century, but it soon disappeared. Three substitutes emerged: social and quasi-political opposition stemming from class struggle; organized political opposition with an active governmental role; and finally, moral opposition, embodied in the three figures of the rebel, the resister, and the dissident. In due course these substitutes also receded, and a new political era began. Today, critical sovereignty survives only in a relatively impoverished form; it has become narrowly negative and even at times regressive. As democracy has weakened, politics has come to be dominated by negativism and intransigence.

7

Negative politics

The age of "deselection"

The most obvious mode of the new form of preventive power is electoral in nature. Contemporary elections are not so much choices of orientation as judgments on the past. The very meaning of elections has changed accordingly. The etymological sense – to choose among candidates – no longer applies; the contest has become one of elimination, or what one might call "deselection." We have entered an era of "democracy by sanction." Electoral competitions can no longer be understood simply as a confrontation between equal candidates. What we find most commonly today is the "disputed re-election." Not enough attention has been paid to what amounts to a significant transformation of the democratic process. In political science, the change has been masked by an interest in "incumbent advantage," which is admittedly an equally important phenomenon. Certain distinctive features of American politics have tended to focus attention on this phenomenon. In the United States the probability that an incumbent will be re-elected is extraordinarily high (currently close to 90 percent for the Senate and House of Representatives).[1]

---

[1] See Stephen C. Erickson, "The Entrenching of Incumbency: Reflections on the US House of Representatives, 1790–1994," *Cato Journal* 14, no. 3 (Winter 1995); Albert Somit, Rudolf Wildenmann, Berhard Boll, and

What is more, this probability has increased over the past twenty years, despite rising rates of abstention and growing citizen disenchantment with government.[2] Quite apart from this fact, however, disputed re-elections are also interesting in their own right. In the early days of democratic government, such situations were rare, for the simple reason that short mandates were originally considered an essential feature of the representative system in both Europe and the United States. As republican elitists, the Founding Fathers still looked upon elective office as a service that ought not to become a profession. The actual conditions of such service (low pay, difficult travel over long distances to the capital) ensured that government service would be relatively unattractive. Thus even without restrictive rules, candidates for re-election were relatively rare in early American history. Hence there was a natural rotation of representatives, due primarily to a high rate of early retirement from government service. The situation in France was comparable. The members of the Constituent Assembly of 1789 went so far as to prohibit members of the first National Assembly from being elected to the second. The principle of barring certain people from becoming candidates during the revolutionary period influenced the way elections were seen. Given the tendency to elect notable citizens, which

Andrea Römmele, eds., *The Victorious Incumbent: A Threat to Democracy* (Dartmouth: Aldershot, 1994).
[2] See Gary W. Cox and Scott Morgenstern, "The Increasing Advantage of Incumbency in the U.S. States," *Legislative Studies Quarterly* 18, no. 4 (Nov. 1993); James L. Merriner and Thomas P. Senter, *Against Long Odds: Citizens Who Challenge Congressional Incumbents* (Westport, CT: Praeger, 1999).

would eventually become part of the country's political mores, and a certain irenic vision of detached elitism, disputed re-elections were rare.

Things began to change when political parties arrived on the scene. The election of Andrew Jackson in the United States in 1828 and the Revolution of 1848 in France mark the turning point. The asymmetry of incumbent and challenger took on a political dimension, as the incumbent was obliged to defend a policy, while the challenger was disposed to attack it. Each candidate derived certain advantages from this state of affairs. The incumbent enjoyed an informational advantage: if an election was a gamble on the future, voters were likely to feel less uncertain about going with the known quantity. On the other hand, the incumbent – structurally in a defensive position – incurred certain liabilities that the challenger did not. The influence of these factors varied with the time and country. The incumbency advantage was and is markedly greater in the United States, owing to the less pronounced ideological division in American politics coupled with material factors such as access to financing, which is usually easier for the incumbent. In Britain and France, sharper clashes on the issues resulted in a larger number of realigning elections.[3]

In recent years, however, the character of disputed re-elections has changed: no longer are they necessarily linked to a clash of rival political camps. What has become the crucial

---

[3] For the United States, see Bruce A. Campbell, *Realignment in American Politics: Toward a Theory* (Austin: University of Texas Press, 1980). For France, see Pierre Martin, *Comprendre les évolutions électorale: La Théorie des réalignements revisitée* (Paris: Presses de Sciences-Po, 2000).

variable for voters is the desire to sanction past policies. In France – a striking fact – every government since 1981 has been turned out by the voters, regardless of its policies. Not all democratic countries are quite this extreme, of course, but a general tendency to punish past policies is evident everywhere. Even in the United States, where the incumbent re-election rate is highest,[4] presidential elections – the most political of all elections (and perhaps the only truly political elections in the United States) – reveal a similar decline in the incumbency advantage. From 1900 to 1980, only two incumbent presidents were beaten: William Howard Taft and Herbert Hoover. Both faced extraordinarily difficult circumstances, moreover: Taft had to contend with a split in the Republican Party, and Hoover was saddled with the Depression. Since 1980, however, three out of five incumbents have failed to win re-election: Gerald Ford, Jimmy Carter, and George Herbert Walker Bush. To put the point a bit too strongly: no one is truly elected any more. Those in power no longer enjoy the confidence of voters; they merely reap the benefits of distrust of their opponents and predecessors.

Evidence for this shift can be seen in the negative focus of recent political campaigns. This shift has been abundantly documented in the United States, where negative

---

[4] A number of political scientists have emphasized the importance of constituency services in explaining the incumbency advantage. See Bruce Cain, John Ferejohn, and Morris Fiorina, *The Personal Vote: Constituency Service and Electoral Independance* (Cambridge, MA: Harvard University Press, 1987). For an overview of the literature on this subject, see Gary King, "Constituency Service and Incumbency Advantage," *British Journal of Political Science* 21, no. 1 (Jan. 1991).

campaigning has taken hold in recent years. Television spots are increasingly "attack ads" directed against the opponent.[5] Comparison of the rival candidates' positions on the issues takes second place. These attack ads make no pretense of offering a reasoned critique of the opponent's positions together with a defense of one's own. Their tone combines personal venom with outright slander. It sometimes seems that the major issue in every election is simply to prevent the opposition from winning. In the United States, negative political advertising is not new. In a sense, attack ads are merely the technological updating of a kind of crude character assassination almost as old as democracy itself. But what was once peripheral, largely restricted to populist movements of one sort or another and likely to turn up only in pathological cases or especially intense contests, has now become the rule. In the early 1980s, negative advertising accounted for no more than an estimated 20 percent of advertising budgets. A line was crossed in 1988, when the elder George Bush was elected: negative advertising consumed 50 percent of what was spent in that contest.[6] In the race between John Kerry and the younger

[5] The extreme degree of negative campaigning in the United States is due to the absence of legal limits on criticism and the possibility of using images of one's opponent.

[6] See Stephen Ansolabehere and Shanto Ivengar, *Going Negative: How Attack Ads Shrink and Polarise the Electorate* (New York: Free Press, 1995), p. 90. See also Michael Pfau and Henry C. Kenski, *Attack Politics Strategy and Defense* (Westport, CT: Praeger, 1990), and Karen S. Johnson-Cartee and Gary A. Copeland, *Negative Political Advertising: Coming of Age* (Hillsdale, NJ: Lawrence Erlbaum Associates, 1991).

George Bush in 2004, the trend continued, leading American political scientists to coin new phrases such as "poison politics" and "negative politics" to describe the change.[7]

What explains these developments? One explanation is obvious: negative campaigning works. Numerous studies have found that negative ads achieve a far higher "penetration rate" than positive ads.[8] Hence it is much more "cost-effective" to destroy one's opponent than to vaunt one's own merits. Advertising consultants gradually overcame whatever moral scruples may have prevented candidates from "going negative," especially since the experts were able to show that the risk of a "boomerang effect" was quite small. Negative advertising works in three ways. First, attack ads crystallize opinion and alleviate doubt. Voters feel hostile to the target of a negative ad even if they have no rational grounds for preferring the other candidate. In 2004, for instance, the unassailable slogan "anybody but Bush" helped Kerry voters overcome doubts about their own candidate. Second, negative ads increase the incumbency advantage, because the effects of slander are asymmetric. It is easier to sow doubt about a challenger, who is less well known than the incumbent and who has no track record in office. The voter feels safer with the person she has already seen in action, even if she didn't especially like what she saw. In some contests, negative ads

---

[7] See Victor Kamber, *Poison Politics: Are Negative Campaigns Destroying Democracy?* (New York: Insight Books, 1997); Kathleen Hall Jameson, *Dirty Politics: Deception, Distraction and Democracy* (Oxford University Press, 1992).

[8] Brenda S. Sonner, "The Effectiveness of Negative Political Advertising," *Journal of Advertising Research* 38 (1998).

can be decisive; in others, they may be just one factor among others. Finally, negative ads discourage undecided voters from going to the polls. These "independents" hesitate between parties as well as candidates. They are in a sense political skeptics. They doubt the usefulness of voting. Negative ads increase their disillusionment with politics in general and make them more skeptical of political promises.

Although negative campaigning has been most evident in the United States, its influence has been felt in most democratic societies. A "democracy of rejection" has developed in many places as a substitute for the old programmatic democracy. If we are to take the full measure of this phenomenon and respond to the challenges it raises, we must first work out a new political philosophy and political science. In the past, democratic theory was mainly concerned with questions of mandate and delegation of authority by an actively engaged and critical electorate. Now voters want mainly to mete out sanctions and revoke authority. Theory needs to explore this new realm of *negative sovereignty*. Elections are not the whole story. Preventive powers are growing in importance generally. The ability to resist and obstruct is an important aspect of contemporary political and social behavior. Hence democratic politics can no longer be analyzed solely in terms of conflicts of interest and compromise, modes of aggregation of individual preferences, or factors shaping public opinion.

Prevention and veto

The modern citizen is not like the club man who deposits a "black ball" to reject an unwelcome candidate. He can participate in preventive actions aimed at forcing government to reconsider its policies. For instance, street demonstrations and pressure groups can be effective means of persuasion. More generally, veto powers exercised in one form or another by social, political, and economic actors have come to play a growing role in modern democracies. Democracy comprises procedures beyond those that authorize and legitimate the actions of government. Accordingly, some political scientists argue that regimes should be characterized not in terms of institutions (presidential or parliamentary system, bipartisan or multi-partisan, etc.) but rather in terms of the capacity of various actors to block systemic change. For these theorists, the political system is defined by the dynamic interaction of so-called "veto players."[9] Although "corporatism" and "deadlock" are regularly denounced in France as peculiarly French pathologies, in fact they have become typical of democratic societies in general.[10]

[9] See the innovative and stimulating analyses in George Tsebelis, *Veto Players: How Political Institutions Work* (Princeton University Press, 2002). Strategic analysis can also be applied to systems in which one or more actors exercises a veto. For the American case, see Charles M. Cameron, *Veto Bargaining: Presidents and the Politics of Negative Power* (Cambridge University Press, 2000). The co-decision system that operates in European institutions can be analyzed in similar terms. Cf. George Tsebelis and Geoffrey Garrett, "Agenda Setting, Vetoes and the European Union's Co-decision Procedure," *The Journal of Legislative Studies* 3, no. 3 (Fall 1997) (with comments by Roger Scully).

[10] What *is* distinctive about France is rather the way in which social actors swerve abruptly from direct confrontation to passive acquiescence owing to the lack of intermediate bodies and opportunities for negotiation.

How are we to understand these changes? To begin with, the transformation of the global ideological context played an essential role. The fall of the Berlin Wall and the subsequent elimination of communism as a structural feature of European politics diminished old political antagonisms. At the same time, the power of political parties and the influence of their programs were reduced. The idea of politics as a choice between radically different social models faded away. Citizens are no longer mobilized by the prospect of a sudden transformation of the system, *un grand soir*. They seem willing to limit their role to that of pure censors and watchdogs. This change in attitude also contributed to the shift from a politics of ideas to a politics of distrust, to revert to the categories invoked earlier in this book.

The advent of negative politics also reflects a genuine triumph of liberalism. Indeed, liberalism emerged triumphant at the end of the twentieth century not as an economic ideology (expressing faith in the virtues of the market) but rather as a political philosophy with a cautious and circumscribed view of politics. In the 1970s, liberalism defined itself primarily, and most rigorously, in relation to the struggle against totalitarianism. Anti-totalitarians denounced the perversion of democracy by totalitarian regimes, and in so doing they contributed to a reconceptualization of the foundations of democracy. Skeptical liberals (who might be described schematically as proponents of a minimalist Schumpeterian view of democracy) came together with strong liberals (such as Hannah Arendt and Claude Lefort) who were trying to work out a new conception of citizenship. At the intersection of these two approaches, Judith Shklar advocated "the liberalism of fear"; writing in the 1980s, her goal was to define a negative politics founded on an aversion to the evil of totalitarianism rather than a purposeful search for the good.[11] In Shklar's view, it was more important to reject the *summum malum* than to search for the *summum bonum*. Yet even this negative approach still embodied a struggle for human emancipation that set it apart from conservative anti-communism. Today's negative politics no longer has this emancipatory dimension. Although a few writers have made vague attempts to inject elements of the anti-totalitarian critique into the anti-terrorist crusade, their intellectual focus remains remarkably narrow.[12] The politics of fear has been reduced to a politics of defensiveness and distrust.[13] The reigning climate of disillusionment has left its mark on negative democracy. Still, one should be careful not to reduce negative democracy to its most grotesque manifestation, a visceral and demagogic form of anti-political populism (about which I shall have more to say later). True negative democracy is a very active form of political engagement, involving the genuine exercise of social power. In order

[11] Judith Shklar, "The Liberalism of Fear," in Nancy L. Rosenblum, ed., *Liberalism and the Moral Life* (Cambridge, MA: Harvard University Press, 1989). "What liberalism requires," Shklar wrote, "is the possibility of making the evil of cruelty and fear the basic norm of its political practices and prescriptions" (p. 30). In a similar vein, see also Michael Ignatieff, *The Lesser Evil: Political Ethics in an Age of Terror* (Princeton University Press, 2004).

[12] See, for example, Paul Berman, *Terror and Liberalism* (New York: Norton, 2003).

[13] See Corey Robin, *Fear: The History of a Political Idea* (Oxford University Press, 2004).

to understand its growing importance, we need to consider why it has been effective.

There is a sociological explanation for the rise of negative democracy: reactive coalitions turn out to be easier to organize than other kinds of coalitions because their heterogeneous membership can be ignored. They do not need to be coherent in order to play their political role. They derive power from the intensity of the reactions to which they give voice. In the streets, in the media, and in other symbolic settings, numbers alone are not the important thing. By contrast, it is much more difficult to organize a true social majority to engage in political action. Positive, deliberate agreement must be reached before such an objective can be achieved. Electoral majorities do not yield that kind of agreement. Political majorities are in essence aggregates, a mere summing up of votes. Each voter may have a specific intention, a specific interpretation of the meaning of his or her vote. Voters thus weigh motives of adherence, sanction, and prevention as they please without even being consciously aware of what they are doing. Their ballots reduce these complex calculations to simple numerical totals. Their only tangible significance is that they can be counted and added up. Rejection is the simplest thing to aggregate. Indeed, all rejections are identical, regardless of what may have motivated them. In a world no longer organized around ideological confrontation, it has therefore become easier and easier to put together reactive political majorities.[14] These have increasingly little in common with action

---

[14] On this point, see the penetrating observations of Étienne Schweisguth, "La dépolitisation en question," in Gérard Grunberg, Nonna Meyer, and

majorities, moreover. One can therefore argue that there is now a structural advantage to negativity. As a result, legitimacy and governability are increasingly distinct in modern democracies. The alternation of political majorities serves as a safety valve, allowing for periodic release of the resulting pressure. It does not eliminate the source of the pressure, however, and each time the valve is opened, disillusionment with the system immediately begins the buildup of pressure all over again.

There are also pragmatic reasons for the development of negative politics. For one thing, it produces immediate results. Negative action fully realizes its motivating intention. The result is indisputable, because it takes the form of a simple, intelligible act or decision. A mobilization to force the government to withdraw proposed legislation produces easily measurable results, for example, whereas action on behalf of some positive goal is subject to constantly shifting judgments because the goals are often ambiguous and intermediate steps are not always easy to evaluate. It is easier to get rid of a vexatious tax than to pursue "fiscal justice." Diderot remarked on this asymmetry in *L'Encyclopédie*: "It has always seemed to me more difficult to achieve strict respect for good laws than to get rid of bad ones."[15] As Hobbes observed, moreover, preventive actions also have "theatrical qualities": they appeal to the imagination and therefore raise expectations of tangible results. Negative actions (prevention, dismissal, rejection, etc.) yield definite results, whereas vesting confidence in a government increases uncertainty: elections are

Paul M. Sniderman, *La Démocratie à L'épreuve* (Paris: Presses de Sciences-Po, 2002), esp. pp. 84–85.
[15] Article on "Corruption."

inherently wagers on the future. This structural uncertainty has only increased as the capacity of political parties to impose social and programmatic discipline has decreased. In temporal terms, negative action is simple: it is immediate. By contrast, an electoral mandate evolves over time; the successful candidate must somehow adjust if conditions change in the future. Voters therefore feel that they need to control what their representatives do. They must become watchdogs if their will is to have any meaning. How that "will" is to be exercised over time remains problematic. Governments can always ignore or deny it. The weaker government oversight is, the greater the desire for immediately effective negative action. One might even try to classify political systems in this respect. The French system turns out to be an extreme case: election, based on an almost "magical" vision of the general will, becomes almost an anointment, but historically this has gone hand in hand with a culture of insurrection, negative politics in its most radical form. The English case is quite different: positive and negative politics are subtly intertwined, with the liberal parliamentary system acting as a buffer.

The recent development of preventive politics should not be seen as a kind of depoliticization. The "negative citizen" is not a passive citizen. If he expresses skepticism and confusion about politics, he nevertheless strongly asserts his presence in the public square. The term "negative politicization" has rightly been applied to this phenomenon.[16] There is a kind of participation in public life, but it is essentially hostile. There is

---

[16] See Jean-Louis Missika, "Les Faux-semblants de la dépolitisation," *Le Débat* no. 68 (Jan.–Feb. 1992).

a kind of commitment, but a commitment to rejection. There is a kind of expression, but in the truncated form of slogans and denunciations.[17] One really should speak of negative *sovereignty*, especially since what is distinctive about preventive powers, and indeed all the other powers of distrust, is precisely the fact of being exercised directly. Negative democracy is thus also a substitute for direct democracy, a kind of *regressive direct democracy*.

Weak democracy

Negative sovereignty has two faces. It manifests itself first of all in the form of preventive powers of one kind or another, as we have just seen. But it also expresses itself in another, weaker form: passive consent. Withdrawal, abstention, and silence are in fact forms of political expression. Indeed, they are ubiquitous forms of political expression, and it would be a mistake to overlook their importance. Absence of reaction to a measure is normally considered a sign of acceptance. "Silence is consent," as the saying goes. The re-election of an incumbent can be interpreted as a failure to exercise the power of prevention because his opponents cannot mobilize or arouse the interest of voters.

---

[17] There is a popular expression in Argentina, *hablar en cacerolio*, which literally means "talking casserole" and figuratively connotes the idea of banging on a pot, noisemaking as a primary form of protest. See Thomas Bouchet, Matthew Legget, Geneviève Verdo, and Jean Vigreux, eds., *L'Insulte (en) politique: Europe et Amérique latine du XIXe à nos jours* (Éditions Universitaires de Dijon, 2005).

What accounts for such "consent by default?" There are several possible explanations. It may stem from absolute or, more commonly, relative indifference: the stakes in the contest may seem small, so that the cost of protest exceeds the benefits of change. One sees this frequently in small groups. One sociologist has applied the term "apparent consensus" to situations in which agreement is the result not of an explicit convergence of opinions but rather of a series of implicit mutual concessions, a feeling that nothing of real importance is at stake, or simply a lack of interest in the issues.[18] Negative consent may also arise when for one reason or another it is difficult to formulate a critique of those responsible for a particular decision. Potential protesters may abstain from opposing the government, for example, if they feel that it is impossible to debate the issue on equal terms or if they fear that the broader public will find their arguments wanting. In routine political interaction, situations eliciting such negative consent are common, but little attention is paid to them because the forces they mobilize are weak and fundamentally without influence. Recognizing the negative sovereignty of the people leads us to view politics in a new way. It is essential to begin by analyzing the most explicit forms of negative sovereignty in both institutions and social movements, but it is also indispensable to pay attention to gray areas of the sort I've just described, to explain why they exist and what their effects are. Sociologists of organization have long recognized the need to move beyond analyses of organizational structure, major

---

[18] See Philippe Urfalino, "La décision par consensus apparent. Nature et propriétés," *Revue européenne des sciences sociales* (Winter 2006).

conflicts, and structured negotiations. Other aspects of organizational life are equally important: small problems of coordination, minor dysfunctions, ambiguous lines of authority, impediments to the integration of individuals into the organization.[19] We need to look at indirect and negative forms of democratic life in a similar light.

Passive democracy may take many subtle forms, but one institutional modality is worth mentioning explicitly: *tacit election*. The term applies to situations in which there is a single candidate for a post, so that election is automatic, without the vote that would normally be required. Technically, the reason for this procedure is obvious: if there is only one candidate, he or she is certain of being elected no matter how many people turn out to vote. To eliminate the balloting is therefore to save time and money. If a vote is merely a ratification of a foregone conclusion, it hardly matters whether the choice is explicit or merely tacit. This rule was first institutionalized in the United Kingdom with the Ballot Act of 1872. The Netherlands and Belgium followed suit in 1898 and 1899, respectively, followed by Switzerland and several other European countries.[20] The rule was vigorously denounced by people who felt that eliminating the symbolic dimension of the election ritual deprived the community of an opportunity to reaffirm the equality of all its citizens before the law. The electionless election was attacked as "spineless democracy"

---

[19] On the importance of weak ties, see Mark Granovetter, "The Strength of Weak Ties," *American Journal of Sociology* 78, no. 6 (May 1973).

[20] I follow the overview of the subject in Jean-François Flauss, "L'élection tacite. Retour sur une vraie fausse curiosité du droit constitutionnel suisse," *Revue Française de droit constitutionnel*, no. 61 (Jan. 2005).

and "democracy by default." It is interesting to note that the tacit election procedure was often introduced by authoritarian or conservative regimes (leaving aside the Swiss case, where the chief reason for the new rule was the desire to reduce the number of elections in which voters were called to participate). Tacit elections were clearly seen as one of several ways to constrain universal suffrage at the margin by limiting the number of appeals to the voters.[21] In England, the system was introduced at the same time as the secret ballot, as if its purpose was to counter the symbolic menace of the latter. This interpretation is unsatisfactory, however. What was indeed troubling about the tacit election system was the way in which it brought out the normally hidden negative aspect of democratic politics. The tacit election was in fact a perfect illustration of the idea that failure to exercise the power of prevention connoted consent. Had even a single citizen come forward as a candidate, an election would have been required. To be sure, there was a high cost to running for office, because many people had to be mobilized, but the option was there. Where public expression subsided into public silence, the tacit election tested the very meaning of democracy.

To be sure, tacit election is not the only weak form of democracy. Other, less visible expressions of tacit consent are common in democratic politics, but tacit election cuts to the heart of the matter. Hence it is not enough to recoil from the idea in horror, as the republicans of the French Third Republic did. To them, tacit election violated a kind of taboo, in part

---

[21] In several of these countries, property qualifications for voting served a similar purpose.

because it touched on a particularly troubling dimension of politics, which they did not want to think about: the exercise of popular sovereignty by an absent people. The mere possibility of tacit election disturbed the enchanted vision of democracy they championed.[22]

This dusty procedural curiosity encapsulates a hard truth about democracy at the dawn of the twenty-first century: an age of weak negative politics has begun. Today's "rejectionists" cannot be compared with the rebels and dissidents of old. Their refusal to participate in the system contains no implicit image of the future. They offer no critique of the existing system as a prelude to further action. Their position lacks a prophetic dimension. In a chaotic and angry way they give voice only to their own inability to make sense of things and find their place in the world. In order to exist they therefore believe that they must vent their wrath on a variety of "rejects": foreigners, immigrants, "the system." Their only hope lies in hate. Counter-democracy has thus been transformed into a banal form of opposition to democracy itself. Instead of oversight and criticism as ways of increasing citizen activity, today's negative politics marks a painful and energy-sapping shrinkage of that activity.

---

[22] See, for example, the jurist Julien Laferrière: "In France, every election deserves to have votes cast ... We cannot accept the idea that a person can be elected if the voters are not called upon to issue an express judgment as to his candidacy." See his *Manuel de droit constitutionnel*, 2nd edn (Paris, 1947), pp. 582–583.

Part 3

The people as judge

Oversight and prevention are two ways of constraining governments, two ways in which society can exert pressure apart from the ballot box. Judgment is a third way of putting power to the test. To judge conduct or action is to subject it to scrutiny. It is a radical extension of the idea of oversight. It raises suspicion to the next level by insisting on a definitive conclusion. It is thus yet another form of popular control of government. The kind of judgment I have in mind extends beyond the strict framework of the law and the courts. It includes detailed and reasoned evaluation, a process of examination leading to the resolution of a question. Voting and judging are two distinct methods of working toward a common goal: coming to a decision that will contribute to the general welfare. Both are *political forms*, and as such they can be contrasted and compared. Each contains an element of "power as the last word." For understandable reasons, citizens might want to pursue both avenues, seeking to obtain as judges what they feel they have not been able to achieve as voters. At times they may be able to exercise judgment directly: when they sit as jurors in a formal proceeding, for example. More broadly, citizens act as judges when they participate in various kinds of investigation, whether through the media or as political activists. Even when judgment is "delegated" to the courts, it retains a societal dimension. For one thing, justice is rendered "in the name of the people." More broadly, it fulfills a collective expectation or responds to pressure from civil society organizations and public opinion. It is not only legally constituted judges who render judgment of the sort I have in mind. Judgment can take many forms, involving numerous types of actors. Those who judge are often aware, moreover, that their decisions play a role in defining the political system itself.

In recent years the judicial and the political have become increasingly intertwined. If we are to make sense of this, we must look more closely at how judgment and voting interact. Historians will naturally want to look at judgment in its political context. In Athens, the people's tribunal played as important a role as the citizens' assembly. Later, the English Parliament established the first real control over monarchy by impeaching the king's ministers. In the United States at the beginning of the twentieth century, certain states adopted a procedure known as "recall," by which voters could remove elected officials from office; the procedure was tantamount to a political trial. These three examples, representing three very different periods of history, show that the word "democracy" has always signified more than just the right to vote for a representative government. Democratic government has always been intimately associated with the idea that society has the right to judge its rulers.

Judgment can be brought to bear in democracy in a variety of ways. The work of the citizen-judge is just one of these. Another involves the application of competing norms. An important but neglected role of trial by jury was to allow citizen juries to correct or amend the strict letter of the law. Jury duty is a form of civic activity that complements voting, and jurors can correct the results of elections by modifying the laws laid down by the very legislators they have elected. Other "quasi-legislative" forms of intervention also exist, and we shall be studying them in subsequent chapters. As we pursue our reflection on the forms and meanings of political judgment, we will need to reconsider what is sometimes described as a "judicialization" of politics. Behind the more prominent role that judges have assumed in recent years lies a new concept of democracy, whose influence needs to be examined carefully.

8

Historical references

The Greek example

Aristotle writes: "A citizen in the strictest sense ... shares in the administration of justice and in offices."[1] More specifically, a citizen is one who exercises the functions of a juror (*dikastes*) and who participates in the assembly (*ekklesiastes*). For the author of *Politics*, judging and voting are inextricable aspects of citizenship. The tribunal of the people (*dikasteria*) and the assembly of the people (*ekklesia*) were both central institutions of Athenian democracy; they complemented each other. Some six thousand citizens came together in the assembly thirty or forty times a year to make decisions about domestic and foreign policy. In the tribunals, juries of 201, 401, or 501 individuals chosen by lot settled disputes over both public and private actions.[2] Both institutions allowed for direct, active participation in civic life.

The relation between these two functions becomes clearer when we look at the activities in which the Athenian tribunals engaged – activities that were fairly political in

[1] Aristotle, *Politics*, 1275. I use the Bollingen translation, edited by Jonathan Barnes, p. 2023.
[2] I follow the account given by Mogens Herman Hansen, "Pouvoirs politiques du tribunal du peuple à Athènes au IVe siècle", in Oswyn Murray and Simon Price, *La Cité grecque d'Homère à Alexandre* (Paris: La Découverte, 1992).

nature. The difference between their role and the role of courts of justice in a modern democracy is immediately apparent. In our political systems, the courts are responsible for resolving civil disputes and judging criminal cases. These matters take up most of their time. There is, to be sure, a more political side of judicial activity: for instance, in resolving disputes between citizens and government agencies and, still more, in judicial review of the constitutionality of laws (where such procedures exist). In terms of numbers of cases, however, this political aspect of the judicial function is relatively limited. Things were quite different in ancient Greece. Matters of private law seldom came before the courts and were settled mainly by arbitration. Magistrates dealt with many criminal cases directly, without a formal trial.[3] The courts heard such cases only on appeal. The real focus of Athenian judicial activity lay elsewhere: it involved the control and sanction of actions that were strictly speaking political in nature. The tribunals spent most of their time reviewing the operations and decisions of the Assembly, the Council, and various city magistrates and officials. Thus their work was essentially political, and for that reason they played a central role in Athenian democracy.

Many of the cases that came before the Athenian people's tribunals were what we would now call "political trials." Significantly, there is no specific Greek word for this type of trial, as though such a word would have been redundant. Defendants in these cases were always people in

---

[3] See Douglas M. MacDowell, *Athenian Homicide Law in the Age of the Orators* (Manchester University Press, 1963), and *The Law in Classical Athens* (London: Thames and Hudson, 1978).

positions of responsibility. They could be prosecuted for several types of crime. Of these the most notorious was corruption, and history has recorded any number of celebrated instances of this accusation (e.g., that Cimon accepted a bribe from Alexander I of Macedon). There were also charges of negligent or imprudent political or military action (for instance, the celebrated trial of Athenian generals accused of failing to rescue the wounded and retrieve the dead after a victorious naval battle at Arginusae in 406 BCE). Charges could also be brought against officials who issued edicts deemed to be unconstitutional or merely contrary to the people's interests. Finally, accusations of impiety (*asebeia*) were also common. In practice these often involved acts that could be construed as offenses against the state or the social order. The "politicians" (to use another word that does not exist in Greek) who were accused of this crime were mainly orators and strategists, which is to say, prominent figures in the Assembly, as well as military commanders, embodying executive power. Accordingly, the people's tribunal played a central role in Athenian politics, and trials were one of the most visible and influential forms of civic activity.[4] Contemporaries recognized this as one of Athens' most distinctive characteristics. The Old Oligarch noted that the citizens of Athens were known for bringing more suits than the citizens of all other

---

[4] On that activity, see Richard A. Bauman, *Political Trials in Ancient Greece* (London: Routledge, 1990); Ron Christenson, *Political Trials in History, from Antiquity to the Present* (New Brunswick: Transaction Publishers, 1991); Martin Ostwald, *From Popular Sovereignty to the Sovereignty of Law: Law, Society and Politics in Fifth-Century Athens* (Berkeley: University of California Press, 1986).

Greek cities combined. In Aristophanes' play *The Clouds*, a character refuses to recognize a point on a map as Athens on the grounds that the map does not indicate the location of the courts.

Athenian political trials can be grouped under two broad heads: nullification of edicts (*graphe paronomon*) and denunciations (*eisangelia*). The *graphe paronomon* procedure could be initiated by any citizen prepared to swear under oath that he regarded an edict of the Assembly as unconstitutional.[5] The notion of "unconstitutionality" was quite broad, since, beyond its juridical meaning, it could also be applied to decisions deemed inopportune or prejudicial to the interests of the city. This procedure was used frequently in the fourth century, often in the place of ostracism, which had been the fate of many of the previous century's political leaders. What was distinctive about the *graphe paronomon*, in fact, was that the person who had proposed the challenged edict was the one who was put on trial. The procedure was thus a way of protecting the people from themselves: the challenged edicts had of course been approved by the assembled citizens of Athens, in some cases unanimously. But the voters may have been misled by the orator who proposed the measure. Hence it was useful to have a procedure that allowed citizens to express themselves in another manner, allowing jurors chosen by lot to sit in judgment and correct their own original decision. The

---

[5] For a detailed account of the procedure and its uses, see Mogens Herman Hansen, *The Sovereignty of the People's Court in Athens in the Fourth Century BC and the Public Action against Unconstitutional Proposals* (Odense University Press, 1974).

idea was to erect a barrier against demagogues and sycophants. Implicit in this practice was a deliberative concept of the general interest, which became apparent only over time and after being *put to the test*. The people's judgment in the *graphe paronomon* was thus a phase in an ongoing process that complemented and corrected the assembly's original decision. In this way Athenian democracy was able to monitor its own inner workings.

The Assembly's agenda also allowed regular opportunities for denunciation. Any citizen could initiate an *eisangelia*, or accusation of malfeasance, which was then open for debate.[6] Charges could be brought for actions deemed likely to undermine democracy, mistakes in military strategy, and betrayal of the general interest. If the Assembly voted to impeach, the case was referred to a people's tribunal. Although the procedure was exceptional, it was not uncommon (some 130 instances have been counted for the period 492–322 BCE). It offered yet another control over Athenian political leaders, and especially military commanders – frequent targets of such charges. Such trials allowed for a second form of democratic oversight: judicial proceedings provided a way of punishing officials whose legitimacy derived from the political process. Athenian democracy thus had two faces, authorization and impeachment, and between the two there was constant tension. The "judicialization" of public life in Athens should therefore not be interpreted as a sign of pathological

---

[6] Mogens Herman Hansen, *Eisangelia. The Sovereignty of the People's Court in Athens in the Fourth Century BC and the Impeachment of Generals and Politicians* (Odense University Press, 1975).

litigiousness or pettifoggery. It was essentially political and essentially democratic. For Aristotle, the ability of citizens chosen by lot to render political judgment of this kind outweighed popular participation in the Athenian Assembly. Why did he draw this conclusion? His reasons are worth examining, for they shed light on some key features of Athenian democracy.

There are several reasons for Aristotle's (relative) preference for judgment over participation in the Assembly.[7] First, as noted above, it was inherently more effective to punish officials for past actions than to authorize future actions. Unlike the citizen who voted in the Assembly, the juror could settle a matter once and for all. He could thus affect the course of events in a definitive and irreversible way. In Athens, moreover, trials fulfilled preventive functions. Charges against officials and especially military commanders were often quite serious. Indictments for corruption and treason were common, even though the facts underlying the charges might seem to suggest lesser offenses. Because of this tendency to bring extreme charges against officials with whom the people became disenchanted, cautionary warnings were often issued. The prosecutors, who might be chosen by lot or elected by this or that official body, knew that their own position was precarious and had a clear idea of what society expected of them. Does this explain why the people's tribunal played such a central role in Athens? Does it suggest that the system

---

[7] In what follows I rely mainly on Jennifer Tolbert Roberts, *Accountability in Athenian Government* (Madison: The University of Wisconsin Press, 1982).

encouraged demagogic appeals to an ungrateful and impulsive populace, which placed ever greater demands on its leaders and impatiently demanded results in a sometimes irrational manner? To some extent these criticisms are accurate, but they ignore the fact that *ex post* judicial judgments complemented *ex ante* controls and delegations of authority. Although this combination of *ex post* and *ex ante* controls defined Athenian democracy, distrust applied after the fact proved to be a more effective control than trust bestowed before the fact. There is also another reason for the centrality of "political" trials and impeachment procedures in Athens: political opinion was divided. When parties and ideas clashed sharply, elected officials sometimes proposed policies that minorities strongly opposed. These minorities then had the option of bringing charges before a court, thus gaining a public hearing for their point of view.

In addition to the above distinction between the *ex post* exercise of distrust and the *ex ante* grant of trust,[8] the distinction between "composite majorities" and "compact minorities" can also help to shed light on the role of judgment in democracy. A court trial may be seen as a kind of "compensation" awarded to minorities. Judgment in Athens had two functions: it imposed a different time scale on the political contract that helped to tighten the bond between rulers and ruled, and it gave minorities a second chance to appeal to the

---

[8] On this connection, see the interesting remarks of Jon Elster, "Accountability in Athenian Politics," in Adam Przeworski, Susan Stokes, and Bernard Marin, eds., *Democracy, Accountability, Representation* (Cambridge University Press, 1999).

general interest and thus corrected some of the dysfunction-ality inherent in majority rule. The corrective function of political trials reinforced the general will in two ways. First, the possibility of demonstrating distrust at any time strength-ened trust, which could only be expressed periodically. Second, political trials undermined the illusion of a unanimous people created by the purely numerical procedure of counting votes, because legal argument required a substantive definition of the general interest (of the common good interpreted as a moral value).

Athenian practice was thus a long way from Montesquieu's reductive understanding of the judge as the mere "mouthpiece of the law," which led to the idea that "the judicial power is in a sense non-existent."[9] For the author of *De l'esprit des lois*, judging and deliberating collectively were two radically different activities. The Athenian example suggests, rather, that they were complementary and that both served as means of controlling political life in Athens.

English impeachment

In English institutions we find a good example of the primacy accorded to judgment in the hierarchy of political powers in the monarchies of old Europe. To put it baldly: in the Middle Ages, the courts were everything. The primary function of the sovereign was to dispense justice, and the emergence of strong royal authority in England and France was of course directly related to the development of a system

---

[9] *De l'esprit des lois*, 11.6.

allowing subjects to appeal the decisions of local courts. There
was no idea whatsoever of an active executive power charged
with the role of organizing society. To govern meant essentially
to administer justice. Even representative institutions were
defined in judicial terms. Until the end of the seventeenth
century, the English representative body was known as the
High Court of Parliament.[10] The law itself was explicitly
described as a "judgment rendered in Parliament." In this
context, the power to judge was the primary power from
which all other powers derived. That is why Parliament sought
to exert control over royal ministers by way of judgment. From
this came the procedure known as "impeachment," which
grew out of a gradual broadening of the medieval concept of
treason.[11] The House of Commons inaugurated the procedure
in 1376, when it brought charges against Lord Latimer and
several London merchants for "frauds and mischief regarding
the King and people." Parliament's decision to impeach was
seen not only as a judicial act but, for that very reason, as a
political judgment as well. The record of the session notes that
Latimer and his confederates were not responding to the
charges of any specific individual but were rather "impeached

[10] On this point, see Charles Howard Mac Ilwain, *The High Court of
Parliament and its Supremacy: An Historical Essay on the Boundaries
Between Legislation and Adjudication in England*, new ed. (Hamden, CT:
Archon Books, 1962). For a broad overview, see Carlos Miguel Pimentel,
*La Main invisible du juge: L'Origine des trois pouvoirs et la théorie des
régimes politiques*, thesis, Université de Paris II, 2000.

[11] See John G. Bellamy, *The Law of Treason in England in the later Middle
Ages* (Cambridge University Press, 1970), and "Appeal and Impeachment
in the Good Parliament," *Bulletin of the Institute of Historical Research* 39,
no. 99 (May 1966).

and accused by the clamour of the commons."[12] In this case, penal and political responsibility were totally intertwined, with the political expressing itself by way of the penal.

Impeachment as a form of political control remained in wide use until the middle of the fifteenth century. It fell into disuse under the Tudors, who succeeded in limiting Parliament's powers of oversight while encouraging the far more arbitrary procedure of bills of attainder, which were often manipulated by the Crown.[13] After a hiatus of nearly two centuries, impeachment made a comeback in the seventeenth century thanks to a leading jurist of the day, Edward Coke, chief justice of the King's Bench. After becoming a member of Parliament in 1621, Coke set out to revive the ancient procedure. He saw it as more than just a way to punish a public official for a crime or misdemeanor, however. His goal was to make ministers accountable for their policies and to punish them for dereliction of duty. In 1624, he secured impeachment of the Lord Treasurer, Lionel Cransfield. In addition to misappropriating funds for his own benefit, Cransfield was punished for having authorized monopolies. The real motive for the impeachment was to obtain the

---

[12] See Theodore Franck and Thomas Plucknett, "The Origin of Impeachment," *Transactions of the Royal Historical Society* 24 (1942), pp. 70–71.

[13] A bill of attainder was not a judicial procedure but an act of Parliament, approved by both houses and sanctioned by the king. It could impose any penalty whatsoever, and usually the death penalty, on any person for deeds not covered by any existing law. With the complicity of a weakened Parliament, the Crown used bills of attainder to punish adversaries. They were sometimes referred to as "legal assassinations."

dismissal of a minister who still had the confidence of the king but had forfeited that of the House of Commons.[14] Coke observed that in such circumstances it was incumbent upon the House to serve as society's "general inquisitor." This way of looking at the matter triumphed in 1621, when impeachment proceedings were initiated against the king's favorite, the Duke of Buckingham. The case is exemplary: the king vigorously supported Buckingham, while Parliament accused him of der-eliction as Lord Grand Admiral. In the end the duke was not impeached, but a decisive step had been taken toward accred-iting the idea that Parliament could indeed judge ministers for their political actions.

Coke had put forward a subtle legal argument. He never openly challenged the royal prerogative yet paradoxi-cally limited its extent by making it so absolute as to reduce it to a totally abstract principle. On the one hand, he solemnly reaffirmed the old adage that "the King can do no wrong." On the other hand, however, he argued that Parliament, in judging royal ministers, should act independently, albeit in the king's name, because the king, if he were to exercise judgment through his own royal courts, would weaken himself, since he would then be both judge and party in the case. James I was thus trapped by the legal fiction of the king-in-Parliament. The consecration of his pre-eminence ultimately reduced his power to a more symbolic function. The judicial power was still exercised in the king's name but outside his effective control.

---

[14] See Jean Beauté, *Un grand juriste anglais: Sir Edward Coke (1552–1634). Ses idées politiques et constitutionnelles* (Paris: Presses Universitaires de France, 1975).

Thus when civil war broke out a few years later, the revolutionaries were able to claim that they were fighting the king in the king's own name. After 1688, the victorious Parliament was able to assume a more direct political role, and use of the impeachment procedure declined rapidly.[15] With the advent of ministerial control through annual votes on taxes and budgets, the rise of great political parties, and the introduction of cabinet government, a new concept of joint political responsibility supplanted the older notion of individual criminal responsibility. Instead of the axe and the chopping block, Parliament wielded the vote of no confidence – progress, to be sure, yet we should bear in mind that the idea of ministerial responsibility retains an essential kinship with the practice of indictment and judgment.

Historically, then, political accountability took the place of criminal responsibility.[16] Ministers were no longer prosecuted for crimes but rather held politically accountable for their acts. Nevertheless, the goal in both cases was to impose punishment, check further action, and make officials accountable. The modern parliamentary system thus grew out of a judicial mind-set.[17] The abolition of older forms of

---

[15] On these matters see John Philipps Kenyon, *The Stuart Constitution, 1603–1688: Documents and Commentary* (Cambridge University Press, 1966).

[16] The last attempted political impeachment targeted Robert Walpole in 1742.

[17] On the development of parliamentarism in England, see the remarkable book by Denis Baranger, *Parlementarisme des origines: Essai sur les conditions de formation d'un exécutif responsable en Angleterre* (Paris: Presses Universitaires de France, 1999).

punishment should not be allowed to obscure this fact. The conditions under which the shift from criminal to political responsibility took place varied from place to place. To this day, the United Kingdom exhibits a greater degree of effective political accountability than any other country. At the opposite extreme is France, which founded its first republic on a regicide and which succumbed to temptation in making the president of its Fifth Republic unaccountable, thereby allowing him to shield government ministers at will.

The recall procedure in the United States

In the United States there exists a procedure known as "recall," which allows voters to remove elected officials from office. Here is yet a third historical example of a judicial means of enforcing political accountability. Recall procedures for all state officials are permitted in some fifteen states, mainly in the West and Midwest, and recall of local officials in thirty-six states.[18] Recall was first authorized in Oregon in 1908 and shortly thereafter in California, Arizona, Colorado, and Nevada (after having been tried out in the city of Los Angeles as early as 1903).[19] The recourse to recall was part of a broader critique of American democracy and political corruption in the early years of the twentieth century. The Progressive Movement also introduced primary elections,

[18] Thomas E. Cronin, *Direct Democracy: The Politics of Initiative, Referendum and Recall* (Cambridge, MA: Harvard University Press, 1995), table and notes on pp. 126–127.
[19] James Duff Barnett, *The Operation of the Initiative, Referendum and Recall in Oregon* (New York: Macmillan, 1915).

initiative petitions, and referendums as further correctives to the defects of representative government. In practice, a recall election began with a drive to collect signatures on a petition demanding the recall of some political official. If a sufficient number of signatures was gathered (usually on the order of 25 percent of registered voters), an election was held. Nearly any public official could be recalled, from the governor of the state to state legislators and local officials, including prosecutors, sheriffs, and in some states judges. Some governors were indeed removed (the latest example being the recall of Gray Davis in California in 2003, leading to his replacement by the actor Arnold Schwarzenegger).[20] Mayors have also been recalled, in Cleveland in 1978, for example, as well as in Omaha in 1987. And thousands of lesser officials have been removed from office in the same way: members of local school boards, officials of "irrigation districts" (whose influence on farmers in states like California and Nevada is significant), and county administrators.[21] One writer has gone so far as to describe recall as "legal ostracism."

How should we interpret these varied uses of recall? It is common to describe the practice as a radical form of direct democracy, comparable to a popular referendum.[22] This description was prevalent, in particular, in the early twentieth century in the United States. To be sure, recall reflects the ultimate source of democratic power: universal suffrage. In my

[20] On the Davis recall, see Larry N. Gerston and Terry Christensen, *Recall! California's Political Earthquake* (Armonk, NY: M. E. Sharpe, 2004).
[21] See Joseph F. Zimmerman, *The Recall: Tribunal of the People* (Westport, CT: Praeger, 1997).
[22] See Cronin, *Direct Democracy.*

view, however, the essence of the institution lies elsewhere, namely, in the type of practice to which it gave rise. In formal terms, a recall is an election in which what is at stake is dismissal from office. It is therefore a vote of no confidence, negating a prior vote of confidence. The two votes are not really symmetrical, however. An election is a choice among two or more candidates. A recall is rather a judgment of the actions of a specific individual. Although a recall is analogous in some respects to a referendum, it does not constitute an alternative to representative government. Indeed, its principal goal is to *restore* "proper representation" by sanctioning public officials accused of dishonesty or incompetence. The citizens who vote in a recall act collectively as a jury, rendering a verdict on the charges brought by the initiator(s) of the recall petition (whose role is similar to that of a grand jury). Hence the citizens who vote in a recall are judges, not ordinary voters.

The quasi-judicial nature of the recall procedure is evident in the form of recall petitions, which resemble indictments. This is evident in the three recall petitions below.[23]

> Text of the petition for the recall of Mayor Davie of
> Oakland in 1917:
> It is apparent that:
> He is absolutely incompetent both in training and ability to
> fill the office.

---

[23] The petitions here are taken from Frederick L. Bird and Frances M. Ryan, *The Recall of Public Officers: A Study of the Operation of the Recall in California* (New York: The Macmillan Company, 1930). Other recall petitions can be found in Zimmerman, *The Recall: Tribunal of the People*.

He insults citizens who appear on city business before the Council, and his actions are making Oakland appear ridiculous.

His gross demeanor and injustice are causing irreparable injury to Oakland.

His control for two years more is too grave a menace to tolerate.

He tears down industry.

He has no constructive ideas.

He talks much but accomplishes nothing.

He talks lower taxes but does nothing to secure them.

He preaches economy but practices extravagance such as securing a $3,000 automobile, a $1,500 job for his son to drive it; an $85.00 chair.

He keeps Oakland in constant turmoil.

His appointed political adviser, Civil Service Commissioner George Kaufman, indicates a desire to create a political machine in the Civil Service.

He ignores petitions to protect health conditions.

He promised to remove Chief Peterson and now is his booster.

Why?

Oakland cannot stand two years more of Davieism.

A Recall is the only possible remedy.

Text of the petition for the recall of Senator Owens of California in 1913:

The undersigned, electors of the State of California, hereby petition for the recall of Senator James C. Owens, of the Ninth Senatorial District, and demand an election of a successor to the office named herein, and in compliance with the provision of Article 23 of the Constitution of the

State of California, a general statement of the grounds on which the removal is sought is herewith submitted:

Senator Owens repeatedly violated his pledges as a Democrat; broke his written promises to Labor; and assisted Big Business at crucial moments by his vote or by staying away.

His party platform favored a State industrial insurance system. He fathered an amendment to Boynton's Workmen's Compensation Bill that would have made such insurance an impossibility; just what insurance companies wanted.

His party platform declared in favor of extending the Women's Eight-Hour law. In committee he voted for every proposition to limit its scope, even to exclude cotton mill employees already included in the law. Stayed away on final passage.

He voted against the Water Conservation Bill, to assist the power companies.

He voted against mining inspection, and against improving working conditions and hours in mines, to please mining corporations.

He introduced Senate Bill 243, which was so bad that the Railroad Commission said officially it should have been entitled: "An Act to Repeal the most important provisions of the Public Utilities Act, respecting railroads."

The last two days he dodged or was absent on 113 roll calls. The above are but a few of the many reasons why Senator Owens should be recalled.

These two petitions, which are typical of recall petitions from the early twentieth century, show the ease with which accusations of different types – moral, professional, and political – were combined in these indictments. The vague and miscellaneous nature of the charges is in itself a good indication of the true nature of the citizens' grievances. It is striking to find that things remained much the same nearly a century later. In the 2003 petition to recall Governor Gray Davis of California, we read:

> The grounds for the recall are as follows: Gross mismanagement of California finances by overspending taxpayers' money, threatening public safety by cutting funds to local governments, failing to account for the exorbitant cost of the energy fiasco, and failing in general to deal with the state's major problems until they get to the crisis stage. California should not have to be known as the state with poor schools, traffic jams, outrageous utility bills, and huge debts ... all caused by gross mismanagement.[24]

Although indicted officials are clearly summoned to appear before the people-as-judge, the charges against them are often a confused mixture of the criminal and the political. Whatever one thinks about the advantages and disadvantages of recall, this basic fact remains. Thus recall is more than just an application of direct democracy to compensate for the defects of representative democracy. Looked at in broader perspective, recall is clearly a "judicial moment" in democratic politics. Hence it should really be analyzed as a form of impeachment rather than a form of referendum. Article Two of the United States Constitution stipulates that the president, vice-president, and other officials may be removed from office

---

[24] Reproduced in Kenneth P. Miller, "The Davis Recall and the Courts," *American Politics Research* 33, no. 2 (March 2005): 140.

on grounds of treason, bribery, or other high crimes and misdemeanors. Impeachment is thus a congressional procedure (indictment by the House of Representatives, trial by the Senate), but it nevertheless targets a fairly specific list of offenses. It has been used fewer than twenty times since 1787.[25] The spirit of the two procedures, impeachment and recall, is similar, yet recall has been used far more often in the states where it exists, because it is simpler and because the grounds for recall are quite broad, with no clear distinction between political and criminal responsibility. It is not nearly as rigorous as a true judicial proceeding, however. Recall is in fact a degraded hybrid of judicial and political processes. It demonstrates the kinship that exists between voting and judgment, as well as the possibility of substituting one for the other. At the same time it shows us how both can be perverted.[26] Peripheral though it is, recall exemplifies some of the hidden realities and dangers of more common democratic practices.

[25] Michael J. Gerhardt, *The Federal Impeachment Process: A Constitutional and Historical Analysis* (Princeton University Press, 1996).

[26] It should be noted that consideration was given at one time to the idea of applying recall to decisions of the courts. Theodore Roosevelt made this idea a plan of his Progressive platform in 1912. For a review of arguments for and against, see Edith M. Phelps, ed., *Selected Articles on the Recall, Including the Recall of Judges and Judicial Decisions*, 2nd edn, revised (New York: The Wilson Company, 1915).

9

Almost legislators

The democratic jury

The people-as-judge also existed in another form: the jury. The history of the institution makes this clear. During the Middle Ages the jury was reintroduced in Europe in order to resolve disputes between knights peacefully, without recourse to the previously widespread practice of judicial combat. Judgment by a small group of peers seemed to be the best way of achieving the desired result.[1] With the rise of the royal courts, however, the institution entered a period of decline. The modern jury did not emerge until the middle of the eighteenth century. Enlightenment thinkers asked how the frequency of judicial error could be reduced. In a period of growing sensitivity to human rights, errors of justice shocked the conscience. Many of the great minds of the age wrote about the issue, including Beccaria, Blackstone, Condorcet, and Voltaire, to mention only the most celebrated. The question to which all of these writers addressed themselves was this: How can judges, fallible human beings, render a judgment with the least likelihood of error? Academies across Europe

[1] For the early history of the jury in England and France, see Thomas Andrew Green, *Verdict According to Conscience: Perspectives on the English Criminal Trial Jury, 1200–1800* (University of Chicago Press, 1985), and Léon Prieur, *Les Origines françaises du jury: Les Assises féodales* (Paris, 1924).

organized competitions on the subject. Everywhere the answer was the same: the jury. For instance, Blackstone marveled at "how admirably this constitution [i.e., institution] is adapted and framed for the investigation of truth, beyond any other method of trial in the world."[2] Twelve people deliberating the facts of the case are less likely to be wrong than one person deliberating alone. It was thus a probabilistic conception of reason and truth that commended the jury to the men of the Enlightenment as an institution essential for protecting the rights and liberties of the individual. In his *Essai sur les probabilités en matière de justice* (1772), Voltaire was the first to attempt to formalize this approach to reducing the likelihood of condemning an innocent person. A few years later, Condorcet gave the most definitive statement of the case in his celebrated *Essai sur l'application de l'analyse à la probabilité des décisions rendues à la pluralité des voix*.[3] Thouret, the great reformer of the French justice system during the Revolution, summed up the reformers' critiques: "Among human institutions, the jury is the closest we have to infallibility."[4]

All this belongs to what one might call the "rationalist" or "probabilistic" history of the jury. Somewhat later, however, another, more political approach emerged in conjunction with

---

[2] William Blackstone, *Commentaries on the Laws of England*, book III, chap. 23.

[3] Paris, 1785. Other leading mathematicians of the day extended Condorcet's results. See especially Antoine Augustin Cournot, "Mémoire sur les applications du calcul des chances à la statistique judiciaire," *Journal de mathématiques pures et appliquées*, vol. III, 1838, and Siméon Denis Poisson, *Recherches sur la probabilité des jugements en matière criminelle et en matière civile* (Paris, 1837).

[4] Quoted in Ernest Lebègue, *Thouret (1746–1794)* (Paris, 1910), p. 232.

the advent of universal suffrage. The jury was now seen as a democratic institution. It is this second aspect of the history of the jury that mainly interests us here. It began with the English Revolution. The celebrated Mayday Agreement (May 1, 1649) expressed radical democratic hopes that jury selection might be coupled with authentic representation of the voice of the people. It was the American Revolution, however, that led to the establishment of the first truly democratic juries. In the United States, popular participation in government took three forms: service in the militia, jury duty, and voting. The jury thus acquired an intrinsic political value: it was one of the ways in which equality manifested itself. Jury duty was a form of civic engagement.[5] Tocqueville emphasized this aspect of the jury in a celebrated passage of his *Democracy in America*: "The jury is above all a political institution ... [It is] the part of the nation charged with ensuring the execution of the laws, just as the houses of the legislature are the part of the nation charged with making the laws."[6] The jury's democratic nature was not merely a consequence of the fundamental principle of equality. It was also a consequence of the way juries worked, namely, by deliberation. The voter expresses his opinion simply by casting

[5] See especially Jeffrey Abramson: "The Jury and Democratic Theory," *The Journal of Political Philosophy* 1, no. 1 (March 1993); "The American Jury and Democratic Justice," *La Revue Tocqueville / The Tocqueville Review* 18, no. 2 (1997); *We, The Jury: The Jury System and the Ideal of Democracy* (New York: Basic Books, 1994). See also the suggestive remarks of Antoine Garapon and Ioannis Papadopoulos, *Juger en Amérique et en France* (Paris: Odile Jacob, 2003) ("the values of the American jury," pp. 177–187).

[6] Alexis de Tocqueville, *Democracy in America*, trans. Arthur Goldhammer (New York: Library of America, 2004), vol. I, part 2, chap. 8, p. 315.

his ballot, whereas the juror participates in an exchange of information and arguments and, in doing so, may come to alter his views. The jury is therefore a more mature form of citizen participation. After the Constitution was drafted in Philadelphia in 1787, this point was stressed in debates about its ratification.[7]

In the United States, the reputation of the jury rested on its being not only a forum for public discussion but also a local institution. Because jurors lived in the same place as the accused, they could be presumed to be familiar with the facts and circumstances of the cases they heard. American political culture placed a high value on proximity in this period.[8] Jury service was also brief, and this was well suited to another aspect of American political culture, namely, the belief that political offices should be accessible to all and be filled on a rotating basis. The jury thus conformed to an American ideal of deliberative and participatory democracy. It helped to make up for some of the defects inherent in the more remote institutions that large-scale representative government required.

Many of these features can be found in French juries as well. In France, too, the hope of minimizing judicial error

[7] It comes as no surprise that the point was stressed especially by anti-federalists. See, for example, no. 15 of the *Federal Farmer* (January 18, 1788), reproduced in Philip B. Kurland and Ralph Lerner, eds., *The Founder's Constitution* (University of Chicago Press, 1987), vol. V, p. 397.

[8] See John Philip Reid, *Constitutional History of the American Revolution*, vol. I: *The Authority of Rights* (Madison: The University of Wisconsin Press, 1986), esp. the chapter entitled "The Jury Rights." This theme was also developed primarily by anti-federalists, who subscribed to an extreme localistic view of politics.

was paramount. The democratic nature of juries was strongly emphasized during the Revolution. The adoption of the jury system was clearly related to other efforts to establish institutions that would embody the sovereignty of the people. Adrien Duport, the main sponsor of judicial reform in the Constituent Assembly, held that, in regard to popular sovereignty, the jury was to the judicial system what the legislature was to the law.[9] Once the jury system was in place, he said, "tyranny can be squarely confronted, because the people will never cease to be free so long as they retain this formidable power to judge."[10] The idea that political freedom rested on two pillars, the right to vote and the jury, was thus central to the revolutionary vision. The twin figures of the citizen – juror and voter – would remain tightly coupled. Under the July Monarchy, which imposed property qualifications on suffrage, it was easier to sit on a jury than to gain access to the ballot box. "May every juror be allowed to vote" was therefore the first slogan that republicans adopted in their campaign for electoral reform. Conversely, conservatives would continue to attack popular juries throughout the nineteenth century, even after it became difficult to criticize universal suffrage openly. Under the Consulate, countless pamphlets denounced "scandalous

[9] On Duport's role and ideas, see Antonio Padoa Schioppa, "La giura all' Assemblea Costituente francese," in Antonio Padoa Schioppa, ed., *The Trial Jury in England, France, Germany, 1700–1900* (Berlin: Duncker and Humblot, 1987) and "Le jury d'Adrien Duport," in *La Révolution et l'ordre juridique privé: rationalité ou scandale?* Actes du colloque d'Orléans (Paris: Presses Universitaires de France, 1988).

[10] Report of November 27, 1790 on the institution of juries.

218

acquittals" by popular juries.[11] The numbers are indeed quite striking. In the first few decades of the nineteenth century, nearly 40 percent of violent crimes ended in acquittal! Statistics on cases of infanticide and abortion tell a similar story. Any number of writers lapsed into reactionary rhetoric to attack the ignorance, capriciousness, and irrationality of common jurors, whose passions resulted in harshly vengeful verdicts as frequently as in unduly lenient ones.[12] There was legislation to restrict juries in ways reminiscent of earlier efforts to exclude certain elements of the population (such as servants and dependents) from "active citizenship." In the late nineteenth century, such restrictions became increasingly common. Gabriel Tarde, one of the leading sociologists of the day, urged his contemporaries to substitute scientific expertise for the judgment of jurors.[13] A whole school of "rationalist anti-democratic" writers participated in this crusade at a time when universal suffrage had become so widely accepted that it could no longer be attacked outright.[14]

---

[11] On this point, see the documentation collected by Yves Pourcher, "Des assises de grâce? Le jury de la Cour d'Assises de la Lozère au XIXe siècle," and Élizabeth Claverie, "De la difficulté de faire un citoyen: les 'acquittements scandaleux' du jury dans la France provinciale du début du XIXe siècle," in *Études rurales*, nos. 95–96, (July–Dec. 1984).

[12] Charles Clauss, *Le Jury sous le Consulat et le Premier Empire* (Paris, 1905), and Adhémar Esmein, *Histoire de la procédure criminelle en France* (Paris, 1881).

[13] See esp. Gabriel Tarde, *La Philosophie pénale*, 4th edn, (Paris, 1890). Raymond Saleilles, a leading jurist of the day, worked toward the same goal.

[14] See Samuel Stern, *Le Jury technique: Esquisse d'une justice pénale rationnelle* (Paris, 1925).

Although these writers denounced "jury-made law," the underlying issue was conflicting social norms: popular jury verdicts were criticized by those who believed that law and morality required a different result.

The production of competing norms

The democratic role of the jury should also be seen in relation to the production of social norms. When jurors acquitted a "guilty" defendant, they were expressing their sense of the gap between the law and the relative importance of the offense. In the early nineteenth century, for example, defendants accused of crimes of passion were often acquitted, while crimes against property were much more likely to end in conviction.[15] Acquittal thus served as a *de facto* corrective to laws approved by the legislature. This "jury nullification" of the law was a direct expression of popular sentiment, which the decisions of jurors made manifest. In practice, jurors enunciated their own understanding of what was just and unjust, established their own hierarchy of the relative seriousness of various crimes (in particular, distinguishing sharply between crimes against persons and crimes against property), and insisted on their right to their own idea of justice, their own normative universe. During the Restoration, for instance, one left-wing deputy described a jury verdict as "the country's

---

[15] For data see Isser Wolloch, *The New Regime: Transformations of the French Civic Order, 1789–1820* (New York: Norton, 1994), pp. 355–379. See also James M. Donovan, "Justice Unblind, the Juries and the Criminal Class in France, 1825–1914," *Journal of Social History* 15, no. 1 (1981).

judgment, intended as a direct form of social protection."[16] Hence, the jury verdict was yet another instance of the conflict between direct democracy and representative democracy, marking another dimension of the jury's political role. Rival definitions of justice and the social order emerged in this context as well. To reduce the tension between different conceptions of justice, the legislature introduced the notion of "mitigating circumstances" in 1832, which allowed juries to impose penalties below the legal minimum for a given crime. The goal was to reduce the number of acquittals, which ranged as high as 30 to 40 percent in some cases. It was also a way of concealing the gap between "popular" and "legal" norms. By 1840, some 68 percent of the verdicts rendered in the criminal courts mentioned "mitigating circumstances."[17] In other words, juries had essentially subverted the measure.

In France, juror activism also took more direct political forms. In political trials during the Revolution and Empire, popular juries usually returned acquittals. Juries broadly opposed attempts by one government after another to use the courts against their enemies. Even during the Terror, nearly three-quarters of political cases ended in not-guilty verdicts. In the Thermidorian period that followed, juries continued to acquit.[18] Not only were jurors undeniably

---

[16] Augustin Marie Devaux in an 1827 debate on jury reform. See *AP*, 2nd series, vol. 49, p. 194.

[17] The change is well analyzed in B. Schnapper, "Le Jury français au XIXe et XXe siècles," in Padoa Schioppa, *The Trial Jury in England, France, Germany.*

[18] See data in Robert Allen, *Les Tribunaux criminels sous la Révolution et l'Empire, 1792–1811* (Presses Universitaires de Rennes, 2005).

independent, they became more so whenever opposition to the incumbent government mounted. Their perception of the political issues of the day differed sharply from that of politicians. Although it is difficult to interpret what this independence meant, it is clear that a wide gap separated the "implicit politics" of jurors from the views of government officials. In cases involving the press, for instance, jurors exercised a corrective function. After 1819 (and again after 1830, following an interruption), press cases were heard by juries – a sign of the importance attached to the jurors' role. Indeed, juries served to regulate the press. They practiced a distinct form of politics, different from the politics of representative government. Once again, we see a "dual democracy" at work. Elites could be quite critical of this dualism, especially after universal suffrage took hold. Their solution? To limit the jurisdiction of the superior courts (*cours d'assises*) and thus reduce the role of juries. A law of 1894 transferred a whole range of offenses from the superior courts to the correctional courts, where they were heard by judges sitting without juries. At the same time, penalties for those crimes were systematically increased. Prior to this law, deceived wives and abandoned mistresses had often been acquitted of murder by juries, to applause from courtroom onlookers. After these cases were transferred to the correctional courts, the number of acquittals fell sharply. The new law closed the gap between the instinctive morality of the lower classes and that of the bourgeoisie. The acquittal rate also declined in more political cases that involved the press or related to the state security and incitement of disobedience in the military. When France experienced a wave of anarchist attacks in the 1890s, the government had nothing to fear from

indulgent juries in crimes relating to public safety.[19] By imposing tighter controls on court decisions, republican elites eliminated a potential rival source of power. And France was by no
means an exception in this respect. As universal suffrage at last
took hold throughout Europe in the latter half of the nineteenth century, juries came under attack everywhere. In Spain
they were abolished, while in Italy, England, and Germany
they came in for spirited criticism.[20] Universally celebrated a
century earlier as one of the most visible expressions of liberty,
the jury had become, in the eyes of the elite, a symbol of the
irrationality of the masses.

The democratic role of the jury was especially prominent in the United States. There, the idea of the jury as
protector of the citizenry against government abuse was a
key element of the national credo. One scholar has described
jurors as "populist protectors" and "political participants."[21]
As in Europe, American juries contributed to the emergence of
"democratic" social norms, as distinct from legal norms (in
regard to self-defense, for example). But for a long time
American juries also exercised a quasi-legislative function.
In the nineteenth century, many states recognized the right
of juries to weigh the law itself. For instance, the (relatively

---

[19] See Jean-Pierre Machelon, *La République contre les libertés? Les
Restrictions aux libertés de 1879 à 1914* (Paris: Presses de Sciences-Po,
1976), pp. 426–447.
[20] See the essays collected in Padoa Schioppa, *The Trial Jury in England,
France, Germany.*
[21] For these expressions, see Akhil Reed Amar, "The Bill of Rights as a
Constitution," *The Yale Law Journal* 100 (March 1991). Recall that juries
play a role in civil as well as criminal cases in the United States.

moderate) Pennsylvania constitution of 1790 stipulated that "the jury shall be judges of laws, as well as fact." This idea, a legacy of the colonial period, was typical of a time when juries were the only "democratic representative institution." In colonial times, when there was no truly representative government, juries were a vehicle for giving voice to local public opinion, which was often at variance with prevailing English law (in cases involving freedom of the press, for example). This practice continued throughout the nineteenth century.[22] On several occasions juries effectively nullified key provisions of fugitive slave laws, for example. The very broad role ascribed to juries also reflected the contemporary emphasis on local power. As a more substantial national government emerged over the course of the nineteenth century, the quasi-legislative function of the jury declined, although the underlying principle remained intact.

Shadow legislators

The jury is not the only example of a discreet social corrective to the normative order established by the representative system. In France, the so-called *conseils de prud'-hommes*, or labor relations boards, charged with regulating workplace conflicts, can also be seen in this light. A principle of parity, mandating equal representation on these boards for workers and employers, was established in 1848, but the system originated much earlier, in 1806, and it helped to

---

[22] Jeffrey Abramson develops this theme at length in *We, The Jury*, pp. 74–95.

legitimate a system of workplace regulation independent of the prevailing liberal legal order. At that time, it was the masters who favored regulation to restore stability to a system that had been disrupted by frequent disputes between masters and employees. As workers gained influence, this distinctive regulatory system took on increasing importance. It fostered a pragmatic sense of workplace justice. In the 1830s, working-men's associations collected and circulated decisions of the labor relations boards. The intent was not merely to compile board rulings but to codify them. Labor historians have described the result as tantamount to a separate code of law governing the workplace. They point out that local labor relations boards established distinctive norms that broke new legal ground compared with prevailing civil law.[23] Note, too, that labor unions in Paris joined together in 1881 to organize a *comité central électoral et de vigilance* to keep an eye on the labor relations boards and coordinate their activity.[24] This was well before the unions thought of joining together in a true confederation of labor: the Confédération Générale du Travail was not organized until 1895.

The unions selected cases in furtherance of a comprehensive legal strategy. The idea was to work toward landmark decisions that would affect the interpretation of key provisions of the laws governing labor. In this way, society itself took an

---

[23] See the very interesting analyses of Alain Cottereau, "Justice et injustice ordinaire sur les lieux de travail d'après les audience prud'homales (1806–1866)," *Le Mouvement social*, no. 141 (Oct.–Dec. 1987).

[24] Pierre Bance, *Les Fondateurs de la CGT à l'épreuve du droit* (Claix: La Pensée sauvage, 1978), pp. 188–191.

active (if peripheral) part in the making of the law.[25] This approach proved particularly fruitful in common-law countries, where court decisions established legal precedents. American unions and other organizations invested heavily in such strategies. They generally took a two-pronged approach. The more traditional procedure was to lobby Congress to influence pending legislation, but the other approach, pursuing landmark cases in the courts, was and remains equally important. The American Civil Liberties Union (ACLU) currently employs fifty lawyers for this purpose.[26] The indirect approach to modifying the law by way of the courts can be more effective than direct support for a political agenda. Judicial activists in a sense become "shadow legislators" who encourage reinterpretation of existing laws. The ACLU has pursued this course in the United States in regard to First Amendment law (which governs freedom of expression). Once again, the people participate in the system not only as voters but also as judges: they choose their representatives, but they also influence the law more directly. Popular sovereignty and the rule of law are complementary: the law is an expression of the will of the people in more than one way. The people make their voice heard through many different institutions and at many different points in time.

[25] For a history of the role of unions in making labor law by lawyers working for the CFDT, see "Le Droit du travail dans la lutte des classes," *CFDT - Aujourd'hui*, no. 23 (Jan.–Feb. 1977).
[26] See the interview with Anthony Romero, executive director of the ACLU, in "Un civisme radical," *Vacarme*, no. 34 (Winter 2006).

10

The preference for judgment

The judicialization of politics

Slippage from the political to the penal is one of the most thoroughly discussed and analyzed aspects of contemporary democracy. Some scholars even speak of a "judicialization of politics." There are many reasons why this is so. Of these, the most noteworthy is surely a change in the nature of political accountability. The phenomenon is complex and multifaceted, and many different factors are involved, but two broad areas deserve closer attention. The first has to do with the nature of political institutions. The application of criminal law to public life has been particularly noticeable in countries with fragile, unstable political systems, as well as countries where institutional contradictions have made it difficult to exercise political responsibility in a transparent manner. In Europe, Italy is the paradigmatic example: Italian judges have exercised political power because the political system has been unable to regulate itself and meet the expectations of society. France, for its part, has suffered from certain constitutional deficiencies. The difficulty of organizing the "dyarchy" at the summit of the state – the prime minister and the president of the Republic – has created a situation in which the president is, in practical terms, unaccountable. Furthermore, the relative weakness of the French Parliament has left the president free of the checks and balances that exist elsewhere.[1] The flaws in the constitution of the Fifth Republic have thus accelerated changes that have affected democracies everywhere.

More broadly, the judicialization of politics is related to a decline of government responsiveness to citizen demands. The less responsive governments are, the more citizens want to hold them accountable. Hence there has been a shift from "competitive representative democracies" to "democracies of imputation." Competitive democracies are organized around the confrontation of parties, platforms, and programs. The advent of post-industrial society has at least temporarily weakened this type of political organization. Ever more opaque decision-making processes and increasingly complex governmental structures have also encouraged the judicialization of politics. It has become harder to find out who is responsible for any particular decision. Thus the imputation of responsibility has itself become problematic. Too many people make policy, and too many agencies carry out decisions, for citizens to gain a clear view of how things work.[2] The advent of "the risk society" has only compounded the

---

[1] On the absence of political accountability in France, see the work of Olivier Beaud, including "La responsabilité politique face à la concurrence d'autres formes de responsabilité des gouvernants," *Pouvoirs*, no. 92 (2000); *Le Sang contaminé: Essai critique sur la criminalisation de la responsabilité des gouvernements* (Paris: Presses Universitaires de France, 1999); and, in collaboration with Jean-Michel Blanquer, *La Responsabilité des gouvernants* (Paris: Descartes, 1999), and "Le principe irresponsabilité. La crise de la responsabilité politique sous la Ve République," *Le Débat*, no. 108 (Jan.–Feb. 2000).

[2] On the problem of imputability in complex societies, see Dennis F. Thompson, "Moral Responsibility of Public Officials: the Problem of Many Hands," *The American Political Science Review* 74, no. 4 (Dec. 1980),

difficulty and spurred the search for better, more efficient ways of ensuring accountability. That is why citizens are sometimes tempted to look to the courts for results that they no longer hope to obtain from the ballot box.[3] If there is no political accountability, people will look for a guilty party in the justice system. It is the sense that normal political processes have failed that shifts attention from the public square to the courthouse.[4]

Greater reliance on criminal accountability to compensate for the deficiency of political accountability has been widely interpreted as a sign that judges in democratic societies exert increasing power. Scholars and the media have described this change as a move toward a "government by judges." An immense literature has grown up around the subject.[5] Some writers worry that the change indicates a decline of popular sovereignty, while others more optimistically see progress toward the rule of law. Attitudes vary from country to country. To take four examples, the United States, France, the United Kingdom, and Italy differ sharply for reasons having to do with

and Mark Bovens, *The Quest for Responsibility: Accountability and Citizenship in Complex Organisations* (Cambridge University Press, 1998).

[3] For an overview of the problem, see Richard Mulgan, *Holding Power to Account: Accountability in Modern Democracies* (New York: Palgrave, 2003), and Robert D. Behn, *Rethinking Democratic Accountability* (Washington: Brookings, 2001).

[4] See Antoine Garapon and Denis Salas, *La République pénalisée* (Paris: Hachette, 1996).

[5] For an introduction to the literature, see Michael H. Davis, "A Government of Judges: An Historical Review," *The American Journal of Comparative Law* 35, no. 3 (Summer 1987) (which points out that the expression was first used in the 1920s), and Séverine Brondel, Norbert Foulquier, and Luc Heuschling, eds., *Gouvernement des juges et démocratie* (Paris: Publications de la Sorbonne, 2001).

the history and institutions of each country.[6] Yet one overall diagnosis applies to all, and in each country related issues come up again and again. Despite all the attention to the increased role of judges and the law in democracies, one central issue is often neglected: the nature of the judicial act. The work of the judge ends in a *judgment*. If there is more judicial government in contemporary democracies, it may be due to a desire for judgment, a diffuse and ambiguous social demand. Judgment is a specific type of public action, a way of articulating the general interest as it relates to a particular case. Rather than reduce the judicialization of politics to a simple question of institutional "competition" between magistrates and representatives, we need to look at the phenomenon as a specific form of political action. The desire for judgment reflects more than mere disenchantment with "electoral politics." It has to do with the fact that a judgment is a special kind of decision. In order to gain a better understanding of this specificity of judgment, we need to compare it with electoral politics. I will organize my remarks under five broad heads: conditions of justification, relation to decision, position in action, form of theatricality, and mode of individuation.

The imperative of justification

Exercising responsibility implies accountability for one's actions. But the way in which one is accountable differs

---

[6] Many factors are relevant to explaining the cross-country differences: whether or not judges are elected, the possibility of having a high court of justice in which parliamentarians sit as judges, etc.

radically depending on whether one is summoned before a court of law or chooses to campaign for votes in an election. "One abandons ambiguity only to one's peril," said Cardinal de Retz. The maxim is most relevant to the world of politics, where the art of dissimulation, the possibility of delay, and vagueness as to one's commitments play a crucial role. It is almost a given of political life that such ambiguity is to be expected. Its function is protective and diversionary. It is, of course, possible that a commitment to "telling the truth" offers a comparative advantage. Yet it is always difficult for voters to judge how sincere and far-reaching such a commitment might be. Things are different in court. The parties to a case are obliged to explain and justify their actions in a public setting. No diversion is possible. The courtroom setting could not be more different from the conditions of a political campaign. In an adversary proceeding opposing points of view are equally represented, and the trial begins only after the facts of the matter have been thoroughly investigated. The parties have no control over the rules of procedure. Questions about the facts cannot be suppressed or avoided. Thus a trial differs sharply from a campaign as to the conditions under which the confrontation of opposing views takes place, the manner of justification, and the nature of the ensuing decision. Hence judicial rhetoric is quite distinct from political rhetoric. The former allows for a more methodical and transparent examination of responsibility. "Chains of imputation," to borrow a phrase from Hans Kelsen, can be examined in a more meticulous and systematic way. And in many cases the courts must give grounds for their decisions.

One should be careful not to idealize the court trial. Legal argument is frequently far from satisfactory in all respects, and the goal of transparency is seldom fully achieved. Still, a trial may well meet many of society's expectations simply by subjecting facts, intentions, and actions to scrutiny in accordance with strict procedural rules. Citizens may therefore believe that it is easier for a politician to escape sanction at the ballot box than in a court of law. They will then turn to the courts for a decision rather than to the political arena. Indeed, they may have higher expectations of the courts than of normal politics. Although they may not say so, many people also feel that judges and juries are better informed than most voters and can therefore approach their task in a more rational way. A court decision thus reconciles the egalitarian demands of democracy with a certain notion of expertise, offering a "third way" between number and reason. A jury verdict may be seen as a more mature decision than the verdict of the ballot box, and because the consequences are more serious, the decision is also weightier and graver. Although it is the electoral process that eventuates in the expression of the general will, the legal process nevertheless remains a crucial part of democratic politics.

An obligatory decision

Court decisions are often compared to other activities of the state. Governing and judging are both ways of intervening in the lives of members of the community for the purpose of promoting the common good. Yet judicial and political decisions are very different in nature. A government decision is often one step in a long series of other actions, a part of a complex policy that creates certain opportunities and looks toward a certain goal. Yet political decisions are also frequently omissions rather than decisions: "Politics is the art of delaying choice"; "There is no problem that time will not resolve in the end." Expressions such as these reveal how many people think about politics. Examples of the preference for non-decision are legion. There is nothing comparable in the judicial realm. A court cannot decline to render a verdict on the grounds that a decision would be delicate or controversial. On the contrary, it is because a difficult issue needs to be resolved that it comes to court. In France, Article 4 of the Civil Code explicitly requires judges to render a judgment even if the relevant law is obscure or ambiguous, or else face charges of obstructing justice.[7] Once a case is laid before a judge, the judge must decide, even if no explicit law applies and he has no recourse other than to invoke natural law.

What distinguishes the decision of a court is that it ends dispute, fixes responsibility, or punishes an action. It marks a definitive end, a final resolution. Thus judgment eliminates uncertainty. Paul Ricoeur writes that "judgment proceeds from the conjunction of the understanding and the will: the understanding weighs the true and the false, the will decides. We thus come to the strong sense of the word judge: it means not simply to opine, evaluate, or hold to be true but in the last instance to take a

---

[7] Article 4 of the Civil Code reads: "Any judge who refuses to judge on the grounds that the law is silent, obscure, or insufficient shall be liable for prosecution on grounds of obstructing justice (*déni de justice*)." The notion of "obstructing justice" is thus inseparable from that of justice. Yet there is no such thing as "obstructing political will."

position."[8] The Indo-European etymology confirms this definition: judgment is an act of establishment, of foundation, of
organization of the world.[9] Beyond the immediate sense of a
judicial act, judgment thus takes a place in a much broader
context. In the Middle Ages, the term *judicium* referred to the
judgment of God. Judgment is thus a transcendent, sovereign
undertaking. It is a radical and extreme form of the human power
to institute the world.[10] A residue of this aspect of judgment
persists to this day, at least in regard to the political. In contrast
to decision by number and to the political principle of self-
determination, judgment reveals the existence of another mode
of action whereby human beings may come together to create a
common world. In the ineluctable dialectic of effective decision
and democratic deliberation, judgment represents a specific
moment in the constitution of the city and a specific mode of
achieving that end.

The active spectator

A political decision is ordinarily a pledge concerning
the future. By contrast, a judgment looks to the past. This is the

---

[8] Paul Ricoeur, "L'acte de juger," in *Le Juste* (Paris: Éditions Esprit, 1995),
p. 186.
[9] See Émile Benveniste, *Le Vocabulaire des institutions indo-européennes*
(Paris: Éditions de Minuit, 1969), vol. II, pp. 99 ff.
[10] On these points see the important articles by Robert Jacob, "Le jugement
de Dieu et la fonction de juger dans l'histoire judiciaire européenne,"
Archives de philosophie du droit (1994), and "*Judicium* et le jugement.
L'acte de juger dans l'histoire du lexique," in Olivier Cayla et Marie-
France Renoux-Zagamé, *L'Office du juge: Part de souveraineté ou
puissance nulle?* (Paris: LGDJ, 2001).

source of its power and efficacy. Hannah Arendt stressed this point in *Responsibility and Judgment* and *The Human Condition*. In the latter work in particular she noted that the meaning of an event does not emerge clearly until it is complete. Hence the actors are always blind, and their understanding is always tentative, incomplete, and biased. Conversely, the spectator can see all the cards; his field of vision is wider. The judge resembles the spectator or historian in this regard. In both cases distance is a necessary condition of *impartiality*. Arendt does not leave it at that, however. To be sure, her position implies a degree of disenchantment with politics, yet she attempts to overcome that disenchantment by placing judgment in a broader context and seeing it in terms of social interaction aimed at elaborating shared values. In this respect the judge is different from the historian. He is a spectator, to be sure, but an *active and engaged spectator*, whose action helps to institute and regulate the life of the city.[11] In terms of the argument that I have been developing in this book, judgment thus defines a category intermediate between positive-electoral politics and preventive sovereignty. Note, moreover, that actors themselves need to incorporate the reflective function of the spectator if they are to exist fully. Where there is no narrative to accompany and interrogate action, there is no

---

[11] On the place of the spectator in the work of Hannah Arendt, see Leora Bilsky, "When Actor and Spectator Meet in the Courtroom: Reflections on Hannah Arendt's Concept of Judgment," in Ronald Beiner and Jennifer Nedelsky, eds., *Judgement, Imagination and Politics: Themes from Kant and Arendt* (Oxford: Rowman and Littlefield, 2001). See also Ronald Beiner, "Hannah Arendt et la faculté de juger," in Hannah Arendt, *Juger: Sur la philosophie politique de Kant* (Paris: Éditions du Seuil, 1991).

action other than in the immediate form of the dream, which history has shown leads nowhere.[12]

Judgment thus suggests a different conception of politics, what one might call a "politics of judgment." To judge is to question oneself and others. To judge is not to transmit a message to others and convey some truth about their situation, as a political activist would do. It is rather a way of putting the normative validity of a community to the test. It is also a reflection on the bonds that define that community.[13] Judgment thus fulfills a properly political institutionalizing function, which the ordinary "politics of the will," carried on through the ballot box and the actions of government, does not. The distinction between the politics of judgment and the politics of the will, though defined in functional terms, also has a sociological dimension. It corresponds to the gap between the "unitary people" and the republican ideal. It attests to the reality of a divided society. It reveals the tension between the citizen and the individual.

Theatricality

All power needs to be staged in order to make its purposes palpable and visible and establish its authority. That is why the various rituals of sovereignty are so important.

---

[12] Only insurrection is unreflective. On this point, see my arguments in *La Démocratie inachevée: Histoire de la souveraineté du peuple en France* (Paris: Gallimard, 2000), in the chapter entitled "La culture de l'insurrection."

[13] I borrow here from Dick Howard, *Pour une critique du jugement politique* (Paris: Cerf, 1998), pp. 291–297 and 302–306.

These rituals indicate the relationship between proximity and distance, emphasize the majesty of the sovereignty, and hint at a protective capacity. A perspicacious observer notes that "all political power ultimately obtains subordination by way of theatricality."[14] Yet in another respect, political activity itself is a form of staging, insofar as it as an aspect of society's self-representation. It requires a public space in which exchanges and confrontation can take place.[15] Historically, democratic politics depended on public space for its very existence. The role of the theater in the ancient Greek *polis* is significant in this regard. The theater was a space in which society could reflect on itself, in which it could make a public display of its mental and civic infrastructure.[16] Yet this dimension of the political has often been hidden, neglected, and even denied. The same cannot be said of the act of judgment, which is a form of theatricality.

A courtroom is a "theater of justice," according to Jeremy Bentham.[17] Everything in it is arranged to create an immediately intelligible scene in which each actor has his assigned place. The public in particular occupies a place of choice. Indeed, the presence of the public is the one great constant. It explains why trials have always and everywhere been major social events. The public dimension has always

---

[14] Georges Balandier, *Le Pouvoir sur scènes* (Paris: Balland, 1980), p. 23.

[15] Hannah Arendt defines politics in phenomenological terms as self-revelation in a place of exhibition.

[16] This is the theme of the classic work of Christian Meier, *De la tragédie grecque comme art politique* (Paris: Les Belles Lettres, 1991).

[17] Jeremy Bentham, *Rationale of Judicial Evidence*, in *Works of Jeremy Bentham*, ed. John Bowring (Edinburgh, 1843), vol. VI, p. 354.

been essential, even when it was merely a masquerade.[18] Courtrooms were designed as theaters of spectacle. Architects have lavished thought on the problem for two centuries, striving to give form to the democratic idea of public justice. The French Revolution experimented with an enormous variety of designs. It is striking to note that most courtroom plans from this period allowed a great deal of space for spectators, who were not treated as mere curious onlookers. Plans often noted an "area reserved for the people," making it clear that the goal was to bring the citizenry into a public space that had its role to play in the expression of the general will.[19] In this connection it is highly instructive to compare courtroom plans with various proposals for parliamentary chambers. Although plans for the chambers often included galleries for the public, these were relegated to a place of secondary importance: the architecture centered on the disposition of the space allotted to the representatives themselves. In parliament, one might say, the elected representatives are everything and the public is nothing. In court, the representation, embodied in the office of the judge, is more modest and merely "functional," but the public, though it must remain passive, nevertheless occupies a central place. What we see in this

---

[18] On this point, see Sadakat Kadri, *The Trial: A History from Socrates to O. J. Simpson* (London: HarperCollins, 2005), and Milner S. Ball, "The Play's the Thing: an Unscientific Reflection on Courts under the Rubric of Theater," *Stanford Law Review* 28, no. 1 (Nov. 1975).

[19] See, for instance, the plan reproduced in Isser Wolloch, *The New Regime: Transformations of the French Civic Order, 1789–1820* (New York: Norton, 1994), p. 360. See also Association française pour l'histoire de la justice, *La Justice en ses temples: Regards sur l'architecture judiciaire en France* (Poitiers: Éditions Brissaud, 1992).

238

comparison, then, are two different "economies of social presence."

A court of justice does more than just decide cases that are brought before it. Its rituals function as a social institution.[20] It helps to restore order and establish social norms. To be sure, there are variations across countries: one might contrast the sacred space of the French courtroom with the American courtroom, which is more like a workshop dedicated to a common project.[21] Nevertheless, the activity of judging animates an aspect of democracy that otherwise goes unfulfilled.

Space for the exemplary

In the end, judgment effectively captures the attention of the public because it deals by definition with particular cases. Not just any particular case, however: the courts deal with exemplary cases, with landmark decisions. They thus set limits to what is possible, check excess, and attempt to make sense of the world in which they operate. Judgment is distinct both from the legislative dimension of the political, which aims for generality, and from the government-action dimension, which involves managing an endless variety of situations. Hannah Arendt observes that judgment "combines the

---

[20] See Pierre Bourdieu, "Les Rites d'institution," *Actes de la recherche en sciences sociales*, no. 43 (June 1982).

[21] On this point, and on the question of judicial ritual in general, see the suggestive remarks in Antoine Garapon, *Bien juger: Essai sur le rituel judiciaire* (Paris: Odile Jacob, 1997).

particular and the general in an enigmatic manner."[22] The tension here reflects an open and constructive conception of the search for the common good. Judgment does not spring immediately from a supposedly unified "reason" or "will," and the growing social demand for judgment reflects a pragmatic and pluralistic vision of the general interest.[23]

The category of "judgment as decision" offers a solution to the aporia discussed by Plato in *The Statesman*. In a passage of this dialogue, Plato notes that the idea that the law is sufficient for government is an illusion.[24]

> Law can never issue an injunction binding on all which really embodies what is best for each; it cannot prescribe with perfect accuracy what is good and right for each member of the community at one time. The differences of human personality, the variety of men's activities, and the inevitable unsettlement attending all human experience make it impossible for any art whatsoever to issue unqualified rules holding good on all questions at all times.[25]

---

[22] Arendt, *Juger*, p. 115.

[23] In this connection, Ronald Dworkin notes that "government by adjudication" is well suited to multicultural societies. See Ronald Dworkin, "Un pontificat laïc," in Robert Badinter and Stephen Breyer, eds., *Les Entretiens de Provence: Le Juge dans la société contemporaine* (Paris: Fayard, 2003).

[24] Cornelius Castoriadis offers a stimulating commentary on this text in *Sur le Politique de Platon* (Paris: Éditions du Seuil, 1999), pp. 155–173.

[25] Plato, *Statesman* 294b, in Edith Hamilton and Huntington Cairns, eds., *Collected Dialogues* (Princeton: Bollingen, 1961), p. 1063. Aristotle draws attention to the same tension in the *Nicomachean Ethics*.

Yet all power aspires to such abstract universalism, to what Plato calls "simplicity," because to achieve such a state would signify an absolute capacity to move the world and govern human beings to perfection. Plato attacks this claim to the power of generality over a reality that consists entirely of particularities. For him, the world is constantly renewed, constantly changing. It is pure diversity in its very essence and complexity and perhaps above all in consequence of its historicity. The nomocratic illusion that Plato deplores ultimately rests, he believes, on (political) presumption and (cognitive) ignorance. If we are to abandon this dangerous and misleading vision of government, must we return to a more modest conception of the art of politics based on pragmatism and the wisdom of a "royal person" attuned to the variety of reality, to the diversity of life's actual circumstances? Plato also rejects this solution. Indeed, he argues that no such leader can exist, for he would have to be a kind of doctor, permanently attentive to a multitude of patients. Here is yet another illusion that must be guarded against. According to Plato, then, politics is torn between unsatisfactory ways of proceeding: rigorous nomocracy on the one hand and pure administrative art on the other. The modern world has inherited this dilemma, and it is precisely the category of judgment that enables us to resolve it. The function of judgment is to link the particular to the general by way of a sanction (or acquittal) possessing a certain exemplary character. Judgment thus helps to establish democracy by bringing facts together with values, by making social situations intelligible in the light of fundamental governing principles. Hence judgment involves a kind of political pedagogy.

The five characteristics or properties of judgment that I have just described tell us something about the specific way in which judgment contributes to the life of democracy. It is not just a consequence of the role of law in safeguarding liberties. Judgment also plays a part in instituting the political system itself.

Voting and judging

Voting and judging are two ways to intervene in the organization of political life. Of course there is an asymmetry between the principle of universal suffrage, which governs the right to vote, and the principle of delegated competence, which underlies the judge's intervention. The difference is not as great as it might appear, however, as a glance at the intermediate figure of the citizen-juror shows. In many respects the power vested in the juror is greater than that vested in the voter. What is more, what takes place in the courts is in many cases more likely to receive publicity than what goes on in parliament. Only a narrow idea of representation and legitimacy would suggest that there is any rigid hierarchy between the two functions. The power of suffrage remains, politically speaking, the "power of the last word," but ordinary democratic activity is a permanent mixture of political decisions and judicial decisions. The specific characteristics of each, which we have just explored, are rather functional in nature. Their complementarity is also functional. That is why the old question of the advantages and disadvantages of electing judges leaves the problem of the social and political function of judgment largely

untouched.[26] It is essential to consider the specific features
of judgment as a political form if we want to understand
why citizens have come to expect more of it.

Take the issue of "competing judgments." There is a
difference between judicial judgment of a politician who mis-
appropriates funds, for example – a judgment that may lead to
his being declared ineligible for office – and political judgment
of the same person at the ballot box, which may follow soon
thereafter.[27] Several cases of this sort arose in France in the
1990s and beyond. In the United States, political scientists have
looked carefully at the effect of corruption charges on electoral
support for tarnished candidates.[28] Voters have re-elected
candidates found guilty of corruption in a court of law, thus
appearing to absolve the sanctioned behavior. Is this interpretation of the vote correct? Did voters really behave amorally or
cynically? If we are to understand their vote, we must see it in
light of both judgment and political representation. The competing judgments of the court and the ballot box may show

[26] Jacques Krynen, ed., *L'Élection des juges: Étude historique française et
contemporaine* (Paris: Presses Universitaires de France, 1999).

[27] See, for example, Eric Doidy, "Ne pas juger scandaleux. Les électeurs de
Levallois-Perret face au comportement de leur maire," *Politix*, no. 71
(2005).

[28] See the seminal article by Barry S. Rundquist, Gerald S. Strom, and John
G. Peters, "Corrupt Politicians and their Electoral Support: Some
Experimental Observations," *American Political Science Review* 71, no. 3
(1977). For a review of the literature on the subject, see Philippe Bezes and
Pierre Lascoumes, "Percevoir et juger la corruption politique. Enjeux et
usages des enquêtes sur les représentations des atteintes à la probité
publique," *Revue française de science politique* 55, nos. 5–6 (Oct.–Dec.
2005).

that voters stand the usual complaint on its head and find the candidate they re-elect to be an effective representative of their interests. Candidates who are elected after being convicted of corruption are generally politicians who have dispensed patronage, and voters are simply demonstrating their gratitude for value received, which in their minds outweighs any moral qualms they may feel in regard to the offense for which the candidate was convicted. In this case, the competing judgments reflect the implicit opposition between "political proximity" and "judicial distance." Voters may suspect the judicial institution of subservience to a remote establishment and of indifference to local concerns. Hence they prefer political judgment to the judgment of the courts. Such cases demonstrate the need for comparing the two types of judgment in democratic systems.

Continuing in this vein, it may be useful to look briefly at what might be called the "general economy of political judgment." Political judgment is organized around procedures of two kinds: at one extreme, re-election; at the other, prosecution. Each has its distinctive characteristics: for instance, what tribunal is the agent of judgment in each case, and what type of legitimacy is invoked? Here again, we may speak of competing forms of democracy. It is important to note the growing importance of *intermediate* modalities of political judgment: for instance, the political media pursue inquiries that bear a certain relationship to judicial proceedings. What types of public debate are involved? How do citizens manifest their presence in the process? Citizens may sit as jurors with only limited expertise. By contrast, opposition political parties may possess the expertise to present a comprehensive indictment of the government's action. Intermediate between these polls, public opinion is like an itinerant judge without a permanent courtroom: it crystallizes around specific events, only to dissolve again as those events fade from memory (in this respect there is of course a close connection with the development of the various powers of oversight that we discussed earlier). The table below may help to fix these various modalities of political judgment in mind.

Table 2.

Forms of judgment	Nature of tribunal	Periodicity of sessions	Types of sanction
Extraordinary trial	High Court of Justice (generally parliamentary in nature)	Very rare	Political and penal (impeachment in USA)
Ordinary trial	Criminal court	Rare/case-by-case	Prison, fine, period of ineligibility
Technical evaluation of an action (intermediate 1)	Expert community	Regular	Loss of reputation
Specific judgment of a policy or action (intermediate 2)	Court of public opinion	Permanent	Loss of reputation
General judgment of policy (intermediate 3)	Tribunal of opposition	Permanent	Change in relative strength of parties
Re-election	Voters	Periodic, predetermined	Failure to win re-election

Democracy today is changing in ways that tend to bring these different forms of judgment together. A certain confusion and aimlessness attend the process, but, on the positive side, a more active citizenry may emerge from it. The crucial fact is that, as different as the various agents of judgment are, together they form a complex system. Regular and appellate courts constitute an increasingly flexible hierarchy. Different investigations may overlap. Sentences are nearly always cumulative. The three modalities that I have characterized as "intermediary" play an essential role in this adaptation. In our earlier discussion of powers of oversight, we saw how experts and public opinion could interact (and there are always many courts of public opinion, with varying points of view). The opposition, construed as a sort of "court" in its own right, also has an important role to play. Indeed, the opposition takes on new meaning if it is seen as a permanent institution prepared to indict and try errors of government. The role of the opposition is more than just to ward off the risk of a tyranny of the majority by standing up for the rights of the minority; it is also to conduct a symbolic trial of the powers-that-be. It is almost as if the old English model of ministers accountable under penal laws to the Parliament survives in a modernized form: the parliamentary minority plays the role of the prosecution and the majority the role of defense before the enduring tribunal of public opinion and the more august yet also more sporadic tribunal of the ballot box.[29] Only in the second tribunal do voting and judgment coincide. Otherwise,

[29] The point is made by Carlos Miguel Pimentel, "L'opposition ou le procès symbolique du pouvoir," *Pouvoirs*, no. 108 (2004).

there is the equivalent of a trial on the one hand and a distinct sanction on the other, although in practice the effects tend to complement each other.

In these various guises, a "power of judgment" has established itself in democratic political systems as yet another dimension of the division and competition of powers. In this perspective, judgment is not a counterweight or a specific independent power. It should be seen rather as one of many ways in which society can act upon itself. It has a place in the general grammar of democratic action. Instead of positing a simplistic opposition between law and politics, we would therefore do better to explain the various types of coordination that regulate the relationship between two forms of action that are both political and to describe their place in the spectrum of counter-democratic institutions.[30] What is really distinctive about the powers of judgment has to do with the type of dialogue they elicit and help to institutionalize. The powers of judgment, along with the powers of oversight and prevention in the counter-democratic sphere and universal suffrage in the electoral-representative sphere, are yet another way of regulating the political system in a democracy.

[30] On this point, see the interesting arguments in Carlo Guarnieri and Patricia Pederzoli, *La Puissance de juger: Pouvoir judiciaire et démocratie* (Paris: Michalon, 1996).

Part 4

Unpolitical democracy

The development of powers of oversight, prevention, and judgment has profoundly changed the way modern political regimes operate. Such regimes can no longer be described solely in terms of their constitutional arrangements. To put the point another way, *democratic activity* now extends well beyond the framework of electoral-representative institutions. Many other practices and structures of the sort explored in the preceding chapters must also be included. The resulting system is complex but, in its own way, coherent. What these various counter-democratic powers have in common is that they describe a new architecture of separated powers and a much more subtle political dynamic than one ordinarily finds in political theory. For instance, many scholars have explored the theme of direct versus representative democracy, yet a more satisfactory account of today's political reality emerges from our study of the various modes of oversight and prevention. Indeed, a whole range of social and political practices make sense only in terms of the dialectic of action and control. Similarly, the distinctions between voting and judgment and between positive and negative powers offer a new interpretive framework for approaching the question of separation of powers in its properly societal context. By attending to the counter-democratic dimension, we can paint a fuller picture of the way in which various forms of social expression help to structure the political field. Our work thus yields a fuller, more complex understanding of democracy's social context.

Our investigation also leads us to look at the history of democracy in a new light. The story is usually told in linear fashion, as a progressive, cumulative triumph, leading, through battle after battle, from the conquest of universal suffrage to the acquisition of ever expanding political rights. The new story is one in which the old and the new clearly overlap. Traditionally, we think of democracy as a radical, self-instituted political system. This old image must be combined with a new one, in which democratic controls are imposed on powers that stand apart from the people. Institutions that might once have been thought to be "pre-modern" turn out to have survived and retained their efficacy. Hence we need to broaden the focus of political history and work toward a more unified account of democratic institutions. This new history should remain attentive to the great diversity of democratic practices and to the specific ways in which institutions evolved. It should avoid the narrow "diffusionist" approach, the assumption of a "democratic seed" that, once planted, automatically gives rise to the modern democratic regime – as if the essence of democracy and the whole future evolution of the political system were somehow encoded in a democratic gene. The new history should also avoid the common assumption that the heteronomous world of the past is sharply divided from democratic modernity. Now that we know that many facets of counter-democracy have carried over from the pre-democratic past to the democratic present, we should be wary of drawing any rigid dividing line. The history of democracy is full of discontinuities and complexities of many kinds.

If we adopt this new approach to history, we begin to see the relation between liberalism and democracy in a new light. This classic distinction, first proposed by Benjamin Constant, needs to be rethought in relation to the various institutions of criticism and oversight that we have been examining. The history of democracy looks different when we do this. In counter-power, however, there is also ambivalence. Counter-democratic institutions seem to elicit two kinds of reactions: positive citizen activism on the one hand, disillusionment with politics (at times coming close to nihilism) on the other. It is important to understand the nature of this ambivalence. It is not simply pragmatic, nor is its source purely psychological. Rather, it is partly structural, having to do with the very nature of counter-democratic power itself. This is a crucial point. Counter-democratic activity is an undeniable sign of political vitality, of direct citizen involvement, but in other ways it is difficult to fathom. Citizen claims to certain powers can lead to political atrophy or even paralysis, as we saw in our account of the transition from critical sovereignty to negative politics. In subsequent chapters we will pursue this analysis further.

11

The sense of powerlessness and symbols of depoliticization

The age of the unpolitical

The recent tendency toward political disintegration has two causes. The gap that counter-powers tend to open up between civic-civil society and the political sphere is one. For *functional* reasons, counter-powers tend to distance themselves from official institutions: the proof of their efficacy lies in their ability to weaken the powers-that-be. The citizen-as-watchdog gains what the citizen-as-voter loses; the negative sovereign asserts himself at the expense of the sovereign *tout court*; the organization of distrust undermines the assumption of trust conferred by election. For structural reasons, therefore, the political sphere tends to become alienated from society, to situate itself externally. Thus when citizens claim counter-powers, legal powers are devalued and minimized. As a logical consequence of the discontinuity that is established between society and the institutions of government, the statesman is automatically degraded to the rank of "politician." To put it more bluntly still, democracy restricts democracy: elected officials are reined in and lose their room to maneuver owing to pressure from the voters themselves. As a result, the dynamics of control take precedence over the appropriation of power. The citizen is transformed into an ever more demanding political consumer, tacitly renouncing joint responsibility for creating a shared world. It is misleading, however, to interpret this development as nothing more than a sign of retreat into private life or growing indifference to the welfare of others, points repeated incessantly by a literature critical of the ravages of democratic individualism and filled with allegations of public "impotence" in the face of the inexorably increasing power of the private sector. On the contrary, the "age of political consumerism" has been characterized by high expectations of political institutions and growing demands upon them. The problem stems from the way in which these demands are expressed, which tends to delegitimate the powers to which they are addressed. This is the source of the contemporary disenchantment with democracy. Disappointment is an almost inevitable consequence of a distrustful citizenry.

A second reason for the political disintegration of recent years is a decline in global awareness of political action. Institutions of oversight and prevention spread by diffusion, and it becomes increasingly difficult to obtain a perception of the political field as a whole. Politics appears to be increasingly fragmented, deconstructed, and opaque. As controls proliferate, it becomes harder and harder to see, much less understand, the big picture. The term "depoliticization" is misleading as a description of this phenomenon. On the contrary, there is ever greater involvement and participation of civil society in political life. The people are omnipresent and no longer content to make their voice heard only on election day. Yet no one believes any longer in the idea of an alternative to the status quo. This, I believe, is why so many people nowadays find the opposition of left and right unsatisfactory when it comes to describing the real stakes of political confrontation. To be sure, skepticism is rampant these days, yet it does not follow that citizens believe that one policy is as good as another. What they are skeptical about is the idea that there is a global alternative to the way things are. Hence they prefer to judge policies case by case. That is why the revolutionary ideal has faded to the point where no one any longer regards revolution as a strategic option. Once upon a time, the belief in revolution was the most incandescent expression of faith in the virtues of direct popular sovereignty, in the prospect of making the world anew. Hence its disappearance cannot be understood solely as a consequence of the collapse of communism or the triumph of moderate reformism. It is the very idea of radicality that has changed. Radicalism no longer looks forward to *un grand soir*, a "great night" of revolutionary upheaval; to be radical is to persist in criticizing the powerful of this world in moral terms and to seek to awaken passive citizens from their slumbers. To be radical is to point a finger of blame every day; it is to twist a knife in each of society's wounds. It is not to aim a cannon at the citadel of power in preparation for a final assault.

Other writers have used terms such as "civil democracy"[1] and "functional democracy"[2] to describe the new relationship between civil society and political society – suspicious

[1] The phrase is derived from "civil religion," which is borrowed from Tocqueville. It is used, for example, in Catherine Colliot-Thélène, "L'Ignorance du peuple," in Gérard Duprat, ed., *L'Ignorance du peuple* (Paris: Presses Universitaires de France, 1998), pp. 36–39.

[2] Jean-François Thuot, *La Fin de la représentation et les formes contemporaines de la démocratie* (Montréal: Éditions Nota Bene, 1998); see esp. chap. 7, "L'espace politique du nouveau sujet démocratique."

and circumstantial rather than prescriptive and comprehensive. These expressions are useful for underscoring the abandonment of the old leitmotif: the alleged decline of the citizenship imperative. Yet they perhaps fail to take sufficient notice of the way in which the idea of social intervention has lately been divorced from the notion that it is politics that structures society and gives it meaning. I therefore prefer the term "unpolitical democracy" (*la démocratie impolitique*) to describe the change. Indeed, the recent rise of what is in essence indirect democracy has gone hand-in-hand with a decline of the political as such. This change is related to other transformations in the modalities of government action. At first, counter-democratic pressures made governments more cautious and less inclined to propose ambitious projects. Everyone knows Louis XIV's famous quip: "Every time I create a job, I create a hundred malcontents and one ingrate." Worries of this sort preoccupy government officials today. They are motivated more by the desire to avoid criticism for controversial actions than by the hope of making themselves popular by risking major reforms. Voters dwell more on the danger of finding themselves worse off than on the hope of improving their situation. This asymmetry of the positive and negative is apparent in the behavior of politicians as well as in the attitudes of citizens.[3] This is the principal dividing line. Strategies of evasion, avoidance, and dilution have

[3] See R. Kent Weaver, "The Politics of Blame Avoidance," *Journal of Public Policy* 6, no. 4 (Oct.–Dec. 1986). See also Michael B. Mackuen, James A. Stimson, and Robert S. Erikson, "Responsabilité des élus devant l'électorat et efficacité du système politique américain: Une analyse contre-factuelle," *Revue française de science politique* 53, no. 6 (Dec. 2003).

THE SENSE OF POWERLESSNESS

proliferated. As the public became quicker to react to government policy, government became more reluctant to act.[4] It is in
this light that one ought to interpret the comment of one
disillusioned French prime minister, who said that governing
had become an "impossible profession."[5]

The horizon of transparency

The sense of powerlessness that many citizens have
with respect to what they see as unacceptable government
timidity should be measured against the foregoing remarks.
It is not simply that politicians are unconcerned with or indifferent to the problem, though indifference is surely part of the
story. The ritual invocation of the need to restore political will
as the means to salvation therefore misses the point. The
problems of today's societies cannot be solved by idealizing a
Gaullist or Churchillian vision or method. In the first place, the
difficulties have been compounded by the rise of negative

---

[4] My approach runs counter to the well-known analyses of the committee of
experts assembled by the Trilateral Commission in the 1970s, who argued
that the "excesses" of participatory democracy would ultimately make
societies ungovernable, "overburdening" governments while
delegitimating authority by way of an accentuation of individualistic
values and a reduction of confidence in leadership. See Michel Crozier,
Samuel Huntington, and Joji Watanuki, *The Crisis Of Democracy*
(New York: NYU Press, 1975). These somber predictions have not been
borne out by the facts. Today, the issue is rather the *insufficiency* of
electoral-representative democracy, which is linked to overdevelopment of
counter-democracy.
[5] Michel Rocard, "Gouverner: métier impossible," *Les Carnets de
psychanalyse*, nos. 15–16 (2004).

democracy. It is this *form* of democracy that constitutes the problem rather than the alleged decline of a supposedly autonomous political dynamic. The impotence is therefore *systemic* and not a consequence of deficient political will or flawed leadership. In the new age – an age of *problematic* democracy – citizens no longer think of conquering power in order to exercise it. Their implicit goal is rather to constrain and limit power, while deploring the ultimate consequences of their own preferred practices. The appropriation of power is no longer the ideal; what people think they want now is to make power transparent enough to permit total control.

Transparency thus replaces the exercise of responsibility as the end of politics. Instead of seeking to achieve political *objectives*, people seek certain physical and moral *qualities*. Disillusioned citizens want to eliminate anything that stands in the way of total transparency. Little by little, a veritable ideology of transparency has emerged as the new democratic ideal, in place of the old, which was to create through politics a society in which people could live together in a shared world. Transparency, rather than truth or the general interest, has become the paramount virtue in an uncertain world. In some metaphorical manner transparency is supposed to eliminate all tension and overcome every difficulty.[6] Not knowing what power is supposed to do, people worry only about what it is supposed to be. It is almost as if

[6] In a paradoxical way, the twenty-first century has come back to naïvely utopian revolutionary ideas of a transformation of human beings and institutions through public appropriation alone. These ideas were linked to the Rousseauian assumption that the general will would emerge as a product of unmediated relations among members of the community.

they dreamed of dissolving power altogether. Their goal is not to limit power, as in the liberal tradition, but to constrain it and thus, in a manner of speaking, to "transfigure" it. But then it can no longer respond to the demands placed on it. Transparency – the new utopia – thus engenders the very disillusionment it was intended to overcome.

Two forms of depoliticization

The development of "unpolitical" counter-democratic forms parallels other key transformations in government. One of the most striking changes in this regard is the substitution of decentralized processes of *governance* for more traditional forms of *government*. Although this change has also contributed to the decline of politics, it is not really of the same nature as the changes discussed previously. It is important to understand the difference in order to appreciate the specific way in which the decline of politics is linked to counter-democracy. Indeed, we need to be clear in order to deconstruct such overly general concepts as "the decline of the political," "the privatization of society," and "the advent of an individualistic society" – concepts that masquerade as indispensable keys to the present but actually make it more difficult to understand what is going on.

Over the past twenty years, a large literature has grown up around the concept of governance.[7] Whole journals

---

[7] James Rosenau's pioneering work is still of major importance. For the French literature, see especially Patrick Le Galès, Pierre Lascoumes, Dominique Plihon, and Marie-Claude Smouts.

are devoted to nothing else.[8] Yet a certain vagueness remains, because the same word is used to denote very different modes of regulation and decision. Thus "governance" can refer to a new age in international relations: the age of "the post-state actor." Or it can refer to corporate governance or the governance of cities or even "public governance." The concept rapidly gained currency because it seemed to describe a series of related changes. Three common features stand out:

Networking: First, decisions involve a number of *actors* of different nature and status. In the international order, for example, one thinks of states, non-governmental organizations (NGOs), and public agencies of various kinds. Public and private operators interact, with each exercising a "governing" function in the sense of exerting pressure or intervening in various ways (through the law, the media, or social interaction, for example). The idea of governance thus posits the existence not of a single legitimate decision-maker but rather of a heterogeneous, interactive network of participants.

Complexity: "Decisions" are not specific choices made at a well-defined point in time. They are rather the result of complex, iterative processes. The very term "decision" tends to lose its significance when applied to the shifting relations among plural actors engaged in an ongoing process of consultation, negotiation, adaptation, and compromise. In firms, pyramidal hierarchies in which the chief management tool is grading of subordinates by superiors are increasingly giving way to more decentralized and flexible modes of cooperation.

[8] See especially *Global Governance* and *Governance*.

Here, the notion of governance refers to a *mode of regulation* characterized by flexible forms of coordination involving several channels of communication that come together in certain nodal points of a network. In the political order, governance applies to situations in which legally empowered authorities are obliged to engage in ongoing dialogue and implicit or explicit compromise with various social agencies. The word thus captures a revolution in the relationship between state and civil society. Broadly speaking, the new modes of regulation tend to dissolve the distinction between administration and politics. The various spheres and organizational levels of social life are governed by increasingly similar processes. Firms, government bureaucracies, and local and regional governments operate in quite similar ways. At the same time, the difference between the international and the national order tends to diminish.

Absence of hierarchy: Rules are no longer derived from a hierarchy of norms organized around the idea of a general will embodied in the state (or an international order defined in similar terms). In this context, "governance" refers to a system of pluralistic, heterogeneous norms combining national and international law with elements of arbitration, convention, and custom in a complex and evolving relationship. The complexity has to do with the variety of agencies involved in the regulation of a series of relevant domains.

There is no doubt that governance in the sense described above is something new and real, but it is difficult to define more precisely, because ultimately it has to be understood in negative terms, that is, in terms of its difference from previous hierarchical systems. There are quite different ways of doing this. On the one hand, governance can be seen as an

expression of social and political disintegration, as tacit assent
to the decline of democratic principles undermined by the
growing influence of the market and legal system.
"Governance" can then be seen as a sort of ideological term
cloaking the wreckage of the republican-democratic ideal. To
adopt this point of view is to accept the idea of a broad crisis of
democracy, of representation, of the idea of the general interest. This pessimistic (or is it disillusioned?) attitude has been
adopted by many authors across a broad ideological spectrum
ranging from anti-globalization activists to neo-nationalist
theorists. On the other hand, there is another way of looking
at the rise of governance, a more neutral approach, which sees
it as a consequence of the growing complexity and fragmentation of contemporary society, which consists of a series of
relatively autonomous subsystems. In other words, the era of
organizations gives way to the era of networks. This leads
directly to the more positive view that societies today are
more capable of horizontal coordination, of organizing themselves without recourse to supervisory authorities. The second
way of looking at governance is probably more widespread
than the first. It is shared by a great many scholars who have
studied changes in public-sector management and the role of
civil-society organizations. It has also attracted the attention of
a writer of the extreme left, Antonio Negri, who sees it as an
opportunity for organizing a new grass-roots movement of
emancipation and subversion.[9] Many scholars take a position

[9] See Michael Hardt and Antonio Negri, *Empire* (Cambridge, MA: Harvard
University Press, 2000), *Multitude: War and Democracy in the Age of
Empire* (New York: Penguin, 2004).

somewhere between these two extremes. Ulrich Beck is a case in point. He looks favorably on the advent of what he calls "subpolitics," by which he means an activation of civil society, because he sees the decline of state-centric politics as a sign of mature democracy. Yet he also deplores the resulting political paralysis.[10]

This brief survey of the literature on governance is enough to suggest what distinguishes the phenomena collected under this head from the forms of indirect democracy that are the subject of the present work. With governance, organizational and regulatory fragmentation in various areas of social life leads to a specific type of depoliticization, which might be described as *decentering* or dissemination. In this perspective, the function of politics is to supply coordination and direction. Depoliticization occurs when the central, unified political subject – the people – disappears. That is why some commentators choose to describe this kind of depoliticization as "post-democracy": the *demos* and nation-state vanish in favor of a new form of regulation.[11] Counter-democracy gives rise to a different type of depoliticization. Here, politics retains its *functional* centrality. The exercise of powers of oversight, prevention, and judgment does not eliminate the "center stage." Indeed, counter-democratic powers exist only in relation to the central power, which they challenge in some ways and reinforce in others. It is striking to note that international

[10] Ulrich Beck, *Risk Society: Toward a New Modernity* (New York: Sage, 1992), and *World Risk Society* (London: Polity, 1992).

[11] To my knowledge, Jacques Rancière was one of the first to use this term in *Disagreement: Politics and Philosophy* (Minneapolis: University of Minnesota Press, 1998).

institutions often seek legitimacy by lending support to counter-powers within civil society. For example, the United Nations and European Union offer accreditation, consultation, and even financing to certain NGOs. In return, the NGOs recognize the role of the international bodies.[12] Nation-states, though generally more cautious in this regard, have resorted to similar methods to accommodate rising counter-democratic powers. But the results that these "strong" powers obtain are quite different from those obtained by "weak" international organizations. At the national level what we find is *destructive legitimation*: governments sacrifice some measure of sovereignty in the hope of regaining the confidence of their citizens. Officials sacrifice a measure of status in order to signal that they are attentive to society's needs. Political institutions retain their centrality, but their power is diminished. In the end, the power of the political to institute the social is undermined. Depoliticization in this sense *drains* politics of its substance.

It is possible to press the analysis of the new "unpolitical democracy" still further. It will be useful, first, to analyze the pathological form of counter-democracy, namely, populism. The recent growth of unpolitical democracy can also be studied in the light of economic transformations that have driven certain new actors into the shrinking political sphere.

---

[12] Thierry Pech and Marc-Olivier Padis, *Les Multinationales du cœur: Les ONG, la politique et le marché* (Paris: La République des idées-Seuil, 2004).

12

The populist temptation

With a meaning as vague as it is ominous, the term "populism" has gained currency in today's political lexicon. Borrowed from Russian, where it first appeared toward the end of the nineteenth century, the word is now widely used to refer to a range of political movements and issues that cannot easily be accommodated within the usual ideological categories. It was regularly applied to a range of extreme right-wing political movements that gained followings in late twentieth-century Europe (and, earlier, to Latin American regimes such as Juan Perón's in Argentina), yet these instances do not exhaust its meaning. To describe a movement as "populist" is to suggest that it is in some way pathological or a danger to liberty without specifying what the nature of the pathology is. In other words, "populism" is a word that serves as both a screen and a crutch. One way to make the term less ambiguous is to think of populism as a democratic pathology in two senses: as a pathology, first, of electoral-representative democracy and, second, of counter-democracy. Populism is not just an ideology. It is a perverse inversion of the ideals and procedures of democracy.

A pathology of electoral-representative democracy

Let us begin by considering the tensions inherent in democratic political representation. Populism claims to resolve the problem of representation by conjuring up an image of a unified, homogeneous people. It radically rejects whatever it assumes to be inimical to such unity and homogeneity: foreigners, enemies, oligarchy, elites. With ever more vehement attacks it seeks to drive a wedge between the people and its supposed enemies. Populists denounce "otherness" in moral terms (by vilifying the "corrupt" and "rotten"), in social terms (by condemning "elites"), and in ethnic terms (by attacking "foreigners," "immigrants," "minorities," etc.). By contrast, they celebrate "the people" as unified and pure, undivided so long as outsiders are kept out. Thus populism attempts to remedy the defects of representation by proposing an essentialist sociology. Its rhetoric also strikes at the representative principle itself. Populists extol the virtues of appealing directly to the people instead of allowing a handful of professional politicians to confiscate the political process for their own benefit. In this sense, most of the anti-parliamentary movements of late nineteenth-century Europe and America could be characterized as "populist" (examples include the Boulangist movement in France and the People's Party of small farmers in the American Middle West).[1] On both continents, we find the same contrast between people and elites: the people are healthy, whereas the elites are cut off from any authentic connection with society. Racist and xenophobic themes found a lamentably logical place in populist rhetoric in both places. Recent work by political scientists has fleshed

---

[1] On populists in the United States, see the classic work by Michael Kazin, *The Populist Persuasion: An American History* (New York: Basic Books, 1995).

out this picture.[2] The revival of populism in the late twentieth century is in part a consequence of a crisis of representation stemming from an increasingly opaque social structure. As the old class structure has disappeared, the role of traditional political parties as the organizers and articulators of class-based political interests has declined. Yet this sociological approach to populism cannot really explain its origins or capture its distinctive features. If the crisis of representation – a pathology of electoral-representative democracy – were a sure gauge of populism, the various forms of totalitarianism would have to be classified as populist, since they, too, depend, albeit in a more radical way, on imagined social unity and incarnation of the people. Hence the criterion is too broad; we need a more precise definition of populism. To that end, I propose to analyze populism as a pathology of counter-democracy.

Populism and counter-democracy

Populism radicalizes the three forms of counter-democracy that I have described in the previous chapters: the

---

[2] The most penetrating recent studies include the work of Paul Taggart and Margaret Canovan. See, for example, Paul Taggart, "Populism and Representative Politics in Contemporary Europe," *Journal of Political Ideologies* 9, no. 3 (Oct. 2004); and Margaret Canovan, "Trust the People! Populism and the Two Faces of Democracy," *Political Studies* 47, no. 1 (March 1999). The essays collected in Yves Mény and Yves Surel, *Democracies and the Populist Challenge* (New York: Palgrave, 2002), are also worth noting. For France, see the studies supervised by Guy Hermet, Olivier Ihl, and Pierre-André Taguieff.

democracy of oversight, negative sovereignty, and politics as judgment. Populism radicalizes each of these to the point where they end up in what I have called "the unpolitical." In this sense, populism might be defined as "the pure politics of the unpolitical," or the consummate anti-politics: absolute counter-democracy. To see this, let us consider populism in relation to each of the three types of counter-democracy.

To start off, populism can be defined as a pathology of oversight and vigilance. An active, positive urge to inspect what the government is doing, to subject it to scrutiny and criticism, becomes a compulsive and permanent stigmatization of the ruling authorities, to the point where these authorities are seen as radically alien enemy powers. In this respect, populism is the faithful heir of Jean-Paul Marat. Marat believed in oversight as a revolutionary ideal. Indeed, he was one of its champions and made it a central theme of his *Chaînes de l'esclavage* (1774): "If we are to remain free, we must always keep an eye on the government. We must watch closely what it is up to, oppose its aggressions, and restrain its excesses."[3] The goal of political action, he noted elsewhere, "is to exert perpetual control over the actions of men who succeed in gaining power. Even when they are your own choice, keeping watch over them is everyone's unremitting duty."[4] But the

---

[3] Jean-Paul Marat, *Les Chaînes de l'esclavage* (1774), in *Œuvres politiques* (Brussels: Pôle Nord, 1995), vol. VII, p. 4421. "If we are to remain free, we always remain on guard against our rulers. The unwary are easily lost, and for any people too much security is a harbinger of servitude to come" (*ibid.*, p. 4355).

[4] Quoted in Patrice Rolland, "Marat ou la politique du soupçon," *Le Débat*, no. 57 (Nov.–Dec. 1989): 134.

newspaper *L'Ami du peuple*, which he began publishing in 1789, would soon go well beyond its original demands – demands that a philosopher as sober as Alain would not have found unacceptable a century and a half later. Marat widened the gulf between the people and power: in no time at all he was unable to imagine the government as anything other than a sinister and implacable machine for conspiracy and intrigue. To him, every government seemed essentially despotic: the vocation of power was inexorably tyrannical, a Machiavellian arsenal. With Marat, "oversight became the citizen's sole form of political activity."[5] Paradoxically, the result was political passivity: weary of being vilified and attacked, power transformed itself into an impregnable fortress so forbidding that no one outside its walls could imagine occupying it. Citizens felt radically alienated. Marat saw only indomitable tyranny; he could not conceive of even the possibility of democratic rule. Populism is the modern heir of Marat's vision. It combines his suspicious nature with a passion for denunciation that has more to do with a will to destroy than with anxious watchfulness. In this respect, populism is in a way the modern embodiment of the "sycophants" of ancient Athens; it takes the spirit of contradiction to its ultimate extreme.[6] Populist movements are also the heirs of a style of

---

[5] On this point, see the stimulating remarks of Patrice Rolland, *ibid.*, 135.

[6] The sycophants of Athens took advantage of the right of every citizen to bring charges against officials in order to conduct a kind of blackmail against the city's magistrates. The sycophants saw themselves as "the people's watchdogs," keen to protect democracy from oligarchic plots, but their adversaries saw them as vulgar demagogues and consummate extortionists. See Carine Karitini Doganis, *Aux Origines de la corruption.*

political derision that permeated the French anti-parliamentary
press in the late nineteenth century. Publications such as *Les
Chambres comiques, La Bombe, Le Balai, La Lanterne,* and
L'Assiette au beurre set the tone for a radically pessimistic and
disillusioned style of journalism, whose goal was not so much
to influence the course of events as to belittle and berate people
in power. In the pages of these broadsheets democratic impatience metamorphosed into hopeless, bitter, and violent
denunciation. In all these ways, populism can be understood
as the power of oversight turned against itself.

Populism can also be seen as a pathology of preventive
sovereignty. In this respect, too, it can be traced back to the
political crisis of the late nineteenth century, when "anti-system"
parties emerged in any number of countries.[7] Revolutionary
sentiment appeared to compete with outright rejection of
politics, but in reality the two attitudes were mutually reinforc-
ing. As we have seen, "critical sovereignty" contributed to the
construction of democracy. Preventive power thus shaped the
evolution of democratic political systems but had yet to trans-
mute itself into a negative and inward vision of politics. In
times of crisis or uncertainty, however, extreme negativism
could assert itself forcefully. In France in the 1950s, for example, the sudden success of the Poujadist movement showed
that latent populist sentiment had remained in the shadows,
ready to erupt at a moment's notice. Poujadism was almost a
caricature of pure negative politics: it was a party propelled by

Démocratie et délation en Grèce ancienne (Paris: Presses Universitaires de,
2007).

[7] See Giovanni Sartori, *Parties and Party Systems: A Framework for Analysis*
(Cambridge University Press, 1976).

tax revolt, and its candidates went before the voters in 1956 without any platform other than pure, visceral opposition to government. They flooded France with posters and brochures containing only the peremptory message, "Throw the incumbents out!"[8] Subsequent incarnations of populism have made this idea of political action commonplace. Populists have no interest in fighting on the usual political battlegrounds. Instead, they warn of decadence and pose as guardians of purity, saviors of the nation from political extremes, and prophets of an apocalypse from which they will emerge victorious. They are joined in this twilight battle by what Elias Canetti calls "the negative masses."[9] In recent years these negative masses seem to have turned exclusively inward. No longer do they pour energy into some promised improvement or future paradise. No moral force spurs them to dignified resistance or purposeful action. To these silent masses – disillusioned, disoriented, and disgusted – populism fails even to supply a language. Yet it knows how to stoke anger and stir protest in the streets and voting booths. Populism's rising power reflects the fact that negative sovereignty finds itself imprisoned in the immediate: it is a force radically bereft of ideas, incapable of active criticism, and reduced to the expression of resigned violence.

Last but not least, contemporary populism has corrosively enlarged the idea of the people as judge. The image of the court as a theater of reasoned argument and expert opinion has

---

[8] Many of these brochures are reproduced in Stanley Hoffmann, *Le Mouvement Poujade* (Paris: Armand Colin, 1956).

[9] Elias Canetti, *Masse et puissance* (Paris: Gallimard, 1966), pp. 55–58.

been transformed by populist movements into a theater of cruelty or a circus. As a result, the very essence of power has been criminalized and ridiculed. All civic activity is reduced to accusation, thus alienating the citizen from government almost as a matter of structural necessity. The state is reduced to its prosecutorial and law-enforcement function, as if this were its only democratic manifestation.[10] The vindictive populist people-as-judge shows little concern for distributive justice, for weighing the various feasible means of achieving greater equality. It suspects the beneficiaries of the welfare state of fraud and lumps them together with immigrants, both legal and illegal. The only justice in which it is interested is the justice of repression, punishment, and stigmatization of those whom it condemns as "undesirables" and "parasites." In this respect the pathology of counter-democracy intersects with the pathology of electoral-representative democracy, the fantasy of solving all of society's problems by creating a healthy, unified social body.

"Ideological" definitions of populism tend to suffer from simplistic value judgments: on the one hand, denunciations of populism as a form of demagogy and xenophobia; on the other hand, praise of populism as an ideology genuinely concerned with "grass-roots society."[11] Our characterization of

---

[10] It is as if the sycophants had become the only true representatives of the people of Athens.

[11] Robert Dahl drew a contrast between "populist" and "Madisonian" regimes in *A Preface to Democratic Theory* (The University of Chicago Press, 1956). In a similar vein, see William H. Riker, *Liberalism Against Populism: A Confrontation Between the Theory of Democracy and the Theory of Social Choice* (San Francisco: Freeman and Company, 1982).

democracy in *functional* terms is both more objective and more precise. Looking at populism as a pathology of electoral-representative democracy was the first step, allowing us to move toward a better definition by emphasizing populism's sociological understanding and its perception of a "crisis of political will." We saw, however, that this approach by itself was inadequate because it failed to distinguish sufficiently between populism and other, more radical pathologies, such as the various forms of totalitarianism, as well as between populism and merely illiberal, authoritarian, or decisionist conceptions of the political. Defining populism as pure counter-democracy – as an absolute distillation of the three types of counter-democracy – yielded a clearer picture. With this definition in mind, we have been able to see populism as a form of political expression in which the democratic project is totally swallowed up and taken over by counter-democracy: it is an extreme form of anti-politics. We can now understand why populism has been such a powerful force in the twenty-first century: it is the political pathology characteristic of an era marked by the rise of counter-democratic forms. It thus triggers the emergence of what I have called "unpolitical" counter-democracy. Populism is an acute manifestation of contemporary political disarray and a tragic expression of our inability to overcome it.

13

Lessons of unpolitical economy

To reiterate a point made repeatedly in previous chapters, it was the inability of electoral-representative politics to keep its promises that led to the development of indirect forms of democracy. A similar phenomenon can be observed in the economic sphere, where frequent market failures gave rise to various mechanisms of oversight. Because market forces continued to evolve as this was taking place, different modes of "indirect regulation" emerged. Negative forms of oversight and control are common in today's economy. The analogy between politics and markets is therefore worth exploring further. A "political" reading of the economy can give us a better grasp of the "unpolitical" side of counter-democratic power.

A word returns

I noted earlier that the word *surveillance* was first used in a political sense by eighteenth-century economists to describe a form of government intervention distinct from both the usual powers of command and the automatic mechanisms of the market. Interestingly enough, when the word came back into use in the 1970s, it was once again thanks to economists. It happened after the first oil shock of 1973, which led to the collapse of the international financial system that had been established at Bretton Woods in 1944.[1] The old system, based on automatic, binding rules, was abandoned, thus raising the question of what was to take its place. What was to be done to stabilize the new system of floating exchange rates? It was at this time that "strict surveillance" was proposed as a possible solution to the problem. First used by the American undersecretary of the Treasury, the expression was incorporated into Article 4 of the revised International Monetary Fund charter in 1975.[2] The same term "surveillance" would later be used to characterize the role of the group of governors of the world's principal central banks (G-10), who were to meet annually. Still later, it was used to describe the meetings of the G-7, the heads of the leading industrialized countries. The idea of effective but indirect government, not derived from any sovereign authority but intended to yield similarly decisive results, thus resurfaced once again in this economic context. Once again, economics and politics hit upon a common concept to describe a power to influence or constrain without command authority. The analogies were more than just verbal.

---

[1] The Bretton Woods conference had established a system of fixed exchanged rates, *de facto* equivalent to the Gold Standard, with American dollars and British pounds sterling serving as reserve currencies alongside gold.

[2] For the history, see Louis W. Pauly, *Who Elected the Bankers? Surveillance and Control in the World Economy* (Ithaca: Cornell University Press, 1997), chap. 6: "The Reinvention of Multilateral Economic Surveillance," and Harold James, "The Historical Development of the Principle of Surveillance," *IMF Staff Papers* 42, no. 4 (Dec. 1995).

The economic function of surveillance

Neo-classical theory assumes that, in order for contracts to work properly, information must flow freely, so that
no agent enjoys a situational rent derived from a monopoly of
information.[3] Hence incentives must be established to insure
that information is disclosed in a timely fashion. This is particularly true of highly complex financial markets, which
depend on large amounts of highly uncertain data. One way
of dealing with this difficulty is to establish self-surveillance:
each party keeps an eye on all the others, resulting in a sort of
mutual control. This is the traditional approach to efficient
financial markets. In many cases it has proved insufficient,
however. Peer-to-peer mutual control has failed to ensure
adequate management of financial risks.[4] It is easy to see
why. The commodity traded on credit markets – namely,
promises of reimbursement – suffers from inherent uncertainty, so that clear and objective measures of risk are impossible to establish. Banks rely largely on collective judgments of
the "business climate" or "state of the market" – judgments
that in fact reflect only the current state of professional opinion. Any mutual control mechanism is thus likely to suffer
from a "mirror effect," which may result in collective

[3] See Éric Brousseau, *L'Économie des contrats: Technologies de l'information
et coordinations interentreprises* (Paris: Presses Universitaires de France,
1993).
[4] Here I am following Michel Aglietta and Laurence Scialom, "Vers une
nouvelle doctrine prudentielle," *Revue d'économie financière*, no. 48
(1998). See also Dominique Plihon, "Quelle surveillance prudentielle pour
l'industrie des services financiers ?" *Revue d'économie financière*, no. 60
(2000).

blindness. It is therefore useful to introduce what economists call a "supervisory party," that is, a third party with coercive powers. Only an outside agent of this kind can restore vertical control and thus limit the risk that the "blind will follow the blind" – a risk inherent in any system based on purely horizontal controls. It is this kind of risk that leads to real-estate and stock-market "bubbles" and market crashes. Proper operation of the market therefore requires more than simply ensuring that everyone obeys the rules, which is the function of the Securities and Exchange Commission in the United States and of the Autorité des Marchés Financiers in France. Public supervision is also necessary. Prudential surveillance can ensure the fluidity and transparency of the system if it is coupled with a capacity to take early corrective action and impose sanctions when necessary.[5]

Looked at in this way, market failures can be compared to dysfunctions in systems of political representation. Defects in the electoral mechanism linking representatives to represented in order to ensure that government serves the general interest create a need for additional systems of surveillance, just as in the case of dysfunctional credit markets. These oversight mechanisms may be institutionalized, or they may simply operate in a more diffuse way through public opinion. The introduction of a supervisory third party is intended to remedy a disorder similar to that caused by market failure. The

---

[5] On European steps to establish institutions of this kind, see Michel Marino, "Quelle architecture pour le contrôle prudentiel en Europe ?" *Revue du Marché commun et de l'Union européenne*, no. 460 (July–Aug. 2002).

insufficiency of horizontal regulation in the markets is comparable to the insufficiency of the electoral bond: in both cases there is a lack of vertical control capable of ensuring that regulation operates in a "time-consistent" manner (to use the jargon of economics). In both cases, moreover, the difficulty of establishing a direct and lasting relationship of trust is counterbalanced by the institutionalization of some form of distrust.

The parallel does not end there. The two other surveillance mechanisms I described earlier, evaluation and denunciation, have also come to play a growing role in the economic realm. Financial rating agencies first appeared in the middle of the nineteenth century, offering evaluations of commercial credit, stocks, and bonds. The first commercial credit ratings were issued in the United States during the financial crisis of 1837. They were a response to a widespread feeling at the time that the market had failed for lack of sufficient independent information. In the twentieth century, firms such as Moody's and Standard and Poor's made financial ratings familiar to all.[6] These firms specialize in independent ratings of bonds and other securities. They are yet another instance of the introduction of a *third-party evaluator* as a way of establishing trust that seller and buyer would otherwise be unable to achieve on their own. Financial market participants exchange information but are also susceptible to rumor and manipulation, so these third-party agencies offer an outside

---

[6] On the history of these agencies, see Gilbert Harold, *Bond Ratings as an Investment Guide: An Appraisal of their Effectiveness* (New York, 1938); Philippe Raimbourg, *Les Agences de rating* (Paris: Economica, 1990).

judgment that is in principle more objective. In the economic sphere they fulfill some of the same functions as journalists and experts in the political sphere. In this vein, the Fitch agency says that its ratings are comparable to editorials, indeed "the world's shortest editorials." The rating agencies thus function as a sort of "visible hand" in conjunction with the "invisible hand" of the market.[7] As such, they typify the role of the power of oversight in economic regulation.[8] Many countries have passed laws requiring that various types of securities be submitted to such rating, a sign of the structural role that the ratings agencies have come to play in financial markets. Ratings have thus acquired a legal status equivalent to debt-to-equity ratios.

Security ratings act as signals, and as such they introduce a new form of economic governance. *Certification* is a second type of oversight power, similar to ratings in some ways but more directly normative. Legally speaking, ratings are merely "information" that may encourage or discourage transactions, whereas certifications are part of a more direct regulatory framework. A certification may determine whether or not a particular security is eligible to be included in a particular portfolio. In the industrial realm, certification may be required in order to obtain authorization to market a particular product.[9] Certification

---

[7] On this function, see Olivier Lichy, "Les agences de rating," *Les Petites affiches* (Sept. 4 and 6, 1991).

[8] Timothy J. Sinclair, "Passing Judgements: Credit Rating Processes as Regulatory Mechanisms of Governance in the Emerging World Order," *Review of International Political Economy* 1, no. 1 (spring 1994).

[9] For pharmaceuticals, see Boris Hauray, *L'Europe du médicament: Politique, expertise, intérêts privés* (Paris: Presses de Sciences-Po, 2006).

requirements for products in certain sectors such as textiles date back as far as the eighteenth century. Liberal economists, Turgot foremost among them, fought hard against such requirements on the grounds that buyers could react quickly if they were deceived as to the quality of a product, so that sellers had an interest in avoiding fraud in order to protect their reputations and hold on to their customers. The distance between this idealized vision of the market and the reality was often great, however. In some markets, therefore, direct surveillance by consumers was therefore supplemented by expert surveillance. In such a setting, certification serves as a "prop to trust."[10]

Audit mechanisms complement surveillance measures. What has been called "an explosion of auditing" can also be seen as a response to the need to restore trust in institutions that the market could not secure on its own. Independent outside evaluations enhance the legitimacy of organizations and firms. The *third-party investigator* ensures full disclosure of information and circumstances needed to judge the quality of a firm's management. The books are examined, and auditors certify that management's declarations accord with the facts. The audit has thus become a crucial tool of corporate governance.[11] Institutions are no longer

---

[10] See Philippe Minard, "Les béquilles de la confiance dans le secteur textile au XVIIIe siècle," in Vincent Mangematin and Christian Thuderoz, *Des mondes de confiance. Un concept à l'épreuve de la réalité sociale* (Paris: CNRS, 2003). In the same work, see also Alessandro Stanziani, "Qualité des denrées alimentaires et fraude commerciale en France, 1871–1905."

[11] Peter Moizer, ed., *Governance and Auditing* (London: Edward Elgar Publishing, 2004).

credible unless they subject themselves to rigorous scrutiny of this sort, which Michael Power has called "rituals of verification."[12] Audits are both an ordeal and an opportunity. At a minimum, an audit serves as a kind of "negative insurance" for an institution. Hence what might seem to be a mere technical operation gives rise to real indirect power.

We also see in the economic sphere yet another form of surveillance that we have already noted in the political sphere: denunciation. In the United States, "whistleblowers" – insiders who come forward to denounce serious dysfunctions within their own organizations – have recently come under the protection of the law.[13] The Sarbanes-Oxley bill, which was passed by Congress in 2002 in the wake of a series of notorious financial scandals, requires American firms that are listed on the stock exchange to establish procedures by which employees can anonymously report irregularities.[14] Ethical lapses, product defects, cover-ups of occupational safety issues, and financial manipulations can thus be brought to the attention of authorities without risk to the whistleblower. The law recognizes that a given individual is both a worker answerable to his or her superiors in the organization and a citizen. Thus the whistleblower is to the firm what the

[12] Michael Power, *The Audit Society: Rituals of Verification* (Oxford University Press, 1997).

[13] For an introduction to the subject, see Roberta Ann Johnson, *Whistleblowing: When It Works and Why* (Boulder, CO: Lynne Rienner Publishers, 2003).

[14] Stephen M. Kohn, Michael D. Kohn, and David K. Colapinto, *Whistleblower Law: A Guide to Legal Protections for Corporate Employees* (Westport, CT: Praeger, 2004).

rebel or resister is to the political system, except that the whistleblower is granted legal status and protection. He or she exercises both oversight power and veto power.[15] It is worth noting that *Time* magazine named as its 2003 "people of the year" three whistleblowers who denounced irregularities at Enron, WorldCom, and the FBI. Several European Union directives have been issued with similar intent. Although ethical concerns are perhaps paramount in whistleblowing, more prosaic "managerial" concerns also play a part. Indeed, whistleblowing yields information that helps to keep institutions and markets operating smoothly. In more general terms, one might even speak of *regulation through denunciation*. Yet there are also less drastic ways for individuals to influence organizations. For instance, many firms are now using blogs to provide a forum where employees can express themselves critically and independently.[16] Many other channels for the transmission of information and suggestions have been tried: hotlines, open forums, mediators, suggestion boxes, etc. For a long time, firms relied on hierarchical, authoritarian management structures, very different from the representative procedures found in the political sphere, but lately they, too, have begun to make room for indirect forms of power. They do this not because they have found virtue but in response to employee pressures and, still more, to the requirements of the market.

---

[15] Gerald Vinten, ed., *Whistleblowing: Subversion or Corporate Citizenship?* (New York: St Martin's Press, 1994).

[16] See Frédérique Roussel, "Quand l'employé fait blog," *Libération*, June 6, 2005.

The market, or the triumph of the veto

Let us continue to explore the parallel between the economic and the political spheres, but now in regard to preventive powers. An analogy is often drawn between consumers and voters: consumers "choose" products just as voters "choose" representatives (and there is an immense literature on the subject). The comparison of the two types of revealed preference and two modes of decision-making has given rise to a key distinction between *markets* and *forums*. Important work has been done on different forms of rationality, including "limited rationality," with Jon Elster playing a pioneering role in this area. Perhaps not enough attention has been paid to one important feature of markets, however: namely, the fact that they are defined by negative interventions. Financial markets offer a striking illustration of this point. It is useful to think of their operation in terms of Albert Hirschman's distinction between "exit" and "voice."[17] Both types of intervention exist in both the political and social realms. Voting itself mixes the elements, combining rejections with aspirations and linking positive and negative sovereignty, to use categories that were introduced earlier. Markets are different: exit is uniformly more important than voice in their operation.[18] In markets there is constant arbitrage between trust and distrust, with priority going to the latter. In conditions of uncertainty, distrust always takes precedence. Because of this asymmetry,

---

[17] Albert O. Hirschman, *Exit, Voice and Loyalty* (Cambridge, MA: Harvard University Press, 1970).

[18] See Mathias Emmerich, "Le marché sans mythes," *Revue de l'OFCE*, no. 57 (April 1996).

most market decisions are driven by negative judgment: in the final analysis, the decision to sell securities is what structures the market.

If the market is the mature expression of a type of negative sovereignty, it is also because negative sovereignty manifests itself in a dispersed, decentralized way, with no need for any *a priori* formalization or aggregation. The market is in a sense the embodiment of prevailing opinion, including the most negative forms of opinion, such as rumor. It is a world in which organized representation has no place, and it is in this sense that market coordination can be likened to an invisible hand. Because its mode of regulation is doubly indirect, many current critiques of the market are problematic. As described above, the market is merely one manifestation – an eminently emblematic manifestation, to be sure – of the phenomenon of decentralized decision-making. The obsession of some market critics with "the horrors of neo-liberalism" thus masks the underlying nature and true scope of the problems raised by "the unpolitical" in today's world. The critics reduce the whole issue to what they take to be an obvious and palpable opposition between political will and laissez-faire economics and between the general interest and particular interests, when what is really at stake is the very notion of the political as it relates to democracy. The market is more the *sign* than the cause of the unpolitical. It is not so much a great hidden power hovering over society and imposing its "will" as the mechanical vector of an anonymous and absolutely negative power that binds everyone yet no one can appropriate. The market is in a sense an acute symptom of negative involvement, the absolutized figure of "civil" democracy, and therefore the most radical example of the separation of the democratic from the political. The "crisis of generality" in today's society is primarily political in nature.

"Unpolitical" economy

These brief remarks suggest the possibility of comparing indirect forms of democracy to a whole range of mechanisms and behaviors that one finds at work in the economic sphere. Indeed, in the economic realm, oversight, evaluation, and auditing are more formalized than any of the watchdog powers we described in the political realm, so one might say that counter-democracy is in this sense more fully developed in the economic than in the political sphere. But it is equally striking to find that "institutionalized" forms of democracy are simultaneously on the decline in the economic realm. For example, the power of trade unions has been severely eroded, and representative principles are less and less evident in the governance of business firms. There has been a dramatic shift away from the image of "progress" as it was conceived in the 1920s. At that time people believed that the mechanisms of representative democracy constituted a prototype for all modern organizations and therefore that those mechanisms would tend to spread beyond the sphere of politics.[19] Reformers took up the great theme of "industrial democracy," which would

[19] Recall that Sieyès had the same intuition as long ago as 1789, when he argued that the division of labor, which he saw as an instance of the representative principle, would eventually extend to all spheres of social life: "In the social state, everything is representation ... The separation of labors belongs to political works as it does to all types of productive labor."

285

occupy them for decades. In France in the 1960s, François Bloch-Lainé, backed by the unions, called for industrial firms to be run by elected leaders answerable to an assembly representing workers, consumers, and stockholders.[20] The German model of "codetermination" (*Mitbestimmung*) derived from a similar line of thought. In the late 1960s, the term *autogestion* (self-management) gave these ideas a new and more radical currency by linking them to new demands for more direct worker involvement in the management of organizations. In all of these instances, the idea was to transfer democratic institutions, which enjoyed a positive image, into various non-political spheres of social life. An old slogan from the nineteenth century – "you can't have a republic in society when you have monarchy in the firm" – remained topical as an indication of the path to follow.

In retrospect, it is clear that this movement culminated in failure. The 1980s marked a definitive turning point. What we have seen since then is not a generalization of the classic representative model but a multiplication of indirect forms of power *in all areas*. And no one seems unhappy about this. For example, no one today would think seriously of defending a proposal to elect a firm's executives as a way of promoting the common good. The idea of nationalizing firms, which was associated in a somewhat different way with the idea of "good governance," has also faded for similar reasons. What has taken its place is a *de facto* consensus in favor of a

Quoted in my *La Démocratie inachevée: Histoire de la souveraineté du peuple en France* (Paris: Gallimard, 2000), p. 13.

[20] François Bloch-Lainé, *Pour une réforme de l'entreprise* (Paris: Éditions du Seuil, 1963).

range of corporate control mechanisms. Powers of oversight and prevention have proliferated. To make clear what I mean, consider the following. In the 1960s, many people thought that the future of economic regulation lay in flexible planning as a substitute for the market. Now, however, reform is seen mainly in terms of increased powers of control.[21] In this new world of "opinion-dominated capitalism," executives are more vulnerable than they were when unions wielded great power inside the firm. What is the significance of this development? For one thing, ideas of legitimacy and efficiency have changed. Many people now believe that they, and society as a whole, can achieve greater influence over the course of events by exercising power indirectly. They also believe that indirect powers are vested in institutions that are impartial and therefore qualified to judge.

As suggestive as the comparison of the economic and political spheres is, we must be careful not to draw naïve and hasty conclusions. A series of financial scandals (Enron, WorldCom, etc.) in the first decade of the twenty-first century demonstrated that evaluation, auditing, and oversight were vulnerable to error and far from adequate safeguards. The age-old question remained: "Who will oversee the overseers?"[22] The problems that indirect powers have faced in the economic sphere give us reason to take a fresh look at their equivalents in the political sphere. It is clear, moreover, that

[21] For a typical example of thinking at that time, see Andrew Shonfield, *Modern Capitalism: the Changing Balance of Public and Private Power* (Oxford University Press, 1965).

[22] Catherine Gerst and Denis Groven, *To B or not to B: Le Pouvoir des agences de notation en question* (Paris: Village Mondial, 2004).

certain indirect political powers, most notably those exercised by the media and judges, have been subject to vigorous challenge, though of course there is nothing in politics to compare with a market recession or crash.

Our comparative approach can be pursued still further. The development of indirect powers in the economic sphere offers a striking illustration of the fact that the "democratization" movement need not have any political dimension at all. Indeed, what we see in the economic sphere is a radicalization of the "unpolitical" character of counter-democratic powers. A good example of this can be seen in the obsessive idealization of the principle of transparency. In economics, transparency truly deserves its name: it describes a project of perfect visibility, a total absence of market frictions, which is to say a utopian form of the market. What oversight and evaluation powers are meant to accomplish is explicitly to introduce the reign of the invisible hand, which is the extreme opposite of politics.[23] Economics is "unpolitical" in a still broader sense: it is possible to imagine an economy of firms and markets ever more closely regulated, controlled, and monitored without ever touching on the political side of the economy, namely, the issue of how wealth is distributed. Indeed, it is striking to observe that the gap between the return to capital and the return to labor, as well as between the compensation of management and the compensation of ordinary workers, widened at the very same time that control and regulation of firms was broadened and extended. It is thus possible for capitalism to be

[23] See Pierre Rosanvallon, *Le Capitalisme utopique: Histoire de l'idée de marché*, new edn (Paris: Éditions du Seuil, 1990).

both more closely regulated and more unjust, both more transparent and more inegalitarian. The difference between liberal control and democratic control, which was discussed in previous chapters, once again needs to be underscored. The economic analogy can thus serve as a magnifying mirror, and it is particularly useful for gaining a better understanding of the nature and effects of counter-democratic powers as well as for focusing attention on the problems of the "unpolitical."

14

Conclusion: the modern mixed regime

Our exploration of the counter-democratic universe has shown that we need to reconsider familiar ideas about the retreat of citizens from the public sphere and withdrawal into private life. It has also encouraged us to take a broad view of the problems and dysfunctions of contemporary democracies and to look at dimensions other than the electoral-representative. In particular, we have seen a contrast between the development of counter-democratic *forms* and the demise of certain political *functions*. What is needed is a new and more complex description of the context in which democratic politics takes place. We have identified three dimensions of democracy, each with its own distinctive characteristics: electoral-representative government, counter-democratic activity, and the institution of civil society by the political (*le travail du politique*). Of these, the first has been studied most frequently and carefully, with an emphasis on the various principles and procedures that govern citizen participation, expression, and representation, along with the legitimation of authority and the various mechanisms by which government is made both responsible and responsive to society. The second dimension of democracy, the counter-democratic, is the subject of this book. It includes a range of practices (which I have categorized as oversight, prevention, and judgment) by which society exerts pressure on its rulers. Counter-democratic practices give rise to informal, parallel forms of authority, or corrective powers (exercised directly in some cases and through ad hoc institutions in others). The third dimension of democracy, theoretical political practice, involves reflective and deliberative activity aimed at elaborating the rules that define a shared world: the definition of principles of justice, arbitration between the interests of various groups, delineation of the relationship between public and private. The development of this third dimension is linked to a demand for a political system whose structure is both visible and comprehensible. These three dimensions serve not only to clarify the analysis of democracy but also to explore the conditions necessary for democratic progress.

New paths of electoral-representative democracy

Electoral-representative democracy is shaped by certain internal tensions. First, there is a tension between suffrage as belonging (that is, inclusion in a political community on essentially egalitarian grounds) and suffrage as a means to governing (access to shared sovereignty, in which the question of the relative competence of individuals remains unresolved). The waxing and waning of this tension between "number" and "reason" has left its mark on the history of universal suffrage, a history that of course also reflects the advent of the "sovereign individual" in modern society. Democratic representation raises a series of fundamental questions. How can the gap between the abstract unity of a sovereign defined by terms such as "people" and "nation" and the actual diversity of social conditions be bridged? How

291

can the "people-as-principle" be made to coincide with the "people-as-society"? How can this abstract sovereign be given form and countenance when represented in an assembly? The whole problem of democratic representation lies in the gap between a political principle – the affirmation of the supremacy of the general will – and a sociological reality. In democracy, the people are an imperious but elusive master. By bestowing sacred status on the will as opposed to the order of nature or history, modern politics entrusted power to the people at a moment when the people's project of emancipation had abolished the old society of orders and corps and thus given rise to a social abstraction. A contradiction thus emerged between the *political principle* of democracy and the *sociological principle*: the political principle consecrated the power of a collective subject whose solidity the sociological principle tended to dissolve and whose visibility it tended to reduce. Indeed, the very notion of popular sovereignty contains yet another source of tension: the idea of representative government has always suffered from a certain ambiguity. At the time of the French and American Revolutions, some observers believed that representative government was fully compatible with the democratic spirit. They viewed it as a mere procedural prop, a "technical" substitute for direct democracy, since the latter was a pragmatic impossibility in a large country. "Representative democracy" was the description applied to this technical surrogate for direct democracy. But others understood representative government as an *alternative* to democracy, which they viewed as dangerous. For many of the framers of the French and American constitutions, the goal was to use representative government to establish a sort of elective aristocracy. Representative government then defined itself *in opposition* to democracy, as a regime of a new type to be added to the classical repertoire.

Subsequent to the age of revolution when democratic regimes were first established, the tensions described above gave rise to a sense of incompletion or even betrayal. Theorists have long argued that such feelings were a consequence of impatience and unsatisfied expectations, which needed to be tamped down if society was to steer a moderate political course. From Madison and Sieyès to contemporary liberal and conservative theorists of democratic realism, a long line of political thinkers has extolled the benefits of modest, temperate government aimed at reducing social dissatisfactions. Intellectual caution coupled with suspicion of mass politics tended to narrow what many saw as the limits of political possibility. In the twentieth century, the threat of totalitarianism encouraged even greater caution and a desire to limit expectations still further. As a result, the democratic ideal has in many cases been pared down to little more than the wish to establish a government capable of defending the liberty of its citizens – a far cry from the old ambition of genuine popular sovereignty. From Kelsen to Schumpeter, a whole series of twentieth-century theorists built theories around the modesty of their aspirations. They sought to substitute a purely procedural definition of political legitimacy for the old metaphysical idea of an active people in command of its own destiny. Lucid though these thinkers were about the abysses lining a road to utopia crowded with legions of the impatient, the desire to find ways of achieving a more effective self-government and a more representative regime inevitably resurfaced. Over the past two centuries, theorists have conceived countless constitutional schemes, and political activists have tirelessly sought new forms of participation. This history continues, as attested by experiments in many countries with ways to enhance citizen participation and improve representation (by such means as barring politicians from holding more than one office at a time, setting term limits, establishing voting procedures, taking direct democratic initiatives, and delegating authority). Constitutional debate, the nature of which varies from country to country, is often vigorous, a sign of the high expectations attached to reforms of this kind.

Increased citizen involvement in decisions affecting people's lives has been a prominent feature of democratic evolution in recent years. Since the 1980s, the term "participatory democracy" has been used to describe a fairly wide range of experiences and practices. Take, for example, the procedures by which the city of Porto Alegre elaborated its well-known "participatory budget." These have little in common with the far more modest forms of participation that one finds in neighborhood associations in other cities around the world. Nevertheless, there has been a general move toward greater public discussion and citizen involvement in the process of governing. In France, numerous measures to promote participation have been adopted since 1990. For instance, a 1999 regional development law mandated the formation of regional development councils including representatives of interested associations. In 2002, another law mandated the organization of neighborhood councils in all cities of more than 80,000 people. The use of public surveys has been extended and broadened.[1] A National Commission of Public Debate was set up in 1995 to enable environmental organizations to "participate in environmental action by government agencies." The status of this commission was later raised to that of "independent authority" under a law of February 27, 2002 significantly entitled "democracy of proximity." At the regional level, numerous "workshops," "assemblies," and "forums" were organized for the purpose of bringing policy-makers and citizens together. At the same time, work in the social sciences led to experiments with consensus-building through conferences, forums, citizen juries, and "deliberative polling."[2] We find similar institutions and practices in many countries at one stage or another of development today. The idea of participatory democracy was honored in particular in the proposed Constitutional Treaty of the European Union (2004). The treaty explicitly distinguished between participatory democracy and representative democracy. The former was defined as "open, transparent, and regular dialogue with representative associations of civil society" (article I.47). The rise of these new democratic forms has unleashed a torrent of publications attempting to define the contours of a new, post-representative

---

[1] See Marie-Hélène Bacqué, Henry Rey, and Yves Sintomer, *Gestion de proximité et démocratie participative: Une perspective comparative* (Paris: La Découverte, 2005), and "Alter-démocratie, alter-économie," *Revue du MAUSS*, no. 26, 2nd semester, 2005.

[2] Michel Callon, Pierre Lascoumes, and Yannick Barthe, *Agir dans un monde incertain. Essai sur la démocratie technique* (Paris: Éditions du Seuil, 2001), and Dominique Bourg and Daniel Boy, *Conférences de citoyens, mode d'emploi* (Paris: Descartes et Cie, 2005).

age, a democracy that would attempt to give flesh to the ideal of a living city.[3]

There are many reasons for this surge of interest in participatory democracy. For one thing, there is social demand for it. Citizens are less and less willing simply to cast their votes and give a blank check to their elected representatives. They want their opinions and interests to be taken into account in a more concrete and persistent way. To shore up their own legitimacy, the powers-that-be look for new ways to exchange views and consult with their constituents. No government is seen as legitimate unless it is prepared to debate and justify its policies. Participation has also become indispensable as an efficient means of administration and problem-solving. The idea of an omniscient state capable of governing rationally from above is now seen as utopian and no longer credible. Decentralization was initially introduced as an administrative necessity: efficiency required hands-on management involving people at the base who were in possession of information not available from any other source. Participatory democracy grew out of this necessity. It was a response to an increased demand for modern forms of governance. In this sense, participation was *functional*. It pertained mainly to local issues. It was also a discreetly depoliticized form of democracy, although its pro-paedeutic and pedagogical aspects could not be denied.[4]

---

[3] See the work of Benjamin Barber, Joshua Cohen, and Carole Pateman.

[4] Clearly, one should distinguish between countries. In Latin America, for example, grass-roots associations and movements were more politicized, since they had to cope with a deficit of state and public institutions (not to mention the fact that many existing institutions dated from a time of dictatorship, when political expression was impossible).

Participation should therefore not be treated as sacrosanct, or as a simple and comprehensive solution to all the problems of democracy. Note, too, that the rise of participatory democracy is closely related to the growth of associations at the local level, resulting in what has been called a "descent toward the local." One scholar who has observed the decline of large national associations and the rise of advocacy groups and other local civil-society associations in the United States has gone so far as to describe the result as "diminished democracy."[5]

The deliberative democracy movement that rose to prominence in the 1990s implicitly acknowledged the limits of participation and proposed a more "qualitative" approach in its stead.[6] It promoted rational discussion, reasoned argument, and citizen forums. From Jürgen Habermas to Bernard Manin, Joshua Cohen, and Jon Elster, many theorists tried to formalize a more procedural approach to democracy built around the idea of a deliberating people.[7] In a whole series of works, theorists attempted to explain how it might be possible to create a better informed, more rational, and more active citizenry. Some proposed combining the ritual of the ballot box

---

[5] Theda Skocpol, *Diminished Democracy: From Membership to Management in American Civic Life* (Norman: University of Oklahoma Press, 2003).

[6] This development has been described as the "deliberative turn."

[7] Work of this sort in the United States stemmed in part from a desire to overcome the narrow focus of rational choice theories, which viewed politics as a mere arithmetic aggregate of interests. On this point see Bernard Manin, "L'idée de démocratie délibérative dans la science politique contemporaine," *Politix*, no. 57 (2002).

with more deliberative activities.[8] There is now a solid literature on the subject. It has added to our understanding of the dynamics of debate, shown how to make deliberation more effective, and explored various ways of bringing a discussion to a conclusion. At the same time, the limits of this approach became clear, and certain problems came into clearer focus. In particular, it was found that in discussion opinions often become polarized, which came as a surprise to theorists who had initially been smitten by the intrinsic virtues of debate.[9] Attention was also drawn to the bias that could be introduced by a consensual as opposed to conflictual conception of democracy. Finally, the risk of underestimating the inequality of the resources available to different groups for participating in collective deliberation was underscored.[10] Without minimizing the importance of recent reflection on and experience with participation and deliberation, we would therefore do well to broaden our horizon in thinking about the possibility of democratic renewal. At the present time one task seems

[8] See the idea of "deliberation day," a national holiday proposed by Bruce Ackerman and James S. Fishkin in *Deliberation Day* (New Haven: Yale University Press, 2004).

[9] It has been shown that discussion often hardens opposition between groups rather than lead to the adoption of a middle-of-the-road proposal. See Cass R. Sunstein, "The Law of Group Polarization," *The Journal of Political Philosophy* 10, no. 2 (June 2002).

[10] See, for example, the remarks of Lynn Sanders, "Against Deliberation," *Political Theory* 25, no. 3 (June 1997). Note, too, the radical opposition of decisionist theorists to the deliberative principle: from Donoso Cortès to Carl Schmitt, they have consistently attacked deliberation as a practice that tends to undermine decisive action and drain the meaning from the antagonisms that they see as constituting the very essence of politics.

essential: counter-democratic powers need to be better organized. There are two reasons for this. First, the risk that counter-democracy will degenerate into a destructive and reductive form of populism needs to be reduced. Second, we need an authentic new understanding of the true nature of politics. Ideas are in short supply, and fresh inspiration is needed.

Consolidating counter-democracy

Historically, counter-democratic powers emerged in haphazard fashion, without any overall focus. They first arose in reaction to certain shortcomings of electoral-representative government. In the eighteenth century, ad hoc counter-democratic institutions were created, but it proved difficult to incorporate such institutions into constitutional governments. As a result, counter-democratic powers suffer from structural instability; the significance of their activity is prone to a certain slippage. It is therefore worth revisiting the question of how they might be given constitutional form. Earlier, we saw how experiments such as the Pennsylvania Council of Censors and the French Tribunate ended in failure. In both cases, the problem lay in the impossibility of creating a "pure institution," narrowly focused on its function and absolutely untouched by politics. This impossibility was structural and not simply circumstantial. Indeed, the idea of purely functional institution turns out to be difficult to sustain in practice. If it were otherwise, goodness, justice, and the general interest would not be such elusive goals. In short, there is no reason to believe that a degree of generality that cannot be achieved through the usual mechanisms of representative government can be attained by the exercise of counter-democratic power. Now, it is by multiplying different forms of representation and sovereignty that democratic institutions are perfected. Hence by the same token, it seems unlikely that counter-democratic powers can be perfected without creating new institutional forms through which they can express themselves. No one can claim to embody the will of the people or speak authoritatively in their name. Similarly, no one can claim to be the sole expression of the people's criticisms and discontents: no person, institution, or group can monopolize this role. Yet some ad hoc institutions do claim such a monopoly, on idealist grounds in some cases, on perverse and partisan grounds in others (populists, for instance, claim that they, and not the discredited powers-that-be, are the "real" incarnation of the people). Counter-democracy is therefore unstable and needs to be closely monitored.

The counter-democratic function must be pluralistic, but its pluralism must find embodiment at different organizational levels, corresponding to different approximations to social generality (ranging from nebulous public opinion to more structured, quasi-representative forms such as those involved in the exercise of what I am calling the power of judgment). If the counter-democratic function is to be firmed up, special attention must be paid to the way in which it is structured at intermediate levels. Between the purely informal power of opinion or militant activism and the strictly constitutional institution there remains a vast area, still largely unexplored. New research, at once theoretical and practical, will be required, and it is beyond the scope of this book to say what needs to be done. But since the book brings us to this threshold, perhaps it is worth taking a moment to open the door just a little. Let us first consider the various types of oversight power. Five types exist today: parliamentary oversight of the executive, combined with investigative powers; public opinion, which is polarized and expressed in a diffuse way through the media; critical intervention by opposition parties; social movements and citizen organizations; and ad hoc democratic institutions. One could use this typology to compare the status of the various types of oversight in different countries and to trace the historical evolution of different political systems.

The range of variation is considerable. As we have seen, certain oversight functions came to be associated with parliament in the nineteenth century, while efforts to establish ad hoc institutions were abandoned after a period of experimentation. Comparison of the present-day role of parliament and current vitality of civil society in different countries would reveal strong contrasts. Yet one would also find strong cross-country parallels. For instance, the Internet revolution has encouraged a tendency toward "privatization" and segmentation of public opinion. As social expression has become increasingly personalized, our perception of the way in which opinion operates as an oversight mechanism has changed. The increasing "democratization" of oversight has encouraged what I have called "unpolitical" attitudes in today's society. The oversight role once ascribed to political parties has simultaneously decreased, with party organizations more and more confined to their role in the mechanics of electoral-representative government.[11] As a

---

[11] The discrediting of political parties is to be understood in these terms, in my view. Its causes are first of all functional: the dissemination and social

result, *nonpartisan* activist organizations are playing a growing role in developing new types of oversight. It is possible, for example, to imagine the organization of *citizen evaluation boards*, whose role would be to judge the actions of certain government agencies. *Citizen watchdog groups* might be established to draw public attention to emerging issues or worrisome trends. Initiatives along these lines have already been taken in regard to issues such as inequality and social segregation. There can be no doubt that democratic progress will depend in part on the mobilization of citizen expertise and direct access to information at the grass roots. But more institutionalized forms of oversight will also need to be considered. There are many avenues to explore. One can even imagine choosing citizens at random to sit on investigative bodies of one sort or another. A range of independent public authorities might be established this way (think, for example, of anti-discrimination commissions and police review boards, which already exist in the United States and France). In any number of forms, counter-democratic surveillance might thus become one pillar of a more active and participatory citizenry.

As I have been at pains to argue, preventive power eventually came to define a negative sovereignty whose dominant characteristics often seemed reactive and destructive. This was the most powerful driving force behind the populist aberration. Yet history suggests that preventive powers can be used in other ways and to other ends. To foster more positive

reappropriation of forms of opposition and control. But it also has to do with the ambiguous position of parties, which occupy a place somewhere between the electoral-representative field and the counter-democratic field.

developments in this direction, we need to look back to the origins of these powers: the intent was to establish forms of criticism and monitoring that would allow political institutions to operate on different time scales. Preventive power involves pluralistic forms of sovereignty in which elections are not the sole source of legitimacy. Judicial review of constitutionality is the most obvious form of institutionalized preventive power. It depends on a hierarchical ordering of the power to interpret the law. The granting to the executive of the power to dissolve parliament is another potent form of preventive power. This, too, is a way of putting the majority to the test: when the bond between social legitimacy and electoral legitimacy is stretched too far, dissolution becomes a way of realigning the two sources of legitimacy. Parliamentary censure of actions by the executive is the mirror image of this type of sanction.

Dissolution and censure are not simple acts of obstruction without coherent purpose. More needs to be done if this "protest dimension" of counter-democracy is to become a useful resource. Can legal powers of prevention be socialized? This was the idea behind the various types of "censorate" that were envisioned toward the end of the eighteenth century. The concept of divided legitimacy that such systems embodied can also be seen at work in procedures designed to disrupt the regular calendar by which political institutions normally operate. Yet these procedures often seem divorced from the concerns of ordinary citizens. How can this flaw be repaired? By electing constitutional judges? During the French Revolution, proposals of this sort were common. Election may not be the most satisfactory solution,

303

however: elections create a strong bond between voters and officials, but the interest it arouses is short-lived and not very deep. A better approach is to impose a *permanent* requirement that the authorities wielding preventive power carefully explain and justify their decisions to the public at large. At the moment, a French president who decides to dissolve parliament is not required to explain his action at all. In many countries, constitutional courts do not have to justify their decisions. The lack of detailed explanation alienates citizens from authorities whose decisions seem peremptory and arbitrary. By contrast, a carefully reasoned argument encourages thoughtful reflection and establishes a strong bond between citizens and authority, while implicitly recognizing the existence of an obligation. Power is obliged to descend from its pedestal and justify its actions. Here, the exercise of counter-democratic power is enhanced not by institutionalization but by pragmatic pedagogy.

Other modes of institutionalization and other ways of exercising preventive power might also be envisioned: for example, one might think of ways to halt governmental action deemed dangerous for one reason or another. A lawsuit might be filed in court, for instance, eventually leading to a special kind of *decision*, a judicial order. In that case, preventive power would still be exercised by an intermediary, namely, the court. Can it be exercised directly? In exceptional circumstances, yes: this is the ultimate significance of social insurrection as well as resistance by isolated individuals. *Normally*, however, preventive power is always delegated. It becomes truly social only when it accepts the obligation to justify itself or render an account of its actions. The structure of preventive power invariably reflects an a priori deconstruction of the political system's normal calendar. In essence, it takes the form of a suspensive veto: democracy puts itself to the test, introducing new agents into the process and operating on a timetable different from that of the normal electoral and legislative calendar. Counter-democratic power broadens our understanding of representation beyond the electoral sphere. It becomes a part of the structure of indirection that is built into representative democracy.[12]

Our third form of counter-democratic power is the power of judgment, which is seldom exercised directly (popular juries sometimes wield this power directly, but seldom in cases without political implications). When the people act as judges, it is usually more a matter of regulating morals or shoring up the social bond than of intervening in the public sphere. As we have seen, however, this is not always the case: in the nineteenth century, cases involving the press, which were intimately intertwined with public debate, were tried by jury. Toward the end of the nineteenth century, the administration of justice in many countries was professionalized. Perhaps the time has come to turn this around. Cases of corruption or misappropriation of public monies might be submitted to juries in order to underscore the gravity of offenses that tend to undermine democratic political systems. In most such cases, however, justice is rendered by judges *in the name of the people*, judges acting as representatives of the community. This representative dimension could be strengthened, but

---

[12] On this point, see my *La Démocratie inachevée: Histoire de la souveraineté du peuple en France* (Paris: Gallimard, 2000), p. 410.

305

once again election might not be the best way to do this. Better results might be obtained by requiring judges to explain their decisions in detail. In this way, judicial decisions are transformed into careful articulations of the public interest. Reasoned judicial argument is more apt than periodic election of judges to socialize the judicial function, because the obligation to justify decisions is permanent rather than sporadic.[13] Once again, counter-democratic powers could be reinforced this way without increasing the risk of a swerve toward populism. Yet the various modifications that have been discussed thus far cannot by themselves compensate for the tendency toward depoliticization (what I have called "the unpolitical"). A way must be found to restore the political function as such.

Repoliticizing democracy

Counter-democracy has its dark side: the unpolitical. This depoliticization has given rise to a vague but persistent feeling of malaise, which paradoxically has grown even as civil society has become more active, better informed, and more capable of intervening in political decisions than ever before. The solution to this problem has to begin by restoring a vision of a common world, a sense that it is possible to overcome fragmentation and disintegration. A sense of helplessness has reinforced the notion of a crisis of meaning and vice versa. The problem today is an absence of meaning rather than an

[13] On this important point, see the essays collected in Chaïm Perelman and Paul Foriers, *La Motivation des décisions de justice* (Brussels: Émile Bruylant, 1978).

absence of will. There is no magic formula for breaking this vicious circle, no simple reform to be implemented, no saving institution to be designed. What is lacking is reflexive social action: action by society on itself. *Democracy is defined by its works*, and not simply by its institutions. It involves a whole range of conflicts and negotiations, a whole set of interpretations of the rules that govern collective life. It also involves the production of a language adequate to our social experience, a language capable of describing social life and therefore of influencing it. These "democratic works," which define the way in which democracy institutes society, can be grouped under three heads: the production of a legible world, the symbolization of collective power, and the testing of social differences.

The production of a legible world: the very definition of political action depends on legibility, which marks the dividing line between mere technical administration and the art of governing. To govern is not simply to solve problems of organization, allocate resources rationally, or set forth a sequential plan of action. To govern means to make the world intelligible, to provide citizens with analytic and interpretive tools to help them make decisions and act effectively. Politics in this sense is fundamentally *cognitive* in nature – a point that needs to be strongly emphasized. Politics *produces* political society (*la cité*) by helping it to represent itself, by obliging it always to face up to its responsibilities, and by enabling it to confront in a clear-sighted way whatever issues need to be resolved. This idea of *active* power is quite different from the idea that power is merely to be drawn passively from society and faithfully reflect its structure. The goal of active power is rather to reveal society to itself, to give meaning and form to a world in which individuals find it increasingly difficult to orient themselves. In this respect, the goals and methods of political action and social science overlap. What the two have in common is the search for ways to overcome the inability of individuals today to see themselves as members of a collectivity; finding one's place in a legible, visible totality has become problematic.[14] It takes work to develop an objective representation of the world in which political subjects can recognize themselves and act accordingly. The work of John Dewey offers a brilliant example of how such concerns can be accommodated. Dewey encourages us to ask why a gap has opened up between the expert and the citizen.[15] Lucidity and liberty, consciousness of constraints and determination to act – these can be linked in a positive way, so as to overcome the fatal alternation between courage fed by illusions and cynical calculation. Here, then, is yet another way of approaching the question of political will. Indeed, the will does not begin with the subject as something to be projected onto and deployed within the external world; it is rather active self-consciousness. Cornelius Castoriadis offers this illuminating comment: "In

---

[14] The history of this dilemma has much in common with the history of sociology, with the various "sociological genres" reflecting different stages and goals of research. The contrasting methodologies of Durkheim and Tarde and, later, of Durkheim and Simmel offer one framework in which to approach this problem.

[15] See Robert B. Westbrook, *John Dewey and Democracy* (Ithaca: Cornell University Press, 1991). Although Dewey's optimistic view of the role of social science is debatable, his overall approach remains essential, in my view.

the realm of action, I act upon myself, for that is what will is: to act upon oneself as activating activity, to reflect upon myself as activity, to will myself or will something with knowledge of what I am trying to accomplish."[16] Kierkegaard earlier voiced a similar sentiment: "The more there is of will, the more there is of oneself."[17] With this we come to the heart of a properly philosophical definition of the citizen as political animal: the citizen has the peculiarity of being both actor and spectator of the political, both subject and object. Hence the goal of democracy is both to make the construction of a common history possible and to delineate a horizon of meaning: it is to end in one movement both man's blindness and his helplessness. Sovereignty is not only the exercise of some power; it is also mastery over oneself and comprehension of the world.

Benjamin Constant, in one of his most famous and often-cited texts, opposed the liberty of the ancients and that of the moderns, the sense of direct citizen involvement stemming from the feeling of belonging to a community as opposed to the autonomy of an individual primarily absorbed in personal preoccupations. For Constant, however, this distinction did not coincide in any simple way with the distinction between public and private, or collective and individual. The difference between the ancient and the modern, he noted, was also a question of a *difference of perception* as to the effectiveness of political action. In Antiquity, Constant observed, "each person's share of national sovereignty was not an abstract

---

[16] Cornelius Castoriadis, *Sujet et vérité dans le monde social-historique* (Paris: Éditions du Seuil, 2002), p. 111.

[17] Quoted in France Farago, *La Volonté* (Paris: Armand Colin, 2002), p. 14.

hypothesis, as it is today. The will of each individual had real influence. The exercise of that will was an intense and repeated pleasure."[18] In the modern world, by contrast, this "compensation" has disappeared: "Lost in the multitude, the individual almost never perceives the influence he exercises. His will never leaves its mark on the whole. He sees no tangible evidence of his cooperation."[19] Constant concludes that "we have lost in imagination what we have gained in knowledge."[20] The whole problem of democratic politics lies here: it cannot substantively exist without effort to make the organizing mechanisms of social life *visible*. This visibility can no longer be taken for granted in either a sociological or a symbolic sense. A society of individuals must construct its own sociological self-representation with the help of both political vision and intellectual elaboration. Neither the people nor the nation can claim palpable existence today. As for symbolism, democratic power also seems to have disappeared, or at any rate to have proclaimed its modesty as a sort of refuge. The monarchies of old were often weak states, or in any event states much less developed than those we have today (Montaigne said that, in his day, a gentleman encountered the state no more than two or three times in the course of a lifetime).[21] Yet the powers-that-be knew how to display themselves

---

[18] Benjamin Constant, *De la liberté des anciens comparée à celle des modernes* (1819), in *Cours de politique constitutionnelle ou collection des ouvrages publiés sur le gouvernement représentatif par Benjamin Constant*, 2nd edn (Paris, 1872), vol. II, p. 547.

[19] *Ibid.*

[20] Benjamin Constant, *De l'esprit de conquête et de l'usurpation* (1814), in *Cours de politique constitutionnelle*, vol. II, p. 207.

[21] Montaigne, *Essais*, book I, chap. 42.

with pomp and circumstance. They took extreme care to culti-
vate appearances, to stage their own magnificence. Power
sought to impose itself, and impress its subjects, by asserting
its authority intermittently while maintaining a permanent
capacity to represent that authority. It thus combined the
"strings of necessity" with the "strings of imagination," to borrow the terms of Pascal's *Pensées*.[22]

Where in today's society can we find the equivalent of
this almost theatrical dimension of politics? There is no denying the fact that we have not yet succeeded in overcoming the
effect that the introduction of democratic order had on the
relation between the visible and the invisible. Faced with this
difficulty, some have called for a more active celebration of
memory, for the enthusiastic preservation of a grand national
narrative, which would use the supposed glory of the past as an
intellectual prop to shore up the present.[23] Alongside these
artificial efforts to resurrect the grandeur of the past, new fears

[22] See the interesting commentary by Joël Cornette in *La Monarchie entre
Renaissance et Révolution, 1515–1792* (Paris: Éditions du Seuil, 2000),
pp. 195–199. On compensating the actual weakness of the old-regime state
with visible action ("spectacular tortures") and careful staging of power
(drums, uniforms, monuments), see Cornette, *Le Roi de guerre: Essai sur
la souveraineté dans la France du grand siècle* (Paris: Payot, 1993), and
Peter Burke, *The Fabrication of Louis XIV* (New Haven: Yale University
Press, 1992). On the juridical and symbolic construction of power as
majesty, see Yan Thomas, "L'Institution de la majesté," and Gérard
Sabatier, "Les rois de représentation. Image et pouvoir (XVIe–XVIIe
siècle)," *Revue de synthèse*, nos. 3–4 (July–Dec. 1991).

[23] This observation explains why a permanent tension exists between the
temptation to idealize memory, or the nostalgia for glory, and another
major modern movement, driven by concern for human rights and
compassion for history's victims.

are repeatedly invoked, as if to conceal the emptiness of every-day life behind a screen of somber terrors and vague imaginings. Decisionist theorists have made a much-discussed comeback in this context. They bring with them a nostalgia for directly perceptible sovereign will and a reverence for emergency sit-uations grave enough to simplify the problem of deciding on a course of action. With a passion for the past or the perverse, some look to the heroes and thinkers of another era – to the legend of Charles de Gaulle or the work of Carl Schmitt – for answers to the political shortcomings of contemporary society. How can a necessary symbolism be restored to politics without recourse to such dubious medicines? How can sovereignty be made visible and palpable without idealizing the old metaphy-sics of the will? How can a measure of theatricality be restored to collective power without draping it in somewhat tattered ancient costume? Only by working to bring about a transfigura-tion of reality. If politics is to be made more visible, we need to remind ourselves constantly of the purpose it is meant to accomplish: to take a people that is nowhere to be found and transform it into a vibrant political community. Symbolization is collective reflection. It is reaffirmation of the decision to write a common history. It is a clear and sober narrative of the failures and hopes that constitute that enterprise. It is the history and memory of the struggles of men and women to institute a society of equals, despite all the difficulties.

The resymbolization of the political is thus part of a permanent questioning of social differences. The goal is to define a community in terms of rules of redistributive justice, principles for expanding the limits of possibility, and clearly delineated norms governing the relation between the individual and the community. Conflict is inevitable in such a project, because debate brings to light the actual transfer of resources that takes place among individuals, groups, and regions, reveals hidden legacies of the past, and discloses implicit regulations. Such a debate has nothing in common with the calm, almost technical kind of discussion envisioned by certain theorists of deliberative democracy. However difficult the exercise, it is nevertheless essential as a way of gaining *practical experience of the general will.* It is a way of ensuring that generalization is not just a deceptive ideal or pious wish but the result of a series of arbitrages and compromises as well as a decisive choice as to the nature of the social bond. The choices to be made involve such things as old-age insurance and the bond between generations; questions of social and occupational security; the allocation of taxes; the measurement and indemnification of unemployment; and issues of long-term development. These practices must, of course, always be related to the type of regime which, taken together, they define. The goal is to expose the reality of the way people live in order to identify problems and then correct them. Restoring substance and meaning to politics does not imply finding a collective redeemer, be it the people, a class, or the masses. It is rather a matter of figuring out how the system that creates social differences and cleavages actually works and finding ways to overcome the obstacles to creating a political system based on reciprocal commitments.

The mixed modern regime

Electoral-representative government, counter-democracy, and political reflection and deliberation are the three pillars of

313

democratic experience. Each contributes to the organization of the political system. Electoral-representative government provides the system's institutional underpinnings; counter-democracy challenges the rules and injects vitality; political reflection and deliberation offer historical and social density. Yet each of these elements can also suffer from certain pathologies and generate certain perverse consequences. Left to its own devices, electoral-representative government tends to transform itself into elective aristocracy, into a governing machine. The specter of populism and of anti-politics hovers over counter-democracy. Political theory tends to be drawn toward the simplifications of decisionism on the one hand and the formalism of deliberative democracy on the other. If the three elements can be brought together in a system, however, they can work together to create a positive dynamic and lay their various demons to rest. The idea of a mixed constitution arose in the Middle Ages in the course of the search for a regime that would combine the best features of aristocracy, democracy, and monarchy to create a polity as generous as it was rational.[24] The idea of a mixed constitution is worth revisiting today, but with a somewhat different twist: democracy itself needs to be understood as a mixed regime, not as the result of a compromise between rival principles, such as liberty and equality, but rather as a composite of the three elements described above. These three elements need to be combined so that they complement and reinforce one another if there

---

[24] See James M. Blythe, *Ideal Government and the Mixed Constitution in the Middle Ages* (Princeton University Press, 1992).

is to be progress in self-government. In other words, democratic progress must be seen as a pluralistic process. There is no "one best way," no single best set of institutions, that is guaranteed to yield the most satisfactory level of participation and the most representative regime. This book has focused on counter-democracy. Future work will need to go back to the roots of democratic political theory in order to develop a systematic account of its main variants and issues.

Looking at democracy in terms of its three dimensions also leads to a new way of envisioning the relation between national democracies and cosmopolitan political forms. Usually one thinks of this relationship in terms of institutional transfer: institutions and regulatory procedures first developed at the national level are reproduced at a higher level of coordination. We have already seen how the concept of counter-democracy provides a framework for exploring the actions of civil society in various realms. In a broader perspective, the notion of a modern mixed constitution can help us to explore democracy on different scales and compare institutional forms at different levels. In each case, a specific mode of "mixedness" is at work, and progress at each level can be defined in terms of mixed institutions of different types. Electoral-representative institutions are still confined mainly to the national level, but counter-democratic institutions have developed at higher levels, as we saw previously. The question of democratic political theory and reflection arises at the international as well as the national level. Even though there is no officially constituted *demos*, the goal is still to construct a common humanity, though of course the demands on individuals are less strenuous at this level.[25] Here, too, differences and conflicts exist, and one wants to make them more visible in order to deal with them more successfully. Progress in this direction should aim to broaden the framework of analysis in order to address simultaneously democracy at the national level, the construction of a cosmopolitan order, and the development of regional groupings such as the European Union. This convergence has generally been approached only in a weak sense, in terms of a generalized dispersion of power or proliferation of forms of governance without government. While certain futuristic thinkers have envisioned a globalization devoid of negative consequences, others look to globalization as the midwife of global revolution. By contrast, the framework I propose can be seen as placing powerful demands on citizens while at the same time providing instruments for achieving progress toward greater democracy.

The scholar and the citizen

The study of politics yields works of two broadly different kinds: normative theories on the one hand and descriptive historical or sociological accounts on the other. In this book I have *practiced* something different: I have tried to develop a new theory of democracy based on detailed

---

[25] On this point, see the distinction I make between "solidarity of citizenship" and "citizenship of humanity" in *La Démocratie inachevée*, pp. 421–422.

observation of what I have called the counter-democratic universe. In doing so, I have built on an approach that can already be seen in embryo in my earlier work on electoral-representative democracy. Two consequences follow from the adoption of this method, one intellectual, the other political. Intellectually, my approach leads to a new realist theory of democracy, in which "realist" is no longer synonymous with disillusionment and resigned acceptance of a certain limited vision of what is possible. Understanding the origins and effects of counter-democracy leads to *realistic* proposals for overcoming our current political disillusionment. By focusing on counter-democratic institutions, we can envision ways of overcoming their limitations and avoiding their perverse consequences. By taking a broader view than usual of the ways in which citizens have tried to shape their own history, a new realm of possibilities is opened up. "Realist" theorists of democracy from Joseph Schumpeter to Karl Popper (to name only two) implicitly propose a minimalist interpretation of the ideal of self-government as "non-tyranny" or as a process for legitimating competing elites. In this perspective, "realism" implies "modesty of ambition," and the very idea of "democratic progress" ceases to have meaning. The approach taken in this book makes it possible to break this association. In this approach, the understanding of democracy no longer begins with its limitations, its risks of failure, its extreme forms. I aim rather to explore the heart of democracy, in its most common manifestations as well as its gray areas.

In political terms, finally, the approach taken here leads to a reconsideration of the role of scholarship. It is no longer necessary to alternate between disillusioned lucidity and naïve enthusiasm or to face a "choice between irony and radicalism," to borrow Thomas Mann's suggestive formulation,[26] or between the "politics of faith" and the "politics of skepticism," to use Michael Oakeshott's celebrated distinction.[27] This book was written in 2005, the centenary of the birth of Jean-Paul Sartre and Raymond Aron. Sartre was the apostle of the twentieth century's culpable utopian dreams, the headstrong fellow traveler of a radical adventure that remained beyond the pale of his critique. Aron was a professor of disillusionment, a model of melancholy lucidity. Expressing the contrary logics of their generation to perfection, each embodied a form of intellectual grandeur. Yet each succumbed to an unfortunate temptation, that of icy reason on the one hand and blind commitment on the other, and in their opposite ways each thus fostered a form of impotence. The author of these lines has sought to escape this impasse by formulating a theory of democracy that is no longer cut off from action intended to breathe new life into democracy.

[26] Thomas Mann, *Betrachtungen ein Unpolitischen* (Frankfurt: Fischer, 1983).
[27] Michael Oakeshott, *The Politics of Faith and the Politics of Scepticism* (New Haven: Yale University Press, 1996).

accountability
  changing nature 227–228
  legal vs. political, differences
    230–231
  need/demand for 16,
    228–229
  replacement of impeachment
    system 206–207
acquittal
  as corrective 220–222
  frequency 219
Act-Up 65
action
  effectiveness, perceptions of
    309–311
  goals of 308–309, 312–313
  relationship with oversight
    80–81
  Western/Oriental modes
    34–36
agencies, government,
  proliferation of 55
Agreement of the Free People of
  England (1649) 2–3
Alain (Émile Chartier) 57–61, 269
Alexander I of Macedon 197
Althusius, Johannes 131–134
American Civil Liberties Union
  (ACLU) 226
Ami des patriotes (newspaper)
  99

Arendt, Hannah 46, 162, 181,
  235–236, 237, 239–240
Argentina 265
  political vocabulary 186
Arginusae, battle of 197
Aristophanes, *The Clouds* 198
Aristotle 84–85, 86–87, 195,
  200, 240
Aron, Raymond 318
Arrow, Kenneth 3
Arterton, Christopher F. 69
Athens 84–85
  assembly of the people 195,
    199–200
  graphe paronomon
    (nullification of edicts)
    198–199
  judicial system 192, 195–202
  as model for modern
    democracies 87
  political trials 196–199
  "sycophants" 269–270
  tribunal 195–199; centrality to
    city life 200–201; relative
    importance to Assembly
    200–201
attainder, bills of 204
audit mechanisms 73–74, 280–281
Aung San Suu Kyi 171
Auvergne 76–77
Aymé, Marcel 42–43

319

juries/jury system (cont.)
    as local institution 217
    political role 221–222
    theoretical arguments for
        214–215
    see also acquittal
Justinian Code 125

Kant, Immanuel 46
Kelsen, Hans 231, 293
Kennedy, John F. x
Kenneth, *Roman Antiquities* 90
Kerry, John 177–178
Kersaint, Armand-Guy-Simon
    de Coetnempren, comte de
    92
Kierkegaard, Søren 309
Knox, John 128, 130

La Boétie, Étienne de 131
La Rochefoucauld, François
    Alexandre Frédéric, duc de
    90
labor law 224–226
Laferrière, Julien 190
Lanthenas, François Xavier 37, 119
Latimer, Lord 203–204
Latin America, political
    institutions 296
Lavicomterie, Louis-Charles de
    91, 137–138
Le Mercier de la Rivière, Pierre-
    Paul 115
Ledru-Rollin, Alexandre 150
Lefort, Claude 168, 181
legibility, as function of politics
    307

legitimacy
    conflict of 107–109, 122
    distinguished from trust 3–4
    expansion of concept 13–14
    first use 115
    of governors vs. actions 116–117
    measures to strengthen 4–5
    new routes to 115–118
    political vs. social 155
    social-procedural 113, 115
    sought by support for
        counter-powers 263–264
    substantial 113–114, 116–117
    through consultation 296
    through impartiality 113–115
    typology 112–115
Leroux, Pierre 101
liberalism
    relationship with democracy
        251
    triumph of 181–183
    see also Great Britain;
        nineteenth century
local associations, growth of 297
Locke, John 33
lot, choice of officials by 84–85
Louis XIV of France 256

Mably, Gabriel Bonnot de 91
Machiavelli, Niccolo 34
macroeconomics 10
Madison, James 6, 293
majority/ies
    changing attitudes to 115–116
    democratic principle of 113
    positive vs. negative 15–16,
        183–184

Mandeville, Bernard 49
Manin, Bernard 297
Mann, Thomas 317–318
Marat, Jean-Paul 41, 105, 106,
    268–269
markets
    comparison with political
        systems *see under*
        economics
    defined by negative
        interventions 283–284
    failure 276–277
    lack of regulation 277–278
    self-surveillance 276–277
Marsilio of Padua 126
Marx, Karl/Marxist theory 47,
    67, 165
Mary I of England ("Bloody
    Mary") 128
media
    conflict with constitutional
        powers 104–120
    exposure of scandals
        43–44
    as expression of public
        opinion 117–118
    means of control 109–110
    as overseer 57, 66–67
    as private institutions 109
Michelet, Jules 106
"Michigan paradigm" 20–21
Middle Ages 25, 54
    industrial action 153
    judicial system 202–204,
        214, 234
    mixed constitution, origins of
        concept 314

popular consent/right to
    resist, doctrine of 125–127,
    166
rural communities 77–78
urban communities 76–77
Mill, John Stuart 14, 80–82, 158
minority/ies
    as oppressor vs. oppressed 116
    protection 156
    role of courts towards
        201–202
Mirabeau, Honoré, comte de 29,
    41–42, 91, 152
mistrust *see* distrust
mitigating circumstances,
    concept of 221
mixed constitution(s) 314–316
"mobilization," usage 33
Mommsen, Theodor 148
monarchomachs 129–131
Montaigne, Michel de 310
Montesquieu, Charles-Louis de
    Secondat, baron de
    6, 49–50, 53, 59, 87, 88–89,
    121, 134, 136,
    145, 202
    De l'esprit des lois 6, 14

Napoleon I *see* Bonaparte
Napoleon III 110
National Commission of Public
    Debate (France) 295
national systems, relationship
    with political theory 315
nationalization 286
negative campaigning 176–179
    advantages 178–179

Printed by Printforce, United Kingdom